The Boxer Catastrophe

NUMBER 583

COLUMBIA STUDIES IN THE SOCIAL SCIENCES

EDITED BY

THE FACULTY OF POLITICAL SCIENCE

OF COLUMBIA UNIVERSITY

The Boxer Catastrophe

by CHESTER C. TAN

OCTAGON BOOKS

A DIVISION OF FARRAR, STRAUS AND GIROUX

New York   1975

Reprinted 1967
by special arrangement with Chester C. Tan

Second Octagon printing 1975

OCTAGON BOOKS
A DIVISION OF FARRAR, STRAUS & GIROUX, INC.
19 Union Square West
New York, N. Y. 10003

LIBRARY OF CONGRESS CATALOG CARD NUMBER: 66-18057
ISBN 0-374-97752-6

Manufactured by Braun-Brumfield, Inc.
Ann Arbor, Michigan

Printed in the United States of America

PREFACE TO THE OCTAGON EDITION

In the present edition I have contented myself with reissuing the book without major alterations. In the twelve years since its first publication, a good deal of interest has been aroused in the subject, with a considerable literature appearing both in China and in the West. Of importance is the *Archival Materials Relative to the Boxers (I Ho T'uan Tang An Shih Liao)*, in two volumes, published by the State Records Office at Peking in 1959. This collection of official documents contains some Imperial decrees with phrases different from those printed in the *True Records of the Ch'ing Dynasty, Reign of Kuang Hsü (Ch'ing Tê Tsung Shih Lu)*, Ch'ang-ch'un, 1937. The discrepancies confirm the suspicion long entertained by scholars that the Ch'angch'un edition of the *True Records* might have undergone some alterations in order to exonerate the Ch'ing dynasty from the charge of extreme xenophobia. A careful comparison of the decrees in the two collections, however, will show that the tampering in the *True Records* is so sparse that it does not in any significant way distort the general picture of the Boxer movement. On the other hand, the *Archival Materials* contains some documents that are of great interest to the historian. For example, in Volume I there is a joint memorial by Chao Shu-ch'iao and Ho Nai-ying, dated May 30, 1900, which proposed that the Boxers be organized into the army. It would help to determine the roles of these two officials if we knew which of them originated the proposal; but the document gives no hints.

Among the recent books on the Boxers, Victor Purcell's *The Boxer Uprising* (Cambridge, England: Cambridge University Press, 1963) makes a serious attempt to solve some of the intricate problems concerning the Boxer movement. He seeks to find out at what time the Boxers changed their "anti-dynastic" position and adopted the slogan "Support the Ch'ing; destroy the foreigner." But he soon realizes that it is impossible to pinpoint the specific moment of the change-over. Available evidence shows that the Boxers adopted the pro-dynastic policy sometime in the latter part of 1899 when Yü Hsien, first as governor of Shantung and then as an adviser to the Imperial Court, played an important role in harnessing the Boxers' anti-foreign sentiments for governmental purposes. Until new materials appear that give us better information, I am afraid that is all we can say about the question of change-over.

The Boxer uprising was primarily an anti-foreign movement devoted to fighting Christianity and foreigners. It was a peasant movement only in the sense that its main support came from the peasants who joined the ranks of the Boxers. Any attempt to view it as a class struggle will have difficulties. For not only the peasants, but the landlords and the scholar-gentry as well, joined the massive movement to rid China of foreign influences. It is hardly convincing to regard the Manchu regime as merely the representative of the landlord class, and even if it were, the theory would still not explain the period in which governmental forces and Boxers combined to fight the foreigners. Theories are surely to be desired if they are solidly founded on facts. Similarly, imagination is helpful, but unless it is restrained by careful research, it will lead to fiction rather than history.

C. C. T.

February, 1967

Preface

ALTHOUGH there is no dearth of books on the Boxer Rebellion, most of them were published immediately after the episode in the form of memoirs or narratives, penned by those who happened to live through some phase of the crisis. The few systematic studies were published before the thirties, the period in which the stream of Chinese documentary material began to flow freely. They were, in fact, based on materials in Western languages.

Since the Boxer uprising was a movement indigenous to China, reliance upon Western sources alone will obviously not furnish an adequate explanation of its origin and nature or the thoughts and acts of the Chinese Government during the crisis. As a result, what Sir Robert Hart wrote in 1901 is still applicable today: " It would be interesting to get a really reliable Chinese account of Palace doings—and Peking doings—during 1900. As it is, we are all guessing and inferring and putting this and that together, but we have not got at the facts yet! It's all a question with no finality in it—*you* may put down your pen, but every new touch will bring a new picture to the eye that looks through the kaleidoscope of history—and the *Aurora Borealis* of circumstance will change unceasingly." [1]

The present work is intended to supply the gap by drawing upon Chinese as well as Western source materials. It is not, however, confined to the mere study of palace doings and Peking doings, though these constitute an important part of it. It studies further the policies and activities of the viceroys and governors, who in this period not only maintained a semi-independent position within their jurisdictions but also exerted enormous influence in the shaping of the national policy. It is impossible to under-

[1] Letter of Sir Robert Hart to Arthur H. Smith, June 18, 1901, in Smith, *China in Convulsion* (New York: Fleming H. Revell, 1901), II, 596.

stand the doings of the Imperial Court without knowing the role
played by these powerful officials.

Also included in this study is the Manchurian crisis created by
the Russian occupation after the uprising of the Boxers. The
Manchurian crisis should be studied in conjunction with the Boxer
uprising, not only because the latter gave birth to the former, but
also because in the course of negotiations the two closely affected
each other. Moreover, a study of the incident will lead to a fuller
realization of the position of the Court and the role of the viceroys
in those difficult days.

Professor Nathaniel Peffer of Columbia University has followed
this study from its inception to its completion. I am greatly in-
debted to him for his wise counsel and constant help. I am deeply
grateful to Professor C. Martin Wilbur for kind advice at every
stage of preparation and for assistance with publication. Professor L. Carrington Goodrich read the manuscript from end to
end and supplied me corrigenda of great value. I am under obli-
gation to Professor Franklin L. Ho for friendly criticism and aid,
and to Professors William T. R. Fox and Arthur W. Macmahon
for helpful comments and suggestions. My sincere thanks are due
to Professor Schuyler C. Wallace, who has given me invaluable
aid in various ways.

It remains to express my gratitude to the Tsing Hua University
Fund for the generous grant which made possible the publication
of this book. I am especially grateful to Dr. Y. C. Mei, President
of Tsing Hua University, for his continuing interest and encouragement.

C. C. T.

February, 1955

Contents

The Boxer Catastrophe

NOTE ON DOCUMENTATION

CITATIONS from Chinese sources, if they are old-style books, are by book (*chüan*) and leaf (*yeh*). If a decree or dispatch is cited, the Chinese date of the document is usually given. Thus,

To Tsungli Yamen, K26/5/4, Chang Chih-tung, *Chang Wên Hsiang Kung Ch'üan Chi*, 160/2

would mean

Telegram to Tsungli Yamen, dated the 26th year of the Kuang Hsü reign (which began in 1875), 5th moon, 4th day, in Chang Chih-tung, *Chang Wên Hsiang Kung Ch'üan Chi*, book 160, leaf 2.

If the full title is not given in the footnote, the reader will find it in the Bibliography, where the books, briefly annotated, are listed in alphabetical order.

In the text all Chinese and Russian dates are converted to the modern Western (Gregorian) calendar.

1

· Imperialism, Reform, and Reaction

THE CHINESE traditionally have been a friendly and sociable people. Confucius said: " To have friends coming to one from distant parts—is not this a great pleasure? " [1] Marco Polo at the end of the thirteenth century, Ricci at the close of the sixteenth century, Schall, Verbiest, and others in the seventeenth and eighteenth centuries all received cordial treatment and even honorable appointments. The Chinese at these periods were, generally speaking, free from prejudice against alien races. Ability and scholarship, whether native or foreign, commanded their respect. They were eager to detect talents and ready to utilize them, even though of alien origin. Confucius well said: " Among the educated, there is no distinction of origins." [2]

And the Chinese could not be said to have been intolerant toward foreign religions. Buddhism had been introduced from India, the Jesuits had flourished at Peking, and the Nestorian Tablet had been erected. For 120 years, from the latter part of the Ming to the beginning of the Ch'ing Dynasty, the propagation of Christianity was openly carried on in China. Now and then there were local attacks against the missionaries, initiated by individual officials who considered some Christian practices mysterious; but the general attitude of those of the Confucian school toward the supernatural was to " respect it but avoid it." It was because of this indifference toward religious matters that Chinese officials never indulged hysterically in religious persecution. It was only when the Pope arrogated to himself the authority of the Chinese

[1] *The Analects*, chap. 1.   [2] *Ibid.*, chap. 15.

Emperor in connection with the matter of ancestor worship and reports came that European religious representatives in the Philippine Islands and Japan had attempted to interfere politically in those countries that the Chinese government decreed the proscription of Christianity in 1706 and 1717.[3]

Nor were the Chinese averse to foreign trade without reason. The Chinese had shown their interest in foreign trade since ancient times, when the products of China were interchanged with those of the Roman Empire. During the Ming Dynasty this interest was embodied in the administrative organizations set up in the vital areas of the Empire to take charge of China's foreign trade. In 1370 the Shih Po Ssŭ (Trade and Shipping Bureaus) were established in Ningpo, Ch'üanchou (Fukien), and Canton to supervise trade with Japan, the Liuchiu Islands, and the South Sea area respectively.[4] Suspended in 1374,[5] the three trade bureaus were reinstated in 1403.[6] Five years later the government found it desirable to add another bureau near the border of Indo-China to oversee the trade with the nations to the southwest.[7] The trade continued for more than a century until 1523 when trouble came from an unexpected quarter. Two Japanese envoys came to pay tribute to the Chinese Emperor, each claiming to be the true representative of his country. When one outbid the other by bribing the superintendent of the Trade Bureau, the other envoy retaliated by plundering Ningpo. A censor, named Hsia Yen, sent in a memorial, pointing out the close connection between foreign commerce and Japanese piracy and recommending the stoppage of trade. The recommendation was accepted by the Emperor, and all trade and shipping bureaus were abolished in that year.[8] But the Chinese interest in foreign trade did not permit the stoppage to

---

[3] See Joseph A. M. M. de Mailla (tr.), *Histoire générale de la Chine,* 13 vols. (Paris: P. D. Pierres, 1777-85), XI, 321 ff.

[4] *Ming T'ai Tsu Shih Lu* (True Records of the Ming Dynasty, Reign of Emperor T'ai Tsu), book 49.

[5] *Ibid.,* books 91-93.

[6] *Huang Ming Ta Chêng Chi* (Important Political Events of the Ming Dynasty), book 6.

[7] *Ming T'ai Tsu Shih Lu,* book 40.

[8] *Ming Shih Chi Shih Pên Mo* (History of the Ming Dynasty from Beginning to End), book 55.

remain long in effect. In 1529 the Viceroy of Kwangtung and Kwangsi memorialized the Throne, pointing out that the strict prohibition in Kwangtung only led to depression and smuggling in Fukien. Moreover, the people of Siam, Cambodia, Java, and Palembang were honest and law-abiding. The Court was convinced and the Trade and Shipping Bureau in Canton was reestablished.[9]

It was under these circumstances that the Europeans entered upon the scene in the sixteenth century. The Chinese Government, though keenly interested in foreign trade, had been forced to stop it in order to safeguard its long coast line against repeated and far-reaching Japanese piracy. The Europeans, unfortunately, only added to the suspicion of the Chinese authorities. The European trade in that early period was in the hands of the Portuguese, whose truculent, lawless conduct made it impossible for the Chinese authorities to accord them a wider sphere of operation than Kwangtung. But it should be noted that the restriction of trade to Canton was in effect before the arrival of the Europeans, and that it was originally due to Japanese piratical activities along the coast of China.

The Manchus, when they came to rule China, did not adopt any " rigid policy of seclusion " toward foreign intercourse, as asserted by some writers.[10] On the contrary, after they had firmly established their rule, the Emperor K'ang Hsi, by the decree of 1684, opened all the ports of China to foreign trade.[11] By this time the British had joined the Dutch in opening trade with China. From 1694 to 1703 the East India Company repeatedly sent their ships to Amoy and Chusan.[12] Then trade conditions in Canton became more profitable, and in 1715 the Company decided to establish a factory with a permanent staff at Canton and to dispatch their

[9] Ku Yen-wu, *T'ien Hsia Chün Kuo Li Ping Shu* (The Merits and Shortcomings of Local Administration throughout the Nation), book 120.

[10] See Paul H. Clements, *The Boxer Rebellion* (" Studies in History, Economics, and Public Law," Vol. LXVI, No. 3 [New York: Columbia University, 1915]), p. 17.

[11] *Ch'ing Shih Kao*, " *Shih Huo Chih*," No. 6.

[12] H. B. Morse, *The Chronicles of the East India Company Trading to China, 1635-1834* (Oxford: Clarendon Press, 1926), I, 86.

ships at stated seasons.[13] From that time on, the history of the British trade was, for all practical purposes, the history of the Canton factories. The Imperial edict of 1757 making Canton the sole staple [14] merely gave official sanction to a state of affairs already established for forty years. It should not be construed therefore as any special effort on the part of the Chinese Government to restrict trade, nor regarded as an action causing too much inconvenience to the foreign merchants.

Though British trade prospered in Canton, the British gradually found unsatisfactory the conditions under which the trade was carried on.[15] To ameliorate these conditions, the British Government in 1793 sent Lord Macartney, and in 1816 Lord Amherst, to Peking to present their case directly to the Chinese Emperor. But whether cordially received or not, these men accomplished nothing. The highhanded manner of the Europeans in the sixteenth and seventeenth centuries remained, of course, a repulsive memory, but even at the later period the conduct of the European sailors in Canton was hardly such as to dispose the Chinese authorities toward expansion of foreign trade.[16]

The abolition of the East India Company on April 13, 1834, opened a new chapter in the history of China's foreign relations. Heretofore the British trade, which occupied the largest share of the trade with China, was carried on in Canton through intermediaries, the Co-hong on behalf of China and the East India Company for England. Having the single purpose of making profit from trade, the Company naturally disliked any disturbance or interruption and would have submitted to the restrictions and

---

[13] H. B. Morse, *International Relations* (London: Longmans, Green & Co., 1910), I, 53.

[14] *Tung Hua Lu*, 11th moon, 22nd year of Ch'ien Lung.

[15] They complained against the taxation imposed upon them, against the monopoly system of the Co-hong, against the debts which the Chinese merchants owed them, against the rules by which life in the factories was regulated, and, last but not least, against the requirement that communications with any Chinese official be transmitted through a Co-hong member. Morse, *International Relations*, I, 86-87.

[16] Numerous cases occurred in which the sailors of the European ships were involved in brawls, sometimes ending in killings, and, worst of all, when crimes were committed in Chinese territory, the Europeans would try by every means to defy Chinese jurisdiction. See Morse, *Chronicles*, Vols. I-V; also *Yüeh Hai Kuan Chih* (Records of the Canton Customhouse).

orders of the local authorities so long as trade could be maintained. Now that this intermediate agency was dissolved, the governments of the two countries were brought into direct contact, and as each held an entirely different set of international principles, it was inevitable that conflicts should arise.

The first dispute occurred in July, 1834, when Lord Napier, newly appointed Superintendent of British trade in Canton, insisted that the time-honored petition form of communication with the Chinese authorities should not be followed, because he was an official of the British Government. The Chinese, on the other hand, could not understand why a traditional form of communication, practiced for more than a hundred years, should now be changed.[17] The dispute did not lead to a great crisis at this time, for Lord Napier soon died of malaria in Macao. But the problem remained; and if the Chinese Government was slow in realizing the inevitability of change in its relations with foreign countries, the Western Powers soon determined that some changes had to be brought about, even if by force.

Thus the Opium War was imposed upon China in 1840 and the Arrow War in 1856. The immediate occasion for the former was, as known to all, the opium trade, while that for the latter was the incident of pulling down a British flag by the Chinese soldiers. But the underlying motive in both cases was the opening of China to trade and the changing of existing conditions under which China's foreign trade was carried on. China, of course, was indignant that the foreigners should interfere with the conception and principle of trade that she had held for centuries. She considered the use of force to support trade a gross injustice and condemned the foreigners as " barbarians." But whatever her feelings might be, she had to submit to the military might of the West.

Upon the conclusion of the Convention of Peking, 1860, most of the important ports of China were opened. Not only were the trade conditions, the subjects of complaint in the thirties, rectified,

17 See Chiang T'ing-fu (T. F. Tsiang) *Chin Tai Chung Kuo Wai Chiao Shih Tzŭ Liao Chi Yao* (Selected Source Materials on Modern Chinese Diplomatic History [Shanghai: Commercial Press, 1931]), I, 8.

but tremendous privileges were secured.[18] By the Chefoo Convention, 1876, more ports were opened to trade,[19] with further privileges granted to the Western Powers. Forty years of diplomacy, agitation, resistance, and war resulted in China's complete yielding to the demands of the Western Powers in the field of trade and residence settlements for foreigners.

European ambitions, however, were not confined to commercial concessions. If the demands for Hong Kong and the Kowloon Point could be explained as being part of the British scheme for opening trade with China, the taking from China of the huge region north of the Amur and east of the Ussuri in 1858-60 was manifestly a political measure to forward Russian expansion toward the Pacific. The early eighties unmistakably demonstrated the political ambitions of the Powers toward the Chinese Empire. One after another, China's dependencies were hacked away. Russia took part of Turkestan in 1881, France seized Tonkin in 1885, and in 1886 Britain annexed Burma. China's protective ring of dependencies was thus broken through. But would the Western Powers stop at the peripheries of the Chinese Empire?

IMPERIALISM RUNS AMUCK

In the meantime, China gradually awoke to the reality of the new forces—the military might and the industrial power of the West—which confronted her. "It is an unprecedented situation in the history of more than three thousand years," exclaimed Li Hung-chang, the statesman and diplomat of the last quarter of the nineteenth century. And so after the suppression of the

[18] By the treaty of Nanking, 1842, China agreed, *inter alia*, to cede Hong Kong, to open five ports to trade, to abolish the monopoly of the Co-hong, to recognize the consular residence with right of direct communication with Chinese authorities, to admit the equality between China and England, and to limit tariff and transit dues. Maritime Customs, *Treaties, Conventions, etc., between China and Foreign States* (Shanghai, 1917), I, 159. The Convention of Peking, in conjunction with the Treaty of Tientsin, 1858, provided, *inter alia*, for the cession of the Kowloon Point, the opening of eleven new ports to trade, the permanent legation at Peking, extraterritoriality and extradition, religious toleration, and the right of inland travel. Maritime Customs, *op. cit.*, I, 212, 238.

[19] By the Chefoo Convention, four more ports were opened to trade and six ports of call were provided for the landing of foreign goods. The West River, however, was not opened until 1897. *Ibid.*, I, 299, 346.

T'aip'ing Rebellion, which overran more than half of the country and lasted for fourteen years, the Chinese Government rallied itself to rebuild the national strength so as to meet the impact of the Western advance. Railway construction had been strongly advocated since 1878, first by Li Hung-chang and then by Liu Ming-ch'uan, but the obstinate objection of the conservative officials prevented it from being adopted. With the advent of the Sino-French War in 1884, however, people began to appreciate the value and importance of railroads. In 1887 came the support of Prince Ch'un, then Minister of the Naval Department, and Marquis Tsêng Kuo-ch'üan, the famous Chinese minister sent abroad. The recommendation of these two, one entitled to speak on the importance of railways from the standpoint of national defense, and the other qualified to explain their value in the economic life of foreign countries, finally converted the Imperial Court to the idea of railways.[20] Similarly, the opening of mines, which had been prohibited at the beginning of the Ch'ing Dynasty, came to be the policy when Emperor Kuang Hsü ascended the throne.[21]

On the military side, under the energetic advocacy of Li Hung-chang, China was to build three navies, the Peiyang squadron, the Nanyang squadron, and the Kwangtung squadron.[22] Warships were bought from the European countries, dockyards were constructed in Shanghai and Foochow, and naval academies were established in Tientsin and Port Arthur. Students were sent to England, France, and Germany to study the manufacture of munitions and military operations. Army systems were reorganized, and new regulations of military drill were drawn up.[23] By 1891 the Peiyang squadron developed to such a degree that a demonstration was held in March. In July of the same year, a squadron of six warships was sent to visit Japan under the command of Admiral Ting Ju-ch'ang.[24]

It was with this preparation that China met the aggression of Japan. This time it was an Eastern Power that China had to cope with, an Eastern Power that had modernized itself since 1870. In

[20] *Ch'ing Shih Kao*, "Chiao T'ung Chih," No. 1.
[21] *Ibid.*   [22] *Ch'ing Shih Kao*, "Ping Chih," No. 3.
[23] *Ibid.*, "Ping Chih," No. 10.   [24] *Ibid.*, "Ping Chih," No. 7.

1874 Japan first demonstrated that in the process of Westernization she was eager to take over Western imperialism as well. In
that year, under the threat of war, Japan assumed sovereignty over
the Liuchiu Islands, a vassal state of China. The episode proved
so successful to the Japanese that they were encouraged a few years
later to challenge China's authority over another of her vassal
states: Korea. Only the conciliatory policy of the Chinese Government prevented war in 1885 when Li Hung-chang signed the Convention of Tientsin, under which both China and Japan were to
withdraw their troops from Korea; Korea was to be left free; and,
in case it should become necessary for either party to send troops
to Korea in the future, previous notice of intention to do so was
to be given, and the troops thus sent were to be withdrawn as soon
as the trouble causing their dispatch had been settled. Japan, however, had no intention of leaving Korea free, nor of abiding by the
convention she had signed. In 1894 when China, upon the request
of the Korean king to help suppress a rebellion, dispatched fifteen
hundred troops to Asan, Japan countered by sending large detachments of troops to Seoul. By the time the Chinese troops reached
Korea, the revolt had been put down by the Korean army. Japan,
however, refused to withdraw her troops simultaneously with the
Chinese; instead, she insisted that reforms should be pressed upon
the Korean Government. She had determined to wrest Korea from
China, and to realize this ambition she was ready for war.

In China there was a strong demand for a stiff policy. It was
manifest that Japan's advance to Korea was a serious menace to
China's security. Moreover, since China had now a navy and a
modernized army, why should she submit to the threat of the
" little island country "? Memorial after memorial was written
for war,[25] and in the Imperial Court there were powerful leaders
advocating a strong policy, men such as Wêng T'ung-ho, the tutor
and confidant of Emperor Kuang Hsü, and Li Hung-tsao, the
Grand Councillor.[26] At last the Emperor and the Empress Dowager were convinced, and Li Hung-chang, who had preferred a

---

[25] Wêng T'ung-ho, *Wêng Wên Kung Kung Jih Chi*, 33/38, 33/66a.
[26] *Ibid.*, 33/58ab.

diplomatic solution to an armed conflict, was instructed not to yield.

The result of the Sino-Japanese War was as unexpected as it was disastrous. The weakness of China, now defeated by a small country in Asia, was shown to all. In the international arena it ushered in the so-called battle of the concessions, in which Western imperialism emerged unabashed. Immediately after the War, Russia and France, having done China a service, together with Germany, in the tripartite intervention on the Liaotung Peninsula, demanded that China should turn to them for a loan. In spite of opposition by Britain and Germany, the loan was concluded with the Franco-Russian Syndicate on July 6, 1895, for the sum of 400,000,000 gold francs at the annual interest of 4 percent.[27] The loan was guaranteed by the duties levied by the maritime customs of China and by the deposit of customs bonds. China was also made to agree that, if she should grant to any one Power any right or privilege concerning the supervision or administration of any revenues of the Chinese Empire, the same right or privilege should be extended to the Russian Government as well.[28] In 1896, when Li Hung-chang was sent to St. Petersburg to represent China at the coronation of the Czar, the Russian Government succeeded not only in concluding a secret treaty of alliance with China but also in obtaining the concession to project the Trans-Siberian Railroad across northern Manchuria directly to Vladivostok.

But Russia was not the only nation that wanted compensation for the service it had done China. On July 20, 1895, France succeeded in securing two conventions from China.[29] By the first convention the China-Annam frontier was delimited in favor of France. By the second convention China agreed to open to trade and residence three new treaty ports on the China-Annam frontier and to allow certain reductions in transit dues. In Article V China

---

[27] John Van Antwerp MacMurray (ed.), *Treaties and Agreements with and concerning China, 1894-1919* (New York: Oxford University Press, 1921), I, 35.

[28] Count Witte, *Memoirs*, ed. by Abraham Yarmolinsky (New York: Doubleday, 1921), pp. 87-93; MacMurray, *op. cit.*, I, 81.

[29] MacMurray, *op. cit.*, I, 20.

gave France a priority in the exploitation of mines in Yunnan, Kwangsi, and Kwangtung and permission to extend the Annamese railway into Chinese territory. To counteract the French advances, Britain on February 4, 1897, concluded a convention with China by which she secured the rectification of the Burma-China frontier in her favor, the opening of ports in Kwangtung and Kwangsi, and the connecting of railways in Yunnan, in case China constructed them, with the Burmese lines.[30]

Germany, another partner in the Liaotung intervention, was by no means left behind. In the autumn of 1895 Germany had asked the Chinese Government to cede a coaling station on the China coast, but the request was declined by the Chinese Government on the ground that it might lead to similar demands from other Powers.[31] At that time the German Government did not press the matter, for it had not decided which place on the China coast should be demanded. But by the end of 1896 the German Government had made up its mind to choose Kiaochow as its object, and in January, 1897, von Heyking, the German Minister at Peking, asked the Tsungli Yamen for the lease of this coaling station.[32] As it was again refused, the German Government began to think of forcible means. It was waiting for a suitable pretext, which was soon furnished by the murder of two German priests in Shantung. Upon receipt of the news, the Kaiser immediately ordered his fleet to seize Kiaochow. Confronted with this *fait accompli*, the Chinese Government first offered an island in place of Kiaochow,[33] then proposed to grant Germany a concession in Kiaochow which was to be opened as a free port;[34] but Germany, fortified by an understanding with Britain[35] and Russia,[36] was insistent upon the lease of Kiaochow. At last China had to accept

[30] *Ibid.*, I, 94.
[31] Hsü Ching-ch'êng, *Hsü Wên Su Kung I Kao*, 8/8-9.
[32] *Ch'ing Chi Wai Chiao Shih Liao*, 125/108.
[33] Wêng T'ung-ho, *op. cit.*, 36/111b, 36/113a.
[34] *Ibid.*, 36/116b.
[35] Salisbury to Lascelles, January 12, 1898, G. P. Gooch and Harold Temperley (eds.), *British Documents on the Origins of the War, 1898-1914* (London: His Majesty's Stationery Office, 1927), I, 4.
[36] See Philip Joseph, *Foreign Diplomacy in China, 1894-1900* (London: G. Allen & Unwin, 1928), p. 205.

the German demands, and on March 6, 1898,[37] a convention was signed by which Kiaochow was leased to Germany for ninety-nine years. Germany also secured exclusive mining rights and concessions of two railways in Shantung and obtained the first option in any undertaking where foreign assistance might be needed.

Angry as she was about the German aggression, China was much more hurt when on March 3 Russia, an ally under the secret treaty signed less than two years before, demanded the lease of Talienwan and Port Arthur for twenty-five years and the right to construct a railway connecting these two ports with the general system of Siberia.[38] Bitter but helpless, the Chinese Government had no choice but to comply with the Russian demands.[39] It also had to accept the British demands for the lease of Weihaiwei for the period of Russian occupation of Port Arthur [40] and, at an earlier time, a lease at Kowloon for ninety-nine years.[41] As for France, China had to grant her the following concessions: (1) the lease of Kwangchowwan for ninety-nine years, (2) the right to construct a railway from the frontier of Tonkin to Yunnanfu, and (3) a representative of French nationality for the head of the Chinese postal office staff.[42]

These concessions, far-reaching though they were, did not fully satisfy the Powers. To safeguard their interests against the encroachment by rivals and perhaps to install themselves in a better position in case of the breakup of China, the Powers applied themselves to the marking out of the country into the so-called spheres of interest. Thus Britain claimed the Yangtze Valley as her sphere; Russia, Manchuria; while France earmarked Yunnan, Kweichow, and Kwangsi; and Japan, Fukien. The assertion of claims to these " spheres " was based upon the leases of territories, railway and economic concessions, and, more formally, the en-

[37] MacMurray, op. cit., I, 43.

[38] MacDonald to Salisbury, March 8, 1898, British Parliamentary Papers, China No. 1 (1898), p. 43.

[39] Wêng T'ung-ho, op. cit., 37/24a.

[40] MacMurray, op. cit., I, 152.

[41] Ibid., I, 130.

[42] Ministère des affaires étrangères, Documents diplomatiques [Livres Jaunes], 1898, pp. 44-50.

forced declarations of territorial nonalienation by China and the agreements between the Powers. Thus China had to declare to England against alienation of the Yangtze regions to another Power; to France against alienation of Hainan and provinces bordering on Tonkin; and to Japan, similar assurance with regard to Fukien.[43] As to the agreements between the Powers, there was the Franco-British Agreement of 1896, by which the two countries agreed to share any special privileges that either secured in Yunnan and Szechuan provinces;[44] the Anglo-German Agreement of 1898, by which the British sphere of interest was defined as the Yangtze Valley and the German one as the province of Shantung and the Yellow River Valley;[45] and the Russo-British Agreement of 1899, by which Russia agreed not to seek any railway concessions in the Yangtze Valley, while Britain gave similar assurance with respect to the Russian sphere north of the Great Wall.[46]

Such was the development of international relations in China after the close of the war with Japan. It was a history of grim advance of imperialism, a series of relentless maneuvers, with the sole purpose of seizing concessions, territorial or otherwise, from China. The Celestial Empire was confronted with a grave danger. Foreigners, abroad and in China, frankly spoke of the partition of the Empire as an event immediately impending.[47] The Chinese statesmen became worried;[48] the Chinese people were alarmed that China might one day be " cut up like a watermelon." What was to be done? Where lay the weakness that caused China to suffer such humiliation and face such danger?

[43] William W. Rockhill (ed.), *Treaties and Conventions with or concerning China and Korea, 1894-1904* (Washington: Government Printing Office, 1904), p. 181.

[44] Later, as France secured the nonalienation agreement on the provinces bordering Tonkin and the right for her nationals to construct railways in Yunnan, Britain tacitly recognized the French claim to a " sphere of interest " in Yunnan, Kwangsi, and Kweichow.

[45] MacMurray, *op. cit.*, I, 266.

[46] Rockhill, *op. cit.*, p. 183.

[47] See Lord Charles Beresford, *The Break-up of China* (New York: Harper & Brothers, 1899); Arthur H. Smith, *China in Convulsion* (New York: Fleming H. Revell, 1901), I, 115.

[48] Wêng T'ung-ho, *op. cit.*, 37/24a.

THE HUNDRED DAYS

As early as the reign of T'ung Chih in the sixties, about the time when Japan began her reforms under Emperor Meiji, China had taken to Western technology. Thirty years of diplomacy and armed conflict with the European Powers convinced her that, in order to defend herself against foreign aggression, it was necessary to strengthen the country somewhat along Western lines. With the suppression of the T'aip'ing Rebellion, there was a general urge to regain her strength, and it was considered time to turn to the West for the secrets of power. Under the direction of Tsêng Kuo-fan, Li Hung-chang, and others, arsenals were established in Shanghai and Tientsin, dockyards were built in Fukien and Port Arthur, warships were bought from foreign countries, the army was trained on Western lines, railroads were introduced, mines were exploited, academies and schools were opened for the study of military and applied sciences, telegraph communications were set up, a shipping bureau was organized, and students were sent abroad to study.[49] But all these were confined to the military and industrial side; nothing was done for institutional or social reforms. Li Hung-chang, according to Liang Ch'i-ch'ao, "knew only military, but not social, affairs; diplomatic, but not political, problems."[50] Being an astute statesman and having most contact with foreigners in his capacity as China's leading diplomat, Li should have known that the strength of the West lay in more than armaments and railroads. Perhaps he had his difficulties. In a conversation with Prince Ito in 1895, when he went to Japan to negotiate the peace treaty, Li, after expressing admiration for the social reforms of Japan, said: "My country is hampered by traditions and customs; one can hardly do what one wants. . . . China also has people who understand modern affairs; but there are too many provinces, with strong sectionalism, just like your country in the feudal period, when one was checked and hindered by others and had no full authority for anything."[51] Whatever difficulty he

---

[49] Liang Ch'i-ch'ao, *Li Hung-chang*, p. 33.
[50] *Ibid.*, p. 4.
[51] Li Hung-chang, *Wu Tz'ŭ Wên Ta Chieh Lüeh*, "First Conference."

might have, the Sino-Japanese War eloquently proved that his modernization was inadequate to save China from the disastrous defeat. It was clear that, if China was to survive and regain her strength, a different approach was indispensable.

The leader of the new reform movement was K'ang Yu-wei, a Cantonese scholar. Canton had been for many generations one of the most important ports in the Far East, and because of its proximity to Hong Kong and Macao it was more susceptible to Western ideas than other places of the country. As early as 1879, at the age of twenty-two, K'ang Yu-wei began to read translations of Western books.[52] He kept on hunting for Western knowledge so that by 1885 he had studied not only the history of Western countries and Western philosophy and politics but also physics and mathematics. He visited Hong Kong and Shanghai and made acquaintance with Chinese who returned from America.[53] His keen eye quickly observed that the Western people had their own civilization and that it was erroneous to speak of them as barbarians.[54] In 1888, when he went to Peking for the metropolitan examination, he first expressed his thoughts in a petition to the Emperor. He pointed out the dangerous position China was in. After breaking through the ring of China's dependencies, he said, " the Powers are now coming to the heart of the country. Japan is plotting against Korea; England is intriguing in Tibet; Russia, building railways in the north, is menacing Peking; and France is nourishing her ambition in the southwestern provinces. . . . Since the dawn of history no country has been able to survive without self-exertion and improvement when confronted with powerful enemies on all sides. With their advanced knowledge and wondrous instruments, their ambitions in China have created an unusual crisis." To cope with the situation, he went on, it was imperative that China should undertake reforms. The conservative view that institutions handed down from our ancestors should not be changed was erroneous. " When the forefathers of the Ch'ing Dynasty ruled China, they did not keep the systems which

[52] Chang Po-chêng, *Nan Hai K'ang Hsien Shêng Chuan*, 4b.
[53] *K'ang Nien P'u*, in *Shih Hsüeh Nien Pao*, II, 183-84.
[54] Chang Po-chêng, *op. cit.*, 4-5.

their ancestors had used in Manchuria." K'ang then described the bright prospect of reform. A small island country like Japan had become powerful after ten years of reform. If China reformed now, " she will become strong and prosperous in ten years, and within twenty years she will be a powerful nation, able to recover her lost territories and to avenge her humiliations." [55]

The petition did not reach the Emperor, for the ministers considered it too unconventional. But the patriotic philosopher was persistent. In April, 1895, when it was reported that China was to sign the peace treaty with Japan, he called together some 1,300 scholars, who had come from various provinces to Peking for the national examination, and drafted a petition to the Throne, to be signed by them all. The petition contained more than eight thousand words, the gist of which was to refuse the Japanese demands, to continue the war, and to begin at once political reforms.[56] But it was too late: before the petition was presented to the Throne, the peace treaty had been signed.

On May 29, after the signing of the Treaty, K'ang wrote another petition. He developed the theme he had discussed in his previous petitions, but he became more and more emphatic on the need of reform. He pointed out that the humiliation of the defeat by Japan was not important; what was important was the danger of partition, for all the Powers were now watching for the chance. " China is confronted with the gravest danger in her history," he declared. The laws and institutions must be changed; for China had been governed under these laws for two thousand years, and the result was her present helpless state. He also proposed concrete measures for reform.[57]

This time the petition reached the Throne, and the Emperor ordered three copies made of the document, one of which was to be sent to the Empress Dowager. On July 19 an Imperial decree was issued to the viceroys and governors of the various provinces, ordering them to push energetically the several measures of

[55] K'ang Yu-wei, Nan Hai Hsien Shèng Ssŭ Shang Shu Chi, 6-14.
[56] Ibid., 2.   [57] Ibid., 4a.

modernization, particularly those concerning industry and rearmament.[58]

But the time was still not opportune for the enthusiastic reformer. He had just passed the national examination and was only a minor official in the Board of Works. To gain the ear of the Court he needed the support of some great minister. Wêng T'ung-ho, the tutor of the Emperor, seemed to admire his scholarship and ability.[59] In an interview K'ang tried to persuade Wêng, but the elder statesman was a cautious man and was not convinced at the time.[60] Finding that there was nothing more for him to do, K'ang returned to Kwangtung in 1896, lectured in Canton, and devoted himself to the writing of books.[61] Meanwhile he had taken a leading part in the Ch'iang Hsüeh Hui (Society for the Study of National Rejuvenation) in Peking, among whose members was Yüan Shih-k'ai who later played such a fatal role in the movement. An affiliated society was set up in Shanghai, where Chang Chih-tung agreed to be a sponsor.[62] A journal was published in Peking and Shanghai to propagate the reform ideas. By 1898 societies, schools, and journals were organized by K'ang's party throughout the country.[63]

In 1897 Germany inaugurated the " battle of the concessions " by occupying Kiaochow, and it seemed that the reformer's prophecy was coming true. Surely no patriot should watch idly while the country was in peril. K'ang rushed to Peking and at once wrote a memorial, which through the assistance of Wêng T'ung-ho was submitted to the Emperor.[64] He boldly stated that if reforms were not undertaken, His Majesty would soon lose not only his throne and life but also his country and people.[65] The Emperor was struck by the courage of the junior official who dared to mention the loss of throne and country. An Imperial decree was issued, ordering a conference to be held between the Tsungli Yamen ministers and the memorializer and that his books be presented to the Throne through the Yamen.

---

[58] Ibid., 33a.   [59] K'ang Nien P'u, II, 191.   [60] Ibid., II, 193.   [61] Ibid.
[62] Ibid., II, 192.   [63] Liang Ch'i-ch'ao, Wu Hsü Chêng Pien Chi, Appendices I, II.
[64] K'ang Nien P'u, II, 194.
[65] Liang Ch'i-ch'ao, Wu Hsü Chêng Pien Chi, 10.

After the conference between the ministers and K'ang, the Emperor was desirous of giving the reformer an audience, but this was canceled on the opposition of Prince Kung on the ground that K'ang was too inferior an official to see the Emperor. Thereupon the Emperor ordered that hereafter if K'ang had any recommendations to make they should be immediately forwarded to the Throne without any obstruction.[66]

On January 29, 1898, K'ang submitted his most comprehensive memorial in which he outlined his reform plans. After reiterating the necessity for full reforms in order to save the country from peril, he proposed that, to silence the opposition of the conservatives, the Emperor should proclaim his determination to reform. All high officials in the government should be summoned before the Emperor and required either to pledge themselves to the faithful execution of the reform policies or to resign from their offices. People throughout the whole country and officials high and low should be permitted to submit their opinions directly to the Throne. A Committee on Institutions, consisting of twelve brilliant minds of the empire, should serve as a consultative organ to map out the master plans of reform for the approval of the Emperor. As the existing boards and ministries were inefficient and hostile to changes, twelve new departments should be established for the administration of the reform measures.[67]

On June 11 an edict was issued proclaiming the Imperial determination for reforms.[68] Five days later K'ang was given an audience in the Summer Palace. He dwelled upon the necessity of " complete and thorough reforms," and pointed out that reconstruction must begin with institutions and laws. The Emperor was captivated; he gave the junior official more than two and a half hours, an unprecedentedly long audience for any single official.[69]

Then began the reforms in earnest in the form of multifarious decrees issued from the Throne. The subjects they touched included the abolition of the traditional essay form examination; [70]

[66] *Tung Hua Hsü Lu,* 142/8; *K'ang Nien P'u,* II, 195.
[67] *Kuang Hsü Chêng Yao,* 24/16-17.
[68] *Tung Hua Hsü Lu,* 143/16.   [69] Chang Po-chêng, *op. cit.,* 26-28.
[70] Decree, K24/5/5, *Ch'ing Tê Tsung Shih Lu,* 419/5.

the establishment of an Imperial University;[71] the Westernization of the army;[72] the modernization of the provincial schools;[73] the abolition of superfluous temples and monasteries;[74] the inauguration of the Special Economic Examination;[75] the permission for junior officials and the common people to memorialize or petition the Throne directly;[76] the sending of students to study abroad;[77] the promotion of commerce, agriculture, mining, and railways under a national board;[78] the amalgamation of six sinecure ministries; and the abolition of the governorships of Kwangtung, Hupeh, and Yunnan, as well as the Director-Generalship of the Yellow River, the Tribute Rice Transport, and other offices pertaining to salt revenue.[79]

It can be readily noted that the decrees were not a coordinated whole. But this lack of planning was not entirely due to the fault or the ignorance of the reformers. Repeatedly K'ang had emphasized the importance of complete reforms and asked that a Committee on Institutions be established so that the whole matter could be carefully deliberated.[80] The opposition of the conservatives, however, rendered it impossible to have such an organ, and the reformers had to accept such reforms as they could. Moreover, in view of the gradual building up of the conservative forces, it was highly improbable that any thorough and comprehensive proposal would not have met a strong opposition.

In fact, the opposition was getting formidable as it was. When K'ang was given a conference with the Tsungli Yamen ministers on January 23, Jung Lu, the confidant of the Empress Dowager, had raised the question: " How could the laws of our ancestors be changed? "[81] On June 16, immediately before K'ang was given an audience, Jung Lu had impeached the reformer before the

[71] Decree, K24/5/8, ibid., 419/7a.　　　[72] Decree, K24/5/21, ibid., 420/7.
[73] Decree, K24/5/22, ibid., 420/9a.
[74] Liang Ch'i-ch'ao, Wu Hsü Chêng Pien Chi, p. 72.
[75] Decree, K24/5/23, Ch'ing Tê Tsung Shih Lu, 420/12b.
[76] Decree, K24/6/15, ibid., 421/15b.　　　[77] Decree, K24/6/15, ibid., 421/17.
[78] Decrees, K24/6/7, K24/6/15, K24/7/15, Tung Hua Hsü Lu, 146/9b; Ch'ing Tê Tsung Shih Lu, 423/6b.
[79] Decree, K24/7/14, Ch'ing Tê Tsung Shih Lu, 424/6b.
[80] Kuang Hsü Chêng Yao, 24/5.　　　[81] Chang Po-chêng, op. cit., 23.

Emperor.[82] During the audience the Emperor sadly complained to K'ang that he did not have a free hand.[83] The day before, Wêng T'ung-ho, the leading minister and tutor of the Emperor, was dismissed with disgrace and sent back to his native province.[84] The same day Jung Lu was appointed Viceroy of Chihli and commander of the northern armies. It was also announced that hereafter officers appointed or promoted to a high rank should appear before the Empress Dowager to express gratitude [85]—meaning that no high official could be appointed without the approval of the Empress Dowager.[86] All these measures were, of course, directed by the Empress Dowager and were designed to curb the power of the Emperor.

The crisis was at last precipitated by an incident in the Board of Rites at the beginning of September. Hsü Ying-k'uei, a president of the Board, had been noted for his hostility to the reformers. Now, ignoring a decree of the Emperor, he refused to forward to the Throne a memorial by Wang Chao, a junior secretary of the

82 *K'ang Nien P'u*, II, 200.   83 *Ibid.*, II, 198.

84 The role which Wêng T'ung-ho played in the reform movement has long been a controversial subject. In the edict issued on December 20, 1898 (*Ch'ing Tê Tsung Shih Lu*, 455/3a), it was charged that K'ang Yu-wei had been recommended to the Emperor by Wêng as being "one hundred times more capable than himself." Wêng denied this (Wêng T'ung-ho, *op. cit.*, 38/66b), and in his *Diary* it was recorded that on May 26 he had told the Emperor that he had no connection with K'ang and that he thought K'ang "unfathomable" (*ibid.*, 37/53a). Some writers believe that this entry was inserted later by Wêng to avoid further persecution by the Empress (Ch'ên Kung-lu, *Chung Kuo Chin Tai Shih* [A Modern History of China], Shanghai, 1935, p. 455). Others maintain that Wêng was at heart opposed to the reformers (Ch'ên Ch'iao: "Wu Hsü Chêng Pien Shih Fan Pien Fa Jên Wu Chih Chêng Chih Ssŭ Hsiang," in *Yen Ching Hsüeh Pao* [Yenching Journal of Chinese Studies], XXV [1939], 67). Whatever Wêng might have thought of K'ang's character, it is certain that the senior minister did help the reformers at the early stage. It was Wêng who asked K'ang to stay in Peking when the latter planned to leave for the south toward the end of 1897 (*K'ang Nien P'u*, 194). And it was Wêng who reported to the Emperor the recommendations made by K'ang in his conference with the Tsungli Yamen ministers (Chang Po-chêng, *op. cit.*, 23). But Wêng was a conservative; he probably could not go to the lengths the young reformers wanted. Indeed, had he stayed in power he might have served as a restraining force. See Wêng T'ung-ho, *op. cit.*, 38/66b; Chin Liang, *Ssŭ Ch'ao I Wên*, 21; Ping-ti Ho, "Wêng T'ung-ho and the 'One Hundred Days of Reform,'" *The Far Eastern Quarterly*, February, 1951.

85 *K'ang Nien P'u*, II, 192, 198.

86 Although the Empress Dowager returned the rule of the country to the Emperor in 1889, she still retained the ultimate power. For any important affair of state the Emperor had to request her approval.

Board. To serve as a warning that the Imperial decrees on reforms were not to be lightly ignored, as they had been ignored by the high officials both in and out of Peking,[87] the Emperor abruptly dismissed all the senior officials of the Board, including two Presidents and four Vice-Presidents.[88] This unexpected stroke, together with the appointment on September 5 of four young secretaries to the Grand Council practically to take over the duties of the Grand Councillors, stirred the conservatives to action. Rumors spread that the Imperial inspection of troops in Tientsin on October 19 would be the occasion on which the Emperor was to be deposed.[89] Indeed, the hostility of the Empress Dowager became so apparent that on September 13 the Emperor wrote a secret decree with his own hand and ordered Yang Jui, one of the newly appointed secretaries in the Grand Council, to deliver it to K'ang Yu-wei. It read as follows: [90]

In view of the present difficult situation, I have found that only reforms can save China, and that reforms can only be achieved through the discharge of the conservative and ignorant ministers and the appointment of the intelligent and brave scholars. Her Graceful Majesty the Empress Dowager, however, did not agree. I have tried again and again to persuade her, only to find Her Majesty more angry. You K'ang Yu-wei, Yang Jui, Lin Hsü, and T'an Ssŭ-t'ung should deliberate immediately to find some ways to save me. With extreme worries and earnest hopes. The Emperor.

Thus the reformers were confronted with an urgent problem and a grave danger. After reviewing the situation, K'ang Yu-wei believed that now only military force could save the Emperor his throne. Of all the generals in the country Yüan Shih-k'ai seemed to be the only person that could do the job. He had demonstrated his bravery and adroitness during his mission to Korea. He was now commanding the most modern army near Tientsin. Moreover, Yüan had joined the Ch'iang Hsüeh Hui, the reform society, in Peking at its inception and had shown an interest in reforms.[91]

[87] Liang Ch'i-ch'ao, Wu Hsü Chêng Pien Chi, pp. 33, 39.
[88] Ch'ing Tê Tsung Shih Lu, 424/17b.
[89] Liang Ch'i-ch'ao, Wu Hsü Chêng Pien Chi, p. 62.
[90] Ibid., p. 65.
[91] K'ang Nien P'u, II, 207.

On September 16 Yüan was summoned to an audience and immediately promoted to a high rank with express authority to train his troops.[92] On September 17 he was given another audience. The following night he was visited by T'an Ssŭ-t'ung, one of the reformers to whom the Emperor had entrusted the mission of resolving the situation. After pointing out the perilous position of the Emperor, T'an strongly urged that Yüan should use his troops to " protect the Emperor, to restore to His Majesty the great power, to eliminate the rebels, and to discipline the palaces." [93] Yüan agreed to execute the plot during the Imperial inspection of troops in Tientsin.[94]

But the hopes of the reformers were soon disappointed. Ambitious as he was, Yüan was a crafty man and had a keen sense of reality. He had under his command only 7,000 troops, while the armies under the command of Jung Lu numbered not less than 100,000.[95] Moreover, practically all the powerful officials, either in Peking or in the various provinces, were loyal to the Empress Dowager. The risks were too great; he decided to disclose the plot to Jung Lu, who immediately informed the Empress Dowager.

On September 19 the Empress Dowager, furious and indignant, hurried back to Peking from the Summer Palace. With characteristic determination she acted quickly. She imprisoned the Emperor in an island palace and resumed the government of the empire. Thus within a hundred days the reform movement ended in dismal failure.

The reformers, from the very beginning, faced formidable opposition. To the conservative literati it was simply heresy to advocate the overthrow of the traditional laws and customs and to substitute for them Western democracy.[96] The West, the con-

---

92 *Tung Hua Hsü Lu*, 148/1.

93 Liang Ch'i-ch'ao, *Wu Hsü Chêng Pien Chi*, p. 108.

94 *Ibid.* According to Yüan Shih-k'ai's *Diary*, T'an demanded an immediate promise. "As the clothing by his waist protruded and it seemed that some weapon was underneath," related Yüan, " I knew he would not leave without result. I therefore told him: ' In October the Imperial inspection will be held in Tientsin. At that time all troops will be assembled. If His Majesty issues an order, who dare disobey and what can not be accomplished? ' " Yüan Shih-k'ai, *Wu Hsü Jih Chi*, in Tso Shun-shêng, *Chung Kuo Chin Pai Nien Shih Tzŭ Liao Ch'u Pien.*

95 Yüan Shih-k'ai, *op. cit.*   96 *I Chiao Ch'ung Pien*, 5/6.

servatives maintained, was superior only in industry and weapons, not in culture and morals.[97] Even Chang Chih-tung, considered a liberal at the time, held that, while Western learning might be used for practical purposes, the classical learning of China must constitute the culture of the nation.[98] Moreover, the conservatives argued, there must be a " distinction between China and the barbarian world." If the Western systems were all adopted in China, the distinction would disappear, and China would no longer be China.[99]

In spite of their organization and propaganda, the reform party did not find a large following among the literati, particularly among the high-ranking officials, whether within Peking or in the various provinces. Indeed, the poor response became the more pronounced when the reformers undertook to abolish the traditional form of the civil service examinations and to sweep away the sinecure offices, thus depriving thousands of their government jobs or opportunities for an official career. The chief support for the reform came from the Emperor, a conscientious ruler trying desperately to save his country from peril. His intelligence saw that the country could only be saved by thorough and radical reforms, but his character lacked the iron will to carry the transformation through. As a politician he was merely a child in comparison with the Empress Dowager, whose cold calculation, quick decision, and unscrupulous maneuvers found no match in the country.

Had the reformers been able to win over the Empress Dowager, it has been surmised, perhaps they would have had a chance of success. The Empress Dowager, it is pointed out, was not opposed to reform; what she opposed was the change of the laws of the ancestors.[100] But the question is, How could there be any political reconstruction without changing the laws of the ancestors? Reforms without fundamental changes had been practiced since the

---

[97] *Ibid.*, 6/17.

[98] Chang Chih-tung, *Ch'üan Hsüeh P'ien* (Exhortation to Study), Part I, chap. 7; Part II, chap. 3.

[99] *I Chiao Ch'ung Pien*, 6/30.

[100] J. Yano, "Mo-so no hen po oyobi šeihen" (The Reform and the Coup d'État of 1898), *Shirin* (Kyoto), VIII, No. 2, 40.

reign of T'ung Chih and had proved sadly futile. The reform movement in 1898 under the leadership of K'ang Yu-wei was not intended to be a repetition of the earlier pattern. Its express aim was a full political and social reform. It would have been entirely contrary to its purpose if the precepts of the Empress Dowager had been accepted.

THE REACTION

The Empress Dowager was no fresh hand in the government of China. Since 1861 she had twice been regent of the country, first during 1861-73 when her son, Emperor T'ung Chih, was a minor, and then during 1875-89 when Emperor Kuang Hsü had not come of age. Of her intelligence there is no doubt, and of her strong will much has been written. Long years of experience in the Chinese Court had brought her the mastery of intrigue. She loved palaces and theatricals, and for these luxuries she once gave up the building of a strong navy.[101] A good actor herself, she was expert at playing on the emotions. She would gain the heart of her ministers with grace and charm, or frighten them with gusts of fury, or disarm them with tears.[102] With a quick perception of what could and what could not be done, she would readily accept what was inevitable.[103] Jealous of power, she could be very cruel toward her enemies.[104]

Upon resuming power in September, 1898, the Empress Dowager immediately set forth to eradicate the reforms. The various offices, lately abolished by the Emperor, were reinstated; the right of memorializing the Throne was again limited to high officials; modern schools in the various provinces were suspended; the traditional form of civil service examination was restored; the National Bureau of Agriculture, Industry, and Commerce was abolished; the journals were suspended and their editors arrested;

---

[101] Wêng T'ung-ho, *op. cit.*, 35/22a, 25b, 33/110b, 34/68b.
[102] See Ch'ü Hung-chi, *Shêng Tê Chi Lüeh; Ên Yü Chi Lüeh.*
[103] Chin Liang, *Ssŭ Ch'ao I Wên*, 10.
[104] Yün Yü-ting, *Ch'ung Ling Ch'uan Hsin Lu*, in Tso Shun-shêng, *Chung Kuo Chin Pai Nien Shih Tzŭ Liao Ch'u Pien*, pp. 456-57.

clubs and associations were strictly forbidden.[105] As to the reformers, " It is not our intention to extend the prosecution," the decree declared. Yet six were executed, and twenty were either exiled or dismissed. Thanks to the timely warning from the Emperor, K'ang Yu-wei managed to escape, as did his chief disciple Liang Ch'i-ch'ao.

There was still one big problem that the Empress Dowager had to deal with. Emperor Kuang Hsü was now deprived of power and practically imprisoned in an island palace. But the Empress Dowager was still not satisfied. The very thought that Kuang Hsü had plotted against her made her wrathful. She could not bear the thought that Kuang Hsü was still Emperor even though only in name. On September 23 the Emperor still performed ceremonies in the palace, but two days later there came a decree proclaiming that His Majesty had been ill since May and that " all medical treatments had proved ineffective." [106] Rumors became persistent that the Emperor would soon be deposed.[107] On January 9, 1899, a decree was issued, announcing the suspension of all Imperial ceremonies and banquets in the coming two months, although the Emperor was to appear before the Empress Dowager to pay his respects.[108] The illness of the Emperor was certainly not so critical that he was unable to perform his duties. But if he was to be got rid of, it was necessary to prepare the public for the eventuality.

The public, however, refused to be prepared this time. The inhabitants of Shanghai sent in a telegram to the effect that the sacred person of His Majesty should be protected and that the Empress Dowager should return the power to the Emperor.[109] The grand old statesman Liu K'un-i, Viceroy at Nanking, also voiced opposition. " The relationship between the Emperor and his ministers has already been fixed," he said, " while the mouths in and out

[105] Ch'ing Tê Tsung Shih Lu, 427/7-8, 11a; see also Liang Ch'i-ch'ao, Wu Hsü Chêng Pien Chi, pp. 87-89.
[106] Ch'ing Tê Tsung Shih Lu, 427/2b.
[107] Yeh Ch'ang-ch'ih, Yüan Tu Lu Jih Chi Ch'ao, 7/73a.
[108] Ch'ing Tê Tsung Shih Lu, 434/15b.
[109] Yün Yü-ting, op. cit.; Yeh Ch'ang-ch'ih, op. cit., 8/18.

of China cannot be easily silenced." [110] Indeed, the British Minister to China had conveyed semi-officially to the Tsungli Yamen " his firm conviction that should the Emperor die at this juncture of affairs, the effect produced among Western nations would be most disastrous to China." [111]

In view of this unfavorable response in and out of China, the Empress Dowager was cautious. [112] She postponed the scheme with regard to the Emperor and on January 24 resorted to the fateful measure of establishing P'u Chün, son of Prince Tuan, as heir apparent to the throne; [113] P'u Chün was to represent the Emperor in the performance of the Imperial ceremonies. This, of course, was intended as a step to the eventual disposal of the Emperor.

The declared purpose of the reformers was to save China from foreign aggression. Now that the reforms were eradicated, what measures would the reactionary party take to deal with the grave situation? Here the reactionaries' answer was unequivocal: a strong policy of no more concessions. They proposed to show that the right way to save China was not institutional reforms, but armed preparations.

Thus they applied themselves vigorously to military reorganization. On September 28 Jung Lu, Viceroy of Chihli, was transferred to Peking and made a member of the Grand Council, while Yü Lu was to succeed him as Viceroy of Chihli and Superintendent of Trade for the Northern Ports. The command of the military and naval forces attached to the Peiyang Administration was, however, retained by Jung Lu. [114] The following day Jung Lu was also directed to take charge of the Board of War. [115] Then on October 11 a decree was issued appointing Jung Lu Imperial High Commissioner and giving him command over the four army corps which constituted the defense forces of the metropolitan area, and which were severally commanded by General Sung Ch'ing, General Tung Fu-hsiang, General Nieh Shih-ch'êng, and General Yüan

[110] Hu Ssŭ-ching, *Kuo Wên Pi Ch'êng*, 3/2; Chang Chien, *Chang Chi Tzŭ Chiu Lu*, 7/5b, 7/7a.
[111] MacDonald to Salisbury, October 13, 1898, *China No. 1 (1899)*, p. 304.
[112] Yün Yü-ting, *op. cit.*   [113] *Ch'ing Tê Tsung Shih Lu*, 457/10.
[114] *Ibid.*, 427/4b.   [115] *Ibid.*, 427/8a.

Shih-k'ai.[116]   Already General Tung was directed to deploy his troops at strategic points along Chinwangtao, while the army of Sung Ch'ing was ordered to guard Shanhaikwan.[117]

On December 7 Jung Lu, upon whom now rested the whole responsibility of national defense, submitted his memorial on the reorganization of the northern armies. To weld them into a grand army and to ensure coordination of their operations, it was necessary, he proposed, that General Nieh's army be stationed at Lut'ai to guard the front, General Tung's army at Chichow and Tungchow to guard the rear, General Sung's army at Shanhaikwan to guard the east, and General Yüan's army near Tientsin to guard the right. To guard Peking itself, a Headquarters Army was to be formed under the direct command of Jung Lu. Thus under a unified command these five armies were to move in close collaboration with one another. As to the Anhui and local troops of Chihli, it was recommended that the former be used to guard the ports and forts while the latter would protect the various localities. For the financing of the new Headquarters Army, which was to cost 200,000 taels, it was recommended that that expense be met by drawing upon the 400,000 taels originally appropriated for the expansion of the modern army and also upon the funds contributed by the various provinces for the Foochow arsenal and dockyard.[118] Under a separate memorial, Jung Lu further recommended that Chihli, Hupeh, and the other provinces that had arsenals and small-arm factories within their jurisdictions be ordered to speed up their production and that military maps of the northern coast be prepared and distributed to the officers of the entire army. All these recommendations were promptly approved by Imperial decrees. On February 18 Yü Lu, Viceroy of Chihli, reported completion of the reorganization and deployment of the Anhui and local troops.[119] By June 27 the Headquarters Army of more than 10,000 was formed.[120] The five armies under Jung Lu now numbered about 60,000. If the 20,000 Anhui and local

116 *Ibid.*, 428/11b.   117 *Ibid.*, 427/3a, 9a.
118 *Tung Hua Hsü Lu*, 150/7b.   119 *Ch'ing Tê Tsung Shih Lu*, 444/4b.
120 *Ibid.*, 445/7b.

troops are added to this figure, the forces amassed in the metropolitan area totaled more than 80,000 men.[121]

Nor did the Imperial Government neglect the navy. The Peiyang Squadron in the north was augmented by five warships and
a number of torpedo boats.[122] On May 23 the Northern and
Southern Squadrons were ordered to drill together, so that they
could have close collaboration in case of emergency.[123]

As to the other provinces, repeated decrees were issued, directing
the authorities concerned to push on military reorganization at top
speed.[124] Special attention was given to three areas: the Yangtze
Valley, the Huai-Hsü area, and the Three Eastern Provinces (Manchuria). The Yangtze Valley, in addition to its important position
in international politics, was a rich source of revenue. To rearm
China, a huge budget was necessary. It was for the dual purpose
of strengthening the defense of the Yangtze and increasing the
national revenues that Kang I, a member of the Grand Council,
was appointed Imperial High Commissioner to investigate the
southern provinces. He started his journey down the Yangtze
in May, and soon found that the armed forces there were far from
being sufficient and that the forts were not adequate for their
purpose.[125] Decrees were promptly issued to direct the authorities
of the Yangtze provinces to rectify the defects. As to the increase
of provincial assessments, the High Commissioner went into such
sources as *likin*, salt revenue, customs, and land tax.[126] He gained
from the foreign press the title of " Lord High Extortioner," [127]
but his work was highly commended by the Empress Dowager as
" stopping extortions and turning to the Imperial exchequer funds
which would otherwise have gone to fill the pockets of provincial
officials." [128] In Nanking and other parts of Kiangsu he increased

---

[121] *Ibid.*, 414/4b.   [122] Decree, K25/3/8, *ibid.*, 440/10b.
[123] Decree, K25/4/4, *ibid.*, 442/14b.
[124] Decrees, K24/11/7, K24/12/4, K25/1/12, K25/2/7, K25/3/22, K25/4/6, *ibid.*,
433/7b, 435/5a, 437/8, 439/7b, 441/6b, 442/6a.
[125] *Ibid.*, 445/1-2.
[126] Memorial by Kang I, K25/5/16, *ibid.*, 445/9a.
[127] See Report by Mr. Mayers, *China No. 1* (1900), p. 352.
[128] *Ch'ing Tê Tsung Shih Lu*, 447/6b.

the annual contribution by 1,200,000 taels, and in Kwangtung by 1,600,000 taels.[129]

The area between the Huai River and Hsüchow was important not only as a communication center between the northern and the southeastern provinces but also because of its strategic position. Close to Shantung and Honan, it stood as the " first gate " to the capital area from the southeast. A strong army stationed there would serve as a reserve that could speedily answer a call either from the north or from the south. For this purpose it was directed on August 30 that an army was to be organized under the command of Jung Lu. The expenses were to be met from the increased revenues which Kang I obtained from Kiangsu.[130]

As to the Three Eastern Provinces, a decree was issued on December 29, 1898, proclaiming that in view of their " proximity to a strong neighbor," a strong army must be quickly trained. The Tartar Generals of the provinces were ordered to exert their utmost to achieve the purpose.[131] In September, 1899, General Ch'ang Shun was appointed to inspect the military reorganization in Manchuria,[132] and in November Li Ping-hêng was sent to the three provinces with a mission similar to that of Kang I.[133]

While all the military reorganizations were energetically pushed, the foreign policy of China took a stiff turn. In March, 1899, a party of three Germans was attacked by the villagers near Jihchao in Shantung. The villagers had already been beaten off, but the German authorities dispatched troops to the area, burned to the ground two villages, and seized the town and held it.[134] Upon receiving the reports, the Chinese Government, while instructing its Minister at Berlin to lodge with the German Government a strong protest against the German action and to assure it of the Chinese intention to protect the Germans,[135] ordered Yü Hsien, Governor of Shantung, to send an armed force to the area at top

[129] Ibid., 452/5a; Kuang Hsü Chêng Yao, 25/25-26.
[130] Ch'ing Tê Tsung Shih Lu, 448/18.
[131] Ibid., 443/2a.   [132] Ibid., 448/21b.   [133] Ibid., 452/12a.
[134] Conger to Hay, April 17, 1899, Foreign Relations of the United States, 1899 (Washington: Government Printing Office, 1901), p. 168.
[135] Decree, K25/2/29, Ch'ing Chi Wai Chiao Shih Liao, 137/14a.

speed. The Governor was directed not to act with undue haste, but at the same time not to be intimidated. He was to deploy his troops for any eventuality.[136] On April 11 the Governor was again instructed not to " accede unendingly to the aggressive demands of the Germans," although he should avoid starting hostilities himself.[137] As the Germans were withdrawn in time, no armed conflict ensued. But it was clearly indicated in this case that, although the Chinese Government was desirous of maintaining peaceful relations with the Powers, it would not hesitate to offer armed resistance if foreign aggression could not otherwise be warded off.

Then there came another case where the firm policy of the Chinese Government found unequivocal expression. In February, 1899, Italy demanded of China the cession of a naval station on Sanmen Bay in the Chekiang Province. The Italian minister followed the demand with an ultimatum, but to the surprise of the world the Chinese Government was resolute in its refusal. China was ready for war, if war was necessary, to put a stop to the unending nibbling at her territory by the foreign Powers. Liu K'un-i, the Viceroy at Nanking, was ordered to resist any landing by the Italian forces. The Imperial Court gave him a free hand in case of emergency, and he was to dispatch all forces to the area at once so as to seize the initiative.[138] A similar decree was sent to the Governor of Chekiang, who was directed to attack, " without hesitation but with all might," any Italian forces who would land to occupy the Chinese territory.[139] In face of the determination of the Chinese Government, Italy at last abandoned her claim and recalled her envoy. For the first time since the Sino-Japanese War, the strong policy of China scored a resounding success.

The success must have heartened the Imperial Court, for on November 21 there was issued the famous decree to the various provinces in which the viceroys and governors were told not to harbor any thought of peace in case unacceptable demands were presented by aggressive Powers. The decree read as follows:

136 Decree, K25/2/26, *Ch'ing Tê Tsung Shih Lu*, 439/24b.
137 Decree, K25/3/2, *ibid.*, 440/3a.
138 Decree, K25/4/8, *Ch'ing Chi Wai Chiao Shih Liao*, 138/26.   139 *Ibid.*, 138/27a.

The present situation is becoming daily difficult. The various Powers cast upon us looks of tiger-like voracity, hustling each other in their endeavors to be the first to seize upon our innermost territories. In view of China's present financial and military strength, we surely would not start any war on our part. But there may occur incidents in which we are forced to face the situation. Should the strong enemies become aggressive and press us to consent to certain things which we can never accept, we have no alternative but to rely upon the justice of our cause, the knowledge of which will strengthen our resolve and steel us to a united front against our aggressors. Recently the viceroys and governors of the various provinces, when facing important international events, often have the word " peace " in their mind with the result that they were not the least prepared. This persistent habit is the worst kind of disloyalty to the Throne and the worst kind of betrayal to the country. It is our special command therefore that, should we find ourselves so hard pressed by circumstances that nothing short of war would settle matters, there will be no possible chance that we would immediately negotiate for peace after the war has been declared. It behooves our viceroys and governors throughout the whole empire to unite forces and act together without distinction or particularism of jurisdictions, to exhort and encourage their officers and soldiers to defeat the enemy and score victory. Never should the word " peace " fall from the mouths of our high officials, nor should they harbor it for a moment in their breasts. With such a country as ours, with her vast area, stretching out for several tens of thousands of *li,* her immense natural resources and her hundreds of millions of inhabitants, if all would prove their loyalty to their Emperor and love of their country, what indeed is there to fear from any strong invader? Let us not think of making peace, nor rely solely upon diplomatic maneuvers.[140]

Thus the foreign policy of China was set. It was not the intention of the Imperial Government to seek war with other countries, but it was its firm determination that China would not shrink from war if the wanton aggression of the Powers could not be stopped otherwise. It was under such strong policy of the Imperial Government that the Boxer uprisings broke out in Shantung and Chihli.

[140] *Ch'ing Tê Tsung Shih Lu,* 543/5a.

2

The Boxer Movement: Its
Genesis and Development

THE POLITICAL AND SOCIAL SETTING

THE REACTIONARIES were firmly installed in the government after the *coup d'état*. They energetically pushed forward the program of military reorganization and were equally energetic in trying to increase revenues badly needed for the rearmament programs. According to the report of the Board of Finance, submitted to the Throne in June, 1899, the expenditures for the year amounted to more than 90,000,000 taels, while the revenues totaled about 80,000,000 taels.[1] It was to make up the deficit that Kang I was sent to the south and Li Ping-hêng to the Three Eastern Provinces.[2] It was for the same purpose that the China Merchants' Steam Navigation Company and the Telegraph Service were required to return a certain percentage of their surplus profits to the national exchequer.[3] Yü Lu, the Viceroy of Chihli, was said to have contributed 300,000 taels, of which the K'aip'ing Mines and the customs *taotai* had to pay a large part.[4] Other provinces were required to send in similar contributions. When the Chinese officials were thus squeezed by their superiors, they did not pay out of their own pockets but passed on the assessment to their subordinates, who in turn had to extort it from the people.

But the people at that time were far from able to pay, since famine, flood, and banditry had added to ordinary hardships during the years 1898-99. In Shantung and Chihli, in particular, flood and famine caused poverty and hunger for thousands of

---

[1] *Ch'ing Tê Tsung Shih Lu*, 444/9a.　　　[2] See above, pp. 29, 30.
[3] *Ch'ing Tê Tsung Shih Lu*, 445/9a.
[4] Ch'ên Kung-lu, *Chung Kuo Chin Tai Shih* (A Modern History of China [Shanghai: Commercial Press, 1935]), pp. 496-97.

people. In January, 1898, it was reported that 48 counties and districts in Shantung were suffering from famine.[5] In August the Yellow River flooded two areas, inundating hundreds of villages.[6] Indeed, the devastation was so great that in practically all places south of the river no seeds could be sown in the spring.[7] What made the situation more unbearable was the corruption and inefficiency with which the local authorities handled the relief.[8] People living in districts a short distance away from the provincial capital received hardly any aid,[9] although the Imperial Government had appropriated large sums of money, in one instance to the amount of over 200,000 taels, and directed large quantities of food to be shipped to the area for relief purposes.[10] The situation was so desperate that large numbers of refugees migrated to Honan.[11] Then in 1899, because of famine and a locust plague, the autumn harvest in Shantung was a failure, so much so that the price of food mounted beyond reach for most people.[12] About the same time famine invaded Chihli, particularly the metropolitan area.[13] The Imperial Court was so disturbed that first Prince Tuan and then Prince Kung (P'u Wei) were appointed to burn incense at the Takao Temple, and monks and priests were employed to pray before the altars.[14]

The social restlessness was intensified and complicated by international factors. Foreign aggression was carried far and wide into the country, which, in the opinion of many, was threatened with partition. The reform party in its publications called the attention of the people to the grave situation caused by foreign aggression. On the other hand, the reactionaries charged that the reform

---

[5] *Ch'ing Tê Tsung Shih Lu*, 414/2b.

[6] *Ibid.*, 423/7a. "In the autumn of 1898 it was officially reported that 34 counties had been flooded in whole or in part by the remorseless Yellow River, which one of its Emperors alike historically and prophetically denominated 'China's Sorrow.' The inundated area was estimated to be at least 2,500 square miles containing perhaps 1,500 villages. The whole population of the devastated regions was supposed to be between a million and a million and a half." Arthur H. Smith, *China in Convulsion* (New York: Fleming H. Revell, 1901), I, 162.

[7] *Ch'ing Tê Tsung Shih Lu*, 437/9a.

[8] *Ibid.*, 435/7a.   [9] *Ibid.*, 436/10b.   [10] *Ibid.*, 452/5a.

[11] *Ibid.*, 434/9a.   [12] *Ibid.*, 450/14a.   [13] *Ibid.*, 450/1b.

[14] *Ibid.*, 450/3a; 451/1a.

movement was under foreign influence which aimed at destroying China's unique culture. As a matter of fact, the people themselves had ample experience of what imperialism meant, particularly in the northern provinces where the Powers had their leased territories. The German authorities in Kiaochow would march their troops into the Chinese territory at the slightest provocation by the people and burn villages to the ground.[15] In south Manchuria, when the Chinese refused to comply with the Russian demands upon their land near Port Arthur, the Russians opened fire, killing 96 and wounding 123.[16] It is not surprising that the Chinese people regarded the foreigners as barbarians who could not be reasoned with and who knew only the language of force.

But it was the conflicts between the Chinese Christians and the village people that often led to serious consequences. Ever since the treaty of 1858 which permitted Christian missionaries, whether Protestants or Roman Catholics, to spread the gospel, popular hostility had steadily grown. The Chinese Christians were forbidden by their religion to perform any ceremonies that were regarded as idolatrous, or to participate in any of the community festivals or amusements where there was a suggestion of honoring false gods. This refusal to conform to the custom of the country was regarded by the Chinese villagers as an unpardonable offense. Their displeasure was the more stimulated because Christian converts, if they were not willing, could not be forced to contribute to the community festivals.[17] Then there was interference by the missionaries, particularly the Roman Catholics, in the lawsuits of their converts. The clergy would exert pressure upon the local magistrate, who, fearful of the serious consequences to his career if the case was taken up by the foreigners with his superiors, would settle it quietly in favor of the Christians, regardless of the merits

[15] See *Foreign Relations of the United States*, 1899 (Washington: Government Printing Office, 1901), p. 41.

[16] Edict, K24/8/24, *Ch'ing Tê Tsung Shih Lu*, 428/10a.

[17] See *I Wu Shih Mo* (Barbarian Affairs from Beginning to End), "T'ung Chih," 2/45-46, 5/11-12; Sir Robert Hart, *These from the Land of Sinim* (London: Chapman & Hall, 1901), p. 6; Smith, *op. cit.*, I, 34-35.

of the case.[18] As a result, the Roman Catholic Church was believed to be a shelter for bad characters, who went there to evade
the laws of the country and who, under the protection of the
missionaries, bullied their countrymen. This feeling, together with
the tales that the orphanages were secret places where children
were mutilated for the purposes of alchemy and that Chinese
women were lured into the Church buildings to be raped,[19] was a
constant source of disturbances in various parts of the country
against the missionaries and converts.

It was under such social restlessness and antiforeign sentiment
that the Boxer riots broke out in the years 1898-99.

STEIGER'S THEORY OF ORIGINS

Before going into the history of the Boxers or I Ho Ch'üan, as
the Chinese called them, let us examine the theories on their origins.
Of these theories two in particular deserve our attention. The
older explanation of the origins was given by Lao Nai-hsüan, a
magistrate in Chihli, who, in a pamphlet published in 1899, maintained that the I Ho Ch'üan—literally, Righteous Harmony Fists—
was a secret society which had been associated with the White
Lotus Society, the Eight Diagram Sect, the Red Fist Society, and
similar heretical and revolutionary organizations. It was suppressed in 1808, but it maintained an obscure existence in many
districts of Chihli and Shantung. Lao's work we shall discuss in
the next section. The other theory was proposed by George Nye
Steiger, who in his *China and the Occident* combated Lao's explanation and asserted that the Boxers were " volunteer militia," recruited " in response to the express commands of the Throne." [20]
The correct name for the organization, he said, " was ' I-ho Tuan,'

<hr>

[18] Memorial by Li Ping-hêng, K22/6/24, Li Ping-hêng, *Li Chung Chieh Kung
Tsou I*, 12/1-20.

[19] Tsêng Kuo-fan, *Tsêng Wên Chêng Kung Tsou Kao* (Memorials of Tsêng Kuo-
fan), 35/29-33; Smith, *op. cit.*, I, 59.

[20] George Nye Steiger, *China and the Occident* (New Haven: Yale University Press,
1927), p. 134. The idea that the Boxers were local militia or legal organizations for
local defense had been espoused by early writers such as Sir Robert Hart, in his *These
from the Land of Sinim*, p. 4, and Ku Hung-ming, in his *Papers from a Viceroy's
Yamen* (Shanghai: Mercury, 1901), p. 17. It was, however, Steiger who presented the
theory in a systematic exposition.

'Righteous and Harmonious Band,' or 'Militia'; the substitution of 'Chuan' for 'Tuan,' as the third character in the name of the organization, was simply a pun which was perpetrated by its opponents."[21] The Boxers were "lawful bodies," he asserted, although they later absorbed the members of secret societies like Ta Tao Hui (Big Knife Society).[22]

A close examination of Steiger's book will show that his explanation is not founded upon sufficient evidence. His attempted refutation of Lao's theory was based upon some assumptions which are far from being conclusive. "It is impossible to believe," he said, "that a secret society, holding heretical doctrines and known to have revolutionary aims, would deliberately go out of its way to institute a campaign of bitter hostility against Christian missions, and thus stir up against itself the activities of the officials and the complaints of foreign diplomats. Such procedure would have been contrary to all that is known of the history of the country."[23] Yet just a year before the emergence of the Boxers, the Ta Tao Hui, a secret society in the same province of Shantung, deliberately showed its hostility against Christian missions by killing two German priests. Indeed, now that the reactionaries were in power and a strong foreign policy was adopted, it might well have been the thought of the secret societies that this was a good time to conciliate the officials and the public by unfurling a popular banner of antiforeignism.

The quotation from a report of Dr. Arthur H. Smith, a missionary in Shantung, that in some villages he had found no connection between a secret society called "Six Times Sect" and the I Ho Ch'üan[24] is certainly no evidence that there was no connection between the Boxers and other secret societies in other districts. Similarly, the lack of reference by Dr. H. D. Porter, another missionary in Shantung, to any secret society in his description of the Boxer bands[25] cannot be taken as a solid basis for Mr. Steiger's theory. Quotations from some missionaries who happened to write what they casually observed are not sufficient to determine the

[21] Steiger, op. cit., p. 134.   [22] Ibid., pp. 130, 141.
[23] Ibid., p. 129.   [24] Ibid., p. 131.   [25] Ibid., p. 132.

character of a widespread movement. Yet it was upon the basis of such evidence that Steiger drew his conclusion. And his statement was as positive as it could be. " The so-called Boxers," he wrote, " were a Tuan, or volunteer militia; they were recruited, in response to the express commands of the Throne, in precisely those provinces whose loyalty was most to be trusted. . . . Whatever the Boxer movement may have become—or may have threatened to become—by the spring of 1900, it was, in the beginning, neither a revolutionary nor an heretical organization; it was a lawful and loyal volunteer militia, whose existence was fully justified by the reasonable apprehensions of the government and the people." [26]

If the I Ho Ch'üan were local militia, it is necessary to explain why they took on such miraculous formulae as were characteristic of the secret and heretical societies. Their charms and incantations, their intricate ritual, and their belief in certain supernatural powers which would render them invulnerable and invincible, all savored heavily of heresy. It is interesting to see how Steiger tried to explain them away:

The decrees of the Empress Dowager, in which she urged the development and improvement of the local militia, had repeatedly ordered that these volunteer bodies be given modern armament and drill. Since the arsenals of the Empire could hardly produce modern weapons in sufficient quantities to supply the needs of the regular imperial and provincial troops, no modern weapons were, for the time at least, available for the militia organizations, which continued to be armed with swords, spears, and a few firearms of the most primitive sort. But although it was impossible to furnish the Tuan with Mauser rifles, it was necessary to comply with the commands of the Throne; this could be achieved by drilling the militia according to the manual adopted for the modern armed troops. Squad and company drill, the " goose-steps " and the " setting-up exercises," which had been introduced into the training of the Peiyang Army by the German and Japanese military instructors, were, therefore, taught to the Tuan and were diligently practiced by them as a means whereby the defenders of the Empire might become equal in prowess to the forces of the " outside Barbarians." It requires little exercise of the imagination to visualize the metamorphosis by which these physical exercises became, in the mind of the Chinese peasant, magic rites which

[26] Ibid., p. 146.

would confer supernatural strength and invulnerability upon all who religiously performed them.[27]

It requires, indeed, a far stretch of imagination to suppose that the Chinese peasants would mistake the Western drills for magic rites. The rites practiced by the Boxers were the rites practiced by the Chinese secret societies for ages. The taking up of them amply testifies to the influence of these societies on the Boxers, if not indeed the metamorphosis from these societies to the Boxers.

The only positive basis given by Steiger for his assertion that the Boxers were lawful and loyal bodies was the Imperial decrees of November 5 and December 31, 1898, ordering the organization of the local militia. To evaluate this assertion and its basis, it is necessary to examine not only the decrees concerned but also the history and functions of the militia. It is only when the nature of these local bodies is clearly understood that the relationship between them and the Boxers can be viewed in the right perspective.

As far as the Ch'ing Dynasty was concerned, the t'uan lien, or militia, had been widely used in the fifties when the T'aip'ing Rebellion swept up from Kwangsi to Hunan. Tsêng Kuo-fan, who was most responsible for crushing the Rebellion, began his military career as the commandant of the militia in his native province.[28] In 1886, when China had concluded a peace treaty with France but was still apprehensive of French ambitions in the provinces bordering Indo-China, it was recommended by a Hanlin official that to save money militia should be organized in Kwangsi to supplement the standing army. The matter was referred to Li Ping-hêng, then Governor of Kwangsi, who, after some investigation, opposed the idea. The militia, he wrote in a memorial, could only be used to protect the villages, or at most to support the army at a distance. They could not be dispatched for " distant operations," and the experience toward the end of the T'aip'ing Rebellion showed that their morale could become so low that they would " quit their posts and disperse." Moreover, " troops to be useful must be intensively trained." The militia, who were drilled twice a month, could hardly be expected to confront a strong enemy.

[27] Ibid., p. 143.   [28] Hsieh Fu-ch'êng, Yung An Pi Chi, 2/7b,

The recommendation of the Hanlin official, concluded the Governor, was therefore " impracticable." [29]

In 1898 the militia was viewed with great favor by the reform party. In his petition to the Throne in 1896, K'ang Yu-wei had advocated the organization of the militia.[30] One able-bodied male out of every twenty would be drafted and trained in camps at times when they were not occupied with farming. The same theme was dwelt upon in an article published in a reform journal in 1898.[31] In September, when the reform movement was well under way, Chang Yin-huan, for some time Minister to Britain and later exiled because of his connection with the reform party, submitted a memorial on the subject. He recommended that the militia system, rather than Western conscription, be adopted. If the militia could be trained by turns, he maintained, they would have practically all the advantages of universal military training. The recommendations were promptly adopted and an Imperial decree was issued on September 5, ordering all the provinces to organize the militia along the lines of Chang's suggestions within the period of three months, except in Kwangsi which was to comply with the order within one month.[32] Two weeks later the *coup d'état* occurred and the reformers were swept away, but the idea of militia training survived.

On October 18, 1898, in response to the Imperial decree, Liu K'un-i, Viceroy at Nanking, submitted his memorial. He did not think the universal military training of the West was practicable for China at the time but that the militia, being a Chinese organization with a long history, could be revived. Moreover, if trained in a military manner, the militia could be used not only for local defense but also for distant operations against possible enemies.[33] The memorial came at a time when the reactionaries rallying around the Empress Dowager were studying military reorganization for the purpose of resisting further aggression by the Powers. The idea of organizing the militia appealed to them, and on No-

---

[29] I i Ping-hêng, *op. cit.*, 3/28.
[30] K'ang Yu-wei, *Nan Hai Hsien Shêng Ssŭ Shang Shu Chi*, 26 ff.
[31] *Hsiang Pao Wên Pien*, II, 21.   [32] *Ch'ing Tê Tsung Shih Lu*, 424/20ᴀ.
[33] Decree, K24/9/4, *Tung Hua Hsü Lu*, 149/2a.

vember 5 the Empress Dowager issued the first decree concerning the militia. It read as follows:

There has never been a time when the relations between the sovereign and people could safely forgo a good understanding and a united effort. It is of course for the local magistrates to initiate measures in all questions of local importance, but no policy can be successfully carried out unless the gentry and the common people cooperate with the Government. If we consider, for example, the question of food-supply reserves, the organization of pao chia [constables], and the drilling of militia, they may seem ordinary matters, but if they are efficiently handled, they may be of great value to the nation. For by reserving grain for the lean years, the people's livelihood is secured, and similarly by the organization of the pao chia, protection is afforded against bandits. As to the militia, they only require to undergo regular training for a sufficient period to know the military tactics; they then could be relied upon in case of emergency. We therefore decree that these matters be started first in Chihli, Mukden, and Shantung and then in other provinces. Generals, viceroys, and governors of the various provinces must advise the gentry and common people, so that these measures may be carried out with the utmost energy. . . .[34]

It is not easy to say, by merely reading the words of the decree, what exactly was the purpose of the organization of the militia. Were they to be used for the defense of the country against foreign enemies, or were they drilled for internal protection? The decree was couched in vague terms: it spoke of emergency without specifying what kind, and the militia were named along with the constables. Considering, however, the original proposal of Chang Yin-huan and the more recent memorial of Liu K'un-i, who pointed out that " if successful, the militia could be dispatched to distant places when necessary," [35] the use of the militia for national defense might well have been within the thought of the Imperial Court. But if that was its intention, it soon found great difficulties. The lack of modern weapons, necessary for any armed engagement with foreign troops, and the reluctance of the villagers to be sent away from their home villages were formidable obstacles. It was with these obstacles in view that a decree was issued on June 19, 1899, explaining more specifically the purpose of the militia.

[34] Ch'ing Tê Tsung Shih Lu, 149/16a. [35] Tung Hua Hsü Lu, 149/2a.

"The militia," it said, "are organized primarily for cleaning out the internal bandits: they were not to be dispatched far away to fight the enemies." There was no need to buy modern weapons, for the locally made guns would be sufficient for the purpose. The viceroys and governors were enjoined not to make too much fuss about the matter.[36]

Whether originally intended for internal protection or external defense, the militia were not organized for antiforeign purposes. To defend the country against foreign aggression was one thing; to create riots against the foreigners was quite another. Although the Imperial Government was zealous in strengthening national defense, it was far from wanting trouble with the foreign Powers, not in the years 1898-99 at least. A careful examination of the various decrees and reports of the provinces on the subject, which were numerous in the *Ch'ing Tê Tsung Shih Lu* (True Records of the Ch'ing Dynasty, Reign of Kuang Hsü), will show no evidence that the Imperial Government had any antiforeign designs in connection with the organization of the militia. On the contrary, the Acting Governor of Kiangsi Province spoke of the militia along with the protection of churches,[37] while Chang Chih-tung, Viceroy at Hankow, actually detailed the militia to guard the churches and to protect the missionaries who traveled out of the cities.[38]

The militia were organized under the supervision of the local governments. Usually a headquarters of the militia was set up in the capital of the province, with branch offices in the localities. The officers of the headquarters as well as the branch offices were selected either by, or with the approval of, the local governments.[39] Under these circumstances it is hard to see how the militia could be the Boxers. The purposes of the two were different: the one was organized for the maintenance of order and peace in their localities, the other for stirring riots against the Chinese converts and the missionaries. Their organizations were different: the one under the sponsorship of the local governments, the other within

---

[36] Decree, K25/5/2, *Ch'ing Tê Tsung Shih Lu,* 444/3a.
[37] Decree, K24/10/17, *ibid.,* 432/7b.
[38] Decree, K25/2/13, *Tung Hua Hsü Lu,* 152/14a.
[39] *Ibid.,* 154/14a; *Ch'ing Tê Tsung Shih Lu,* 439/14.

the control of the secret societies. The militia were a legal body organized in accordance with the Imperial decrees; the Boxers were rioters to be suppressed by government troops. The Boxer societies were not formed in response to the Imperial decrees, for before November 5, 1898, the date of the first decree ordering the organization of the militia, they had already existed and operated.[40] The fact that the local authorities and the Imperial Government repeatedly attempted to place the Boxers within the militia so as to control them more effectively should prove that the two were different entities.[41]

THE VIEWS OF LAO NAI-HSÜAN

The theory of Lao Nai-hsüan should not be dismissed lightly, for the author was not only a scholar but also a competent official with a firsthand knowledge of the Boxer movement. He had been magistrate of Wuch'iao, a district in southeastern Chihli, for ten years. In June, 1898, after serving in another district for two years, he was transferred back to Wuch'iao. It was about this time that the Boxers began to be active in southeastern Chihli. Their activities drew his attention, and he made a study of their origins. In September, 1899, he published his famous treatise *I Ho Ch'üan Chiao Mên Yüan Liu K'ao* (Study of the Origins of the Boxer Sect). He found that the I Ho Ch'üan was a branch of the Eight Diagram Sect, whose early leader Kao Shêng-wên, a native of Honan Province, had been executed in 1771. His descendants and disciples, however, survived and together with other secret societies continued to operate in the provinces of Honan, Shantung, and Kiangnan. In 1808 a decree was issued by Emperor Chia Ch'ing, ordering strict suppression of the secret societies and severe punishment of their leaders. In spite of this, however, it was reported in 1818 that the I Ho sect spread to Chihli and practiced the " I Ho Boxing." Many of its members were again executed, but the Society maintained an obscure exist-

[40] See below, p. 47.
[41] *Ch'ing Tê Tsung Shih Lu*, 418/2b; *Chih Tung Tien Ts'un*, 1/11.

ence in many districts in Chihli and Shantung and ultimately emerged in 1898 as an active anti-Christian organization.[42]

Lao based his statement upon the Chinese documents which he found in the *Jén Tsung Jui Huang Ti Shêng Hsün* (Edicts of Emperor Chia Ch'ing).[43] It should be noted that in those documents the exact name of I Ho Ch'üan appeared and that the practice of boxing was reported as a feature of the secret society in 1815. Lao also supported his exposition with current evidence. The Boxer monk Wu Hsiu, captured in Chingchou, and another Boxer leader, Ta Kuei, captured in Kuch'êng, all admitted belonging to the Eight Diagram Sect. Other Boxers in the several other districts of Chihli also declared their allegiance to the secret society.[44] Furthermore, the rules of the Boxer Society were typically those of the secret societies; for instance, those who joined the Society must strictly obey orders, the violation of which would be punished by execution and even extermination of whole families.[45]

The theory of Lao Nai-hsüan has been well accepted in China, for besides the same name and the same practice of boxing, the charms and incantations of the Boxers clearly indicated their connection with the secret societies. It is quite common that heretical societies, in spite of frequent suppressions by the government, continued to exist. It had been the traditional policy of the Ch'ing Dynasty with respect to these societies to execute only the chieftains, but let the followers disperse. This was called the policy of magnanimity, and magnanimity was considered good government. In fact, the secret societies, with their long history, usually infiltrated deep into the various levels of society. If an extensive purge had been undertaken, a very great number of people would have been involved. Whatever the motive, this policy never did exterminate the secret sects, with the result that many of them maintaind their existence for ceuturies.[46]

---

[42] Lao Nai-hsüan, *I Ho Ch'üan Chiao Mên Yüan Liu K'ao*, 1-5.   [43] Book 99.

[44] Lao Nai-hsüan, *op. cit.*, " Postscript."   [45] *Ibid.*

[46] See J. Yano, "Shin cho no sho han ran to Shina han ran no seishitsu" (The Characteristics of Rebellions in China, Especially under the Ch'ing Dynasty), *Shirin* (Kyoto), XI (1926), 24-42.

It is difficult to say to what extent the Boxer movement was initiated by the heretical sects. For if they played an important role in organizing the movement, their illegal status made it impossible for them to reveal themselves. There are no records as to exactly how and when the I Ho Ch'üan was first organized. Our evidence indicates that they began as volunteer associations. It is quite possible that the secret societies operated in the background. But whoever the initiator may have been, it is beyond argument that the Boxer movement was dominated by the heretical elements. This of course did not prevent the movement from becoming a popular front against the foreigners and the Christians. That was a time when the Chinese hatred of the foreigners was intense and widespread. The Boxers' slogan of "upholding the Ch'ing Dynasty and exterminating the foreigners" caught the imagination of the people, and the antiforeign sentiment of the people must at the same time have inspired the direction of the Boxers. It is difficult to trace exactly the stimulation and reaction in this kind of interaction, for the development of the Boxers was as multifarious as it was spontaneous. At any rate the movement soon galvanized the populace of the northern provinces and spread like wildfire. It absorbed various elements of society and infiltrated various organizations, whether secret or official. At last it recruited the high officials and princes of the blood in the Imperial Court and thus precipitated the great catastrophe. The history of the Boxers as traced below will bear out these generalizations.

THE BOXERS IN SHANTUNG

Shantung, the native province of Confucius, had been noted for the honor and respect accorded to the sages and their teaching. But it had also been the place where foreign aggression showed itself most clearly. The seizure of Kiaochow by the Germans and the occupation of Weihaiwei, first by the Japanese and then by the British, together with the arrogance of the German troops, intensified the hatred of the villagers against foreigners. Then the frequent overflowing of the Yellow River, devastating an area as wide as 30 to 40 counties and depriving as many as over a million people of food and shelter, made life so hard that secret societies flourished and banditry became rampant. Under such conditions it was easy for the discontented to vent their wrath upon the foreigners or the Chinese Christians who were regarded as just as bad as the " foreign devils."

Early in July, 1896, the secret societies were reported active in Shantung. The following memorial by Li Ping-hêng, then Governor of the province, is interesting in that it sheds light not only on the policy of the government but also on the nature of the societies:

The Big Sword Society is the same as the heretical sect of the Golden Bell. It has a long history and, in spite of its suppression by the local officials, continues to exist. Last year, as the coast was not peaceful, the people, believing that the sect was invulnerable against guns and cannons, flocked to it, with the result that its members spread everywhere. Now, while the stupid consider it a means of protecting their lives and families, the dishonest seize the opportunity to indulge in their violence. And when incited by the outside bandits, they would assemble and create riots. If, before having an opportunity to disperse, they were executed indiscriminately, there is danger that they would become desperados and create greater disturbances. . . . The riots now stirred up by the secret societies have their origin in the conflicts between the people and the Christians. . . . The reason they could not live together peacefully is that the Christians, with the support and protection of the missionaries, bullied and oppressed the common people. . . . The local officials, afraid of incurring foreign hostility, usually settle the cases in favor of the Christians. Feeling that their grievances cannot be redressed through the local authorities, the people resort to self-defense, and the result is riots and burning of the churches and chapels.[47]

Li therefore recommended a policy of pacification and the result was, as we know, the continued growth of the secret societies until their activities culminated in the murder of two German priests and the German occupation of Kiaochow.

In May, 1898, it was reported that there were volunteer associations organized along the border between Shantung and Chihli, declaring hostility against the Christians. The Imperial Court ordered Wang Wên-shao, Viceroy of Chihli, and Chang Ju-mei,

<hr />

[47] Li Ping-hêng, *op. cit.*, 12/19-20.

Governor of Shantung, to investigate and to maintain order. A memorial was submitted by Chang, who reported that the associations were called I Ho T'uan, but that there were no riots.[48] This was the first time that the Boxers were reported in the Chinese documents, and six months before the Imperial decree ordering the organization of the militia. The Governor apparently wanted to minimize the matter, for the bills which the Boxers distributed actually declared their intention to kill the Christians.[49] In October the Boxers began to act. They gathered their men around Weihsien and Kuanhsien, the bordering districts between Shantung and Chihli. During the night of October 25, they attacked the house of Chao Lo-chu, a Chinese Christian, in Kuanhsien and forced the whole family away. Within six days they assembled as many as 1,000 men with 40 to 50 horses.[50] Government troops were dispatched to the scene, and instructions were issued by Yü Lu, Viceroy of Chihli, that the local officials should put down the riots and disband the Boxers.[51] In another telegram Yü Lu added that suppression and pacification should both be adopted and that, while the leaders should be arrested, the followers might be dispersed.[52]

While the Boxers in Chihli were being disbanded, riots broke out over the border in Shantung. The Boxers of Kuangp'ing, in collaboration with the others in the vicinity, went to Kuanhsien, killed two Christians and wounded a third, and set fire to a chapel and over one hundred houses of the Christians. On their way to Chihli, they also burned down a chapel and twenty houses in Weihsien.[53]

With the aid of the Chihli troops, which were promptly dispatched upon the request of the Shantung Governor,[54] the Boxers were caught in Weihsien. The leader Yao Lo-ch'i and fifteen accomplices were captured, four Boxers were killed, and the rest

---

[48] Ch'ing Tê Tsung Shih Lu, 418/2b.
[49] Lao Nai-hsüan, Ch'üan An Tsa Ts'un, book 2.   [50] Chih Tung Tien Ts'un, 1/3.
[51] Ibid., 1/4.   [52] Yü Lu to Ta Ming Tao, K24/9/21, ibid., 1/6.
[53] Ta Ming Tao to Yü Lu, K24/9/27, ibid., 1/11.
[54] Chang Ju-mei to Yü Lu, K24/9/21, ibid., 1/4.

were dispersed.[55] Upon receipt of the report of the Chihli Viceroy, the Imperial Government issued a decree in which the authorities of Chihli and Shantung were ordered to make special efforts to forestall and suppress the riots, so that they would not lead to uncontrollable disturbances.[56]

With Yü Hsien succeeding Chang Ju-mei as Governor of Shantung in March, 1899, the Boxer movement took a new turn. Yü Hsien was an able official, but like his former superior Li Ping-hêng, he was strongly antiforeign.[57] In April the I Ho Ch'üan activities became pronounced in Shantung, particularly in the district of P'ingyüan. In the various villages of the district the Boxers set up their establishments and were armed with big swords and spears, guns and cannon. They carried charms and recited incantations; they boasted their invulnerability against any weapons. When the magistrate Chiang K'ai attempted suppression, they declared defiantly that they had the blessings of the Governor.[58]

In October the Boxers, under the direction of a certain Chu Hung-têng, intensified their activities. Gathering about three hundred men in P'ingyüan, they looted the homes of Christians, and when six of them were arrested they challenged the district force. Reinforced from Tsinanfu, the government troops fought the Boxers, killing twenty-seven in the field and dispersing the rest.[59]

When Yü Hsien received the report of the conflict, he became very angry. On the ground that innocent lives had been lost in the affray, he discharged the district magistrate, removed the local commander, and had the head constable, who had arrested the rioters, put in prison.[60] The conduct of Yü Hsien was immediately taken as a sign of encouragement for the Boxers. Their

---

[55] Yü Lu to Tsungli Yamen, K24/10/5, *ibid.*, 1/11.

[56] Decree, 24/10/6, *Ch'ing Tê Tsung Shih Lu*, 431/10a.

[57] When the Imperial Court decreed that the Christians were also Chinese subjects and should not be maltreated, Yü Hsien reported that the Christians were arrogant in the villages, bullying the good citizens, and that there was no such thing as maltreatment of Christians. Decree, K25/2/25, *ibid.*, 439/23a.

[58] Chiang K'ai, *P'ing Yüan Ch'üan Fei Chi Shih*, 2-3.   [59] *Ibid.*, 11.

[60] *Ibid.*, 12; *Ch'ing Tê Tsung Shih Lu*, 453/46.

activities broke out with renewed intensity, and plundering and pillaging spread far and wide. In Tsinan, Tungch'ang, and Ts'ao-chou as well as in Chining and Linch'ing, there were a number of Boxer bands, each consisting of several hundred men. No troops were sent down from the provincial capital, nor were requests for suppression answered by Yü Hsien.[61] At last diplomatic pressure was brought to bear, and Yü Hsien, on December 7, 1899, was summoned to Peking for " an audience," while Yüan Shih-k'ai was ordered to Shantung as Acting Governor.

The policy of Yüan Shih-k'ai toward the Boxers in Shantung has been a subject of controversy. According to some writers, Yüan handled the situation with ruthless severity and thus swept the Boxers out of his territory, while to others, Yüan's policy toward the rioters " was marked by no greater display of severity than had been showed by Yü Hsien." [62] It is interesting to find out the true nature of Yüan's policy, for there lies the answer to the question why the Boxer movement was stopped in Shantung but not in Chihli.

Yüan, the young commander, whose career was assured the minute he betrayed the plots of the reform party to Jung Lu, was a man of different type from Yü Hsien. He had been recommended by Li Hung-chang as a man of " high calibre, brilliant and tactful." [63] His residence in Korea as China's representative made him no stranger to international politics. Now on his way to Shantung to take up his new post, he received Lao Nai-hsüan, the author of the theory that the Boxers belonged to the heretical societies. He apparently was impressed by Lao's theory, for he discussed with the author the ways of suppression and highly praised the recommendations the latter made.[64] Upon assuming office the Acting Governor issued a proclamation ordering vigorous suppression of the Boxer societies. The contents of the document may be summarized as follows:

(1) All counties and districts must vigorously suppress the Boxers.

---

[61] Chiang K'ai, op. cit., 16. [62] Steiger, op. cit., p. 157.
[63] Li Hung-chang, Li Wên Chung Kung Ch'üan Chi, " I Shu Han Kao," 17/15.
[64] Lao Nai-hsüan, Ch'üan An Tsa Ts'un, book 3.

The local officials will be severely punished if Boxer establishments are found within their jurisdictions.

(2) The village headmen and constables are liable to 1-3 years of imprisonment if they do not report any Boxer establishment set up in their village. If the constables or any Yamen employees connive with the Boxers, they will be promptly executed.

(3) If fathers or elder brothers let their sons or younger brothers join the Boxers, the sons or younger brothers will be executed, while the fathers or elder brothers will be imprisoned for three years.

(4) Establishments where the Boxers assemble and drill will be destroyed. If the establishment is set up in some person's premises, the property of that person will be confiscated.

(5) If any person informs the government of any family allowing the Boxers to set up an establishment on their premises, one half of the property of the family will be awarded to the informant, the rest to be confiscated. If any person captures a leader setting up a Boxer establishment, he will be awarded the whole property of the family.

(6) The neighbors of any Boxer establishment, if afraid of revenge by the Boxers, may secretly report to the village headmen or constables. If they know of a Boxer establishment and do not report, they will be severely punished if cases of arson or murder occur. Those who harbor the Boxers will be punished as Boxers.

(7) These rules are to be applied to those who join the Boxer societies hereafter. Of those who have joined before, only the leaders and the ones who are guilty of burning and plundering are punishable; the rest may be pardoned if they redeem themselves.

(8) Those who make false accusations will be punished.[65]

These measures were indeed severe and thoroughgoing. If they had been carried out vigorously throughout the empire, the Boxer movement might have been nipped in the bud. The Imperial Court, however, had different opinions. On December 26, 1899, a decree was issued in which the Shantung Governor was directed to give strict orders to his subordinates that, in case of conflicts between the common people and the Christians, they should handle them equitably and " in no way should rely solely upon military force, lest the people be frightened into disturbances." [66] Three days later, another decree was issued, admonishing that Yüan should not " stubbornly stick to the policy of extermina-

[65] Hsi Hsün Hui Luan Shih Mo Chi, 4/234.
[66] Ch'ing Tê Tsung Shih Lu, 455/11b.

tion, but should make a distinction between different cases, so that the people would not be forced to more desperate deeds." The Governor was cautioned to be "extremely careful." If he did not handle the situation well and thus caused disturbances in the important province, he would "be held responsible." [67] On January 3, 1900, a third decree was sent to Yüan, cautioning the Governor again and ordering that he must not stubbornly resort to violent measures. He should handle the situation on the basis of persuasion and pacification.[68]

Under these grim warnings, Yüan had to do something to appease the Imperial Court. A memorial was therefore submitted on January 13. After calling attention to the banditry and the false invulnerability of the Boxers, Yüan discussed the fundamental and immediate measures in dealing with the situation. For the fundamental solution, he said, an understanding must be promoted between the common people and the Christians. Proclamations had been issued in Shantung explaining that Christians, though believing in a Western religion, were still Chinese subjects, and that the propagation of Christianity was permitted by treaties. Christians must not bully the common people, and the common people must not mob the Christians. As to immediate action, Yüan continued, the first thing was to maintain order. To do this the bandit elements must be liquidated, while the ignorant people who had been led astray should be permitted to redeem themselves.[69]

In spite of these apparent compromises, Yüan was firm with the Boxers. To those who had been "led astray" he indeed gave a chance to reform and redeem themselves, but the ringleaders were ruthlessly dealt with. The Boxers in Yüch'êng, Shihp'ing, and Hsiachin were dispersed by force, and their leaders were captured. In Ch'ingp'ing the government troops opened fire on several hundred Boxers, killing a number and capturing eleven. In Lin-i, Yüan's force pursued a group of over one hundred Boxers, killing four and capturing four.[70] Thus by virtue of the unswerv-

[67] Ibid., 455/14a.   [68] Ibid., 456/4a.
[69] Yüan Shih-k'ai, Yang Shou Yüan Tsou I Chi Yao, 2/1.
[70] Hsi Hsün Hui Luan Shih Mo Chi, 2/122-23.

ing determination of Yüan Shih-k'ai, the Boxers were suppressed in Shantung, which was saved from the calamities its neighboring province suffered.

THE BOXERS IN CHIHLI

When the I Ho Ch'üan were first reported in 1898, they were grouped around the districts on the southern border between Shantung and Chihli. They apparently took advantage of the borderland to evade the government forces of either province, for by shifting back and forth from one province to the other, the pursuing force of either province would be baffled by the question of jurisdiction. During the governorship of Yü Hsien in Shantung, the Boxers were active on both sides of the border. In August, 1899, more than 500 Boxers were assembled around K'aichou, in Chihli, and numerous riots with pillaging and plundering were reported.[71] Assistance was requested of Yü Hsien, who, however, counseled calm and careful investigation as " many rumors have been found unfounded." [72] The Chihli force at this time acted energetically; they captured six Boxers, executed five, and wounded a number. The rest of the Boxers were dispersed.[73]

The lack of cooperation from Shantung was a great advantage to the Boxers, who, when pursued by the Chihli force, could conveniently withdraw to their Shantung shelters.[74] By December, 1899, the Boxer activities were so increased in the districts of Fuch'êng, Chingchou, Kuch'êng, Wuch'iao, and Tungkuang that the five magistrates called a conference and resolved that the program of six points recommended by Lao Nai-hsüan for the suppression of the Boxers be adopted and submitted to the Viceroy of Chihli for approval.[75] On December 13 Yü Lu ordered that Lao

---

[71] Ta Ming Tao to Yü Lu, K25/7/14, *Chih Tung Tien Ts'un*, 1/17.
[72] Yü Hsien to Yü Lu, K25/7/17, *ibid.*, 1/22.
[73] Yü Lu to Ta Ming Tao, K25/8/8, *ibid.*, 1/26.
[74] Lao Nai-hsüan, *Ch'üan An Tsa Ts'un*, book 3.
[75] The six points were: (1) to make known to the people that the Boxers were secret sects so that they would not be deceived and join them; (2) to condone those who joined the Ch'üan by mistake; (3) to execute the ringleaders; (4) to stabilize the situation by strong reinforcements; (5) to prove the falsity of the Boxers' protestation of patriotism and of their invulnerability against weapons; (6) to memorialize the Throne for a decree to suppress the heretical sects. *Ibid.*, book 2.

Nai-hsüan's pamphlet on the origins of the Boxers be printed and distributed to the districts where the Boxer societies were active.[76] The Viceroy, however, did not say anything about the six points. When Yüan Shih-k'ai inquired if the Viceroy had approved Lao's recommendations and requested the Throne to issue a decree expressly ordering suppression of the Boxers,[77] Yü Lu replied that the Boxers could not be any great trouble, that the six points recommended by Lao could not be used in their entirety, and that therefore it would not be wise to submit them to the Throne.[78] On January 10, 1900, Yüan again proposed that the Viceroy should report the actual situation to the Throne so that " the erroneous view be stopped." [79] But again the Viceroy evaded the question by replying that he had just communicated with the Tsungli Yamen.[80]

It is hard to say what would have been the result if Yü Lu had memorialized the Throne on the suggestions of Yüan Shih-k'ai, for about that time the Court unmistakably showed its disinclination to take any drastic measures against the Boxers. However, because of the hesitation of Yü Lu, a chance was lost to counteract the reactionary influence at an early stage. It should be noted that Yü Lu was not a man of strong determination: he had neither the iron will nor the defiant tactics of Yüan Shih-k'ai. Moreover, he was handicapped by two factors. First, the proximity of his province to Peking rendered him more susceptible to the pressure of the reactionary party. Secondly, he did not have the benefit of united counsel from his chief lieutenants, for T'ing Yung, the Provincial Judge, was sympathetic with the Boxers.[81] Yü Lu, however, did try to suppress the Boxers by force, for six battalions were dispatched to the troubled districts for that purpose.[82] But his moderate measures soon proved of no avail against the strong surge of the Boxers.

[76] *Chih Tung Tien Ts'un*, 1/42.
[77] Yüan to Yü Lu, K25/11/20, *ibid.*, 1/50.
[78] Yü to Yüan, K25/11/20, *ibid.*, 1/50.
[79] Yüan to Yü, K25/12/10, *ibid.*, 1/61.
[80] Yü to Yüan, K25/12/10, *ibid.*
[81] Liu Ch'un-t'ang, *Chi Nan Chi Pien Chi Lüeh*, 1/1; *Chih Tung Tien Ts'un*, 2/25.
[82] Yü Lu to Lo Jung-kuang, K25/11/9, *Chih Tung Tien Ts'un*, 1/39.

And so from Hochienfu as well as the two counties of Shên and Chi, in the southeast of Chihli, the Boxers spread northwestward to Tientsin, Ichoufu, and Paotingfu, burning, pillaging, and kidnaping; and in some places they assembled as many as several thousand men.[83] The available government force proved deplorably inadequate to cope with the situation;[84] in spite of the effort of the local officials, many of whom showed genuine interest in the suppression, the Boxer movement grew rapidly.

That the Boxers could spread rapidly in defiance of the local authorities was not without reason. They apparently had friends in the Imperial Court, whose support, though subtle, was unmistakable. On January 12, 1900, a decree was issued declaring that societies were of different kinds and that people drilling themselves for self-defense or organizing themselves for the protection of their villages should not be regarded as bandits. Any indiscriminate execution would, instead of easing the situation, " add fuel to the fire." [85] On April 17, 1900, it was again decreed that the villagers of the various provinces, in organizing the T'uan for the preservation of themselves and their families, were acting in accordance with the ancient principle of " keeping mutual watch and giving mutual help." If they were peaceful and law-abiding, they should be left alone.[86] Although it was enjoined that people should not stir up strife against the Christian converts, the decrees immediately gave rise to a widespread impression that the Boxer societies were regarded with favor by the Imperial Court. The Boxers openly expressed their gratification and claimed that the decrees gave them protection.[87]

The first major conflict between the Chihli troops and the Boxers occurred in the district of Laishui, where more than 1,000 Boxers were assembled. In May, 1900, riots broke out at the Kaolo Village, where 75 houses of Christians were burned down and 68 Christians killed. Troops were dispatched to the scene and promptly arrested 20 Boxers. The troops then attacked the main

---

[83] *Ibid.*, 1/50, 2/10.
[84] *Ibid.*, 1/69.   [85] *Tung Hua Hsü Lu*, 157/11a.
[86] *Ch'ing Tê Tsung Shih Lu*, 461/7b.
[87] Liu Ch'un-t'ang, *op. cit.*, 2/28.

body of the Boxers. In the first encounter 18 Boxers were killed and 7 captured; but when the government forces advanced further, they were ambushed, with the result that the commander Yang Fu-t'ung was killed. This was the first time that the Boxers had killed a government commander. It was a challenge to the government, and the people watched eagerly to see how the government would take the test. Again Viceroy Yü Lu showed timidity: he recommended the arrest of the leaders, but the dispersion of the followers; he would not, he said, " resort to severe measures unless the Boxers resist again." [88] And again the Imperial Court ordered moderation. " Rash actions," it decreed, " may lead to catastrophes." [89]

After this the Boxers pushed on fearlessly. Their objects now were the railroads and telegraph lines, the symbols of foreign exploitation. Among the Boxers there must have been many who hated these new means of communication which had deprived them of a living. On May 27 it was reported that the Paotingfu Railway had been attacked and the telegraph lines cut. For more than 100 miles from the Liuli River to Ch'anghsintien, all the stations, bridges, and factories were burned.[90] On May 28, Fêngt'ai, the second railway station on the Tientsin line, about ten miles from Peking, was burned; rail communication between Peking and Tientsin was thus cut off.[91] The situation now became so serious that Yü Lu for the first time recommended strong action. On June 6 he telegraphed to the Tsungli Yamen that the Boxers had become so aggressive that " persuasion can no longer disperse them. The commanders, if hesitant and tolerant, will certainly lead to calamities." The only thing to do now, he urged, was to request the Throne to order General Nieh and other commanders speedily and ruthlessly to put down the Boxers.[92]

But it was too late. The Boxers were rapidly approaching Peking, and international complications soon gave a new turn to the matter.

---

[88] Yü Lu to Tsungli Yamen, K26/4/25, *Chih Tung Tien Ts'un*, Introduction /8.
[89] Tsungli Yamen to Yü Lu, K26/4/27, *ibid.*, Introduction /9.
[90] *Ibid.*, 2/49.   [91] Hsü to Yü Lu, K26/5/1, *ibid.*, 2/2.
[92] Yü Lu to Tsungli Yamen, K26/5/10, *ibid.*, Introduction /11.

3

The Manchu Court and
the Boxers

THE REACTIONARY PARTY AND THE FOREIGN POWERS

THE REACTIONARIES who assumed control of the government after the *coup d'état* in 1898 had special reasons for disliking the foreigners. " The tendency shown by the Government," reported Sir Claude MacDonald, British Minister to China, " is to look with suspicion upon all officials who have had dealings with foreigners. . . . The Manchu party evidently considers foreigners are responsible for K'ang Yu-wei's views, and consequently distrusts all those who have associated in any way with foreigners." [1]

On September 25, upon the report that Chang Yin-huan, who had attended the Diamond Jubilee of Queen Victoria as China's envoy, was to be executed, Sir Claude MacDonald immediately addressed a letter to Li Hung-chang, " pointing out the horror with which such sudden executions were regarded by all Western nations, and the bad effect the secret and hasty condemnation of an official of Chang's rank, who was so well known in Europe, would produce, and begged his Excellency to use whatever influence he possessed to prevent such hurried action." [2] Thanks to the British Minister's intervention, Chang was saved from death, but was later banished to the frontier of Chinese Turkestan.[3] The incident tended to confirm the suspicion of the reactionaries and added to their hatred of the Powers.

Then, when there were persistent rumors that the Empress Dowager would proceed to extreme steps with regard to the Emperor, the British Minister conveyed semi-officially to the

[1] MacDonald to Salisbury, October 13, 1898, *British Parliamentary Papers, China No. 1* (1899), p. 304.
[2] MacDonald to Salisbury, September 28, 1898, *ibid.*, p. 288.
[3] He was executed in 1900 during the height of Boxer activity.

Tsungli Yamen his firm conviction that, should the Emperor die at this juncture of affairs, the effect produced among Western nations would be most disastrous to China.[4] The British Minister's intervention may have saved the Emperor's life, but it also carried with it a further addition to that legacy of hate and resentment which the reactionary elements in the Imperial Court were storing up against Europe.

The sanctuary accorded K'ang Yu-wei by the governments of Britain and Japan was also a source of exasperation to the Manchu Court, particularly the Empress Dowager, whose hatred of the reformer was so great that she put a price of 100,000 taels on his head.[5] The principles of international law could give no satisfactory explanation to the revengeful lady, who refused to understand why a " criminal " deserving the severest punishment in his own country should be harbored by foreign states.[6]

Finally P'u Chün, the son of Prince Tuan, was set up as Heir Apparent on January 24, 1900, with the intention of having him ascend the throne before long. But again the Manchu Court was frustrated, for none of the foreign diplomats sent in congratulations. The refusal on the part of the diplomatic corps to acknowledge the event deterred the reactionary party from carrying out their plan, and this particularly infuriated Prince Tuan, who was impatient to see his son enthroned.[7]

BETWEEN SUPPRESSION AND PACIFICATION

In spite of the reactionaries' hatred of the foreign Powers, the Imperial Government under Tz'ŭ Hsi did not at the early stage adopt any antiforeign measures. Although it was vigorous in strengthening national defenses and was determined to resist any further foreign encroachments, its policy was still to protect the foreigners. On October 6, 1898, in connection with the antiforeign riots in Szechuan, a decree was issued enjoining the Chinese

---

[4] MacDonald to Salisbury, October 13, 1898, *China No. 1 (1899)*, p. 304.

[5] *Ch'ing Tê Tsung Shih Lu*, 432/10; 458/11a.

[6] See Chang Chih-tung, *Chang Wên Hsiang Kung Ch'üan Chi*, 80/14, 16.

[7] Yün Yü-ting, *Ch'ung Ling Ch'uan Hsin Lu*, in Tso Shun-shêng, *Chung Kuo Chin Pai Nien Shih Tzŭ Liao Ch'u Pien*.

people not to mistreat foreigners. Local officials were ordered to give effective protection to Christian chapels, to treat the foreign missionaries with courtesy, and, in case of disputes between the people and the Christians, to settle them judiciously. The same protection should be accorded to foreigners traveling in China. "If, after this decree, riots still occur because of ineffective protection, the local authorities concerned will be severely punished and the viceroys and governors also will be held responsible." [8] Nine days later another decree was issued reiterating the same orders.[9] When riots against the Chinese Christians broke out in Kuangp'ing, Shantung, in November, Governor Chang Ju-mei was promptly ordered to make special efforts to put them down.[10] Then on January 3, 1899, when attacks upon the churches in Szechuan and Hupeh were reported, the provincial authorities were ordered to suppress the disturbances at the start, so that they would not spread to other places.[11] Indeed, as a token of its conciliation, the Imperial Government agreed, on March 15, 1899, to give official status to the Roman Catholic missionaries. Bishops were to rank with viceroys and governors, and were entitled to visit and correspond with them on equal terms; archdeacons and deans with *ssŭ* (i.e., provincial treasurers and provincial judges) and *taotai;* and ordinary missionaries with prefects and magistrates.[12]

The change of policy was first indicated in April when Yü Hsien succeeded Chang Ju-mei as Governor of Shantung. On April 5, in an edict to Governor Chang, the Imperial Court still gave the following instructions:

It was reported that the people and the Christians in Shantung could not live peacefully with each other, but came to frequent conflicts. It must be due to the maltreatment of the Christians, who, having suffered from injustice, create trouble when an opportunity occurs. . . . The Governor is hereby directed to order the local officials to explain assiduously to the literati and the common people that Christians are also children of the Throne, and that, living as neighbors, they should cultivate their friendship. . . . When legal disputes arise, the local officials

[8] Decree, K24/8/21, *Ch'ing Tê Tsung Shih Lu*, 428/1.   [9] *Ibid.*, 429/1b.
[10] *Ibid.*, 431/10a.   [11] Decree, K24/11/22, *ibid.*, 434/10b.
[12] Decree, K25/2/4, *Tung Hua Hsü Lu*, 152/4a.

should settle them judiciously, regardless of whether Christians are involved or not. It is hoped that all trouble will thus be nipped in the bud.[13]

The decree was issued just before Yü Hsien assumed office as Governor of Shantung but was answered by him. True to his character, the new Governor immediately found fault with the Christians. " The conflicts between the people and the Christians in Shantung," he wrote in a memorial, " have had a long history. At first the common people looked down upon the Christians, but later when the foreigners were strong and we were weak, the Christians became increasingly arrogant. They domineered in the villages and bullied the good people. There is absolutely no such thing as maltreatment of the Christians." [14]   As to how much this memorial of Yü Hsien influenced the opinion of the Court there is no direct evidence, but from then on there was an unmistakable change of tone in the decrees dealing with antiforeign riots. On November 3, when the government troops came into armed conflict with the Boxers in P'ingyüan, Shantung, a decree was issued condemning the action of the magistrate as being impetuous and improper.[15]   Later, upon the report of Yü Hsien, the magistrate and the local commander were cashiered.[16]

That was the time when Italian warships were reported cruising near the Shantung coast. The Imperial Government was much concerned over the situation, for the Italians, frustrated in March in their demand for a base in Sanmen Bay, might renew their efforts. In a national crisis it is but natural that a government, with a view to rallying all elements to the national defense, should avoid trouble with its own people. It is significant that in the decree of November 21 the Imperial Court, while ordering Yüan Shih-k'ai, who was then commanding the new army near Tientsin, to dispatch his troops to Shantung, at the same time, and for the first time, instructed Yü Hsien to deal with the anti-Christian riots on the basis of suppression as well as pacification.[17]

In December Yü Hsien was removed from Shantung under

[13] Decree, K24/2/25, *Ch'ing Tê Tsung Shih Lu*, 439/23a.   [14] *Ibid.*, 439/23.
[15] Decree, K25/10/1, *ibid.*, 452/3a.   [16] Decree, K25/10/18, *ibid.*, 453/4b.
[17] Decree, K25/10/19, *ibid.*, 453/6a.

diplomatic pressure, but the Court had no intention of changing the policy of the ex-Governor with regard to the Boxers in the province. From December 26, 1899, to January 3, 1900, three decrees were issued to Yüan Shih-k'ai, the new Governor of Shantung, ordering him not to resort to force in dealing with the Boxers.[18] Strong language was used to warn Yüan that he would be held responsible for any consequences if he insisted upon his ruthless policy of suppression.

As far as foreigners were concerned, the Imperial Court still held fast to the policy of effective protection, as witnessed in the case of the murder of Mr. Brooks, a British missionary, in Shantung. Upon report of the incident, the Court, on January 4, issued an edict ordering the immediate capture of Brooks's murderers and the punishment of the officials who had neglected their duties.[19] But apparently in the mind of the Court it was one thing to protect foreigners and another thing to suppress the Boxers. If the Court stuck to the policy of protection with regard to the foreigners, at the same time it did not depart from the policy in force since the governorship of Yü Hsien that the Boxers were not to be suppressed by force. On January 11 a decree appeared which was viewed with great apprehension by the foreigners. It read as follows:

Recently in all the provinces brigandage has become daily more prevalent, and missionary cases have recurred with frequency. Most critics point to seditious societies as the cause, and ask for rigorous suppression and punishment of them. But societies are of different kinds. When worthless vagabonds form themselves into bands and sworn confederacies, and relying on their numbers create disturbances, the law can show absolutely no leniency to them. On the other hand, when peaceful and law-abiding people practice their skill in mechanical arts for the self-preservation of themselves and their families, or when they combine in village communities for the mutual protection of the rural population, this is only a matter of mutual help and mutual defense. Some local authorities, when a case arises, do not pay attention to this distinction, but listening to false and idle rumors, regard all alike as bandit societies, and involve all in one indiscriminate slaughter. The result is that, no

---

[18] *Ibid.*, 455/11b, 14a; 456/4a.
[19] Decree, K25/12/4, *Ch'ing Tê Tsung Shih Lu*, 456/5a.

distinction being made between the good and the evil, men's minds are thrown into fear and doubt. This is, indeed, " adding fuel to stop a fire," or " driving fish into the deep part of the pool to catch them." It means, not that the people are disorderly, but that the situation is handled badly. . . . Let the viceroys and governors of the provinces give strict orders to the local authorities that in dealing with cases of this kind they should only inquire whether so-and-so is or is not a bandit, whether he has or has not stirred up strife, and should not consider whether he belongs or not to a society, whether he is or is not an adherent of a religion.[20]

About this time Lao Nai-hsüan, the magistrate of Wuch'iao, sent his *Study of the Origins of the Boxer Sect* to his friend Yüan Ch'ang, a member of the Tsungli Yamen. Yüan tried to submit the book to the Throne, but was discouraged by the senior members of the Yamen.[21] About the same time Yü Hsien had been recalled to Peking. His presence there must have contributed much to the government's decision to adopt a policy of nonsuppression. It should be noted that this was also the time when the reactionary party, anxious to enthrone the new Heir Apparent, was vexed by the refusal of the foreign diplomats to acknowledge his new status. That Yü Hsien had the ear of the Manchu Court was beyond doubt, for before long he was awarded a new appointment as Governor of Shansi.[22]

On January 27 identical notes were sent to the Tsungli Yamen by the British, American, French, German, and Italian ministers at Peking, protesting against the decree of January 11, and asking that another decree be issued ordering the complete suppression and abolition of the " Fist of Righteous Harmony " and the " Big Sword Societies." [23] Receiving no satisfactory answer, the five ministers reiterated their demands on March 2 and 10,[24] but all to no avail. The Imperial Government determined to pay no more

[20] *Tung Hua Hsü Lu*, 157/11; *China No. 3* (1900), pp. 9-10.

[21] In December, 1899, Lao sent his book to Yüan Ch'ang. On January 24, 1900, Yüan wrote to Lao that he was unable to submit it to the Throne. Yüan to Lao, K25/12/24, K26/1/14, Yüan Ch'ang, *Yüan Chung Chieh Kung Shou Cha*, I.

[22] *Ch'ing Shih Kao, ts'ê* 68/38. On December 6, 1899, Yü Hsien was ordered to proceed to Peking. On March 14, 1900, he was appointed Governor of Shansi.

[23] *China No. 3* (1900), p. 13.

[24] *Ibid.*, pp. 21-23, 25-26.

attention to the foreign demands and held to its own policy. The decree issued on April 17 was in substance the same as that of January 11, although the people were now enjoined not to stir up disturbances.[25]

In the beginning of May the Imperial Court even contemplated the organization of the Boxers into a militia. Some official memorialized the Throne, suggesting that since the I Ho T'uan practiced boxing for the purpose of self-defence and, despite the use of anti-Christian slogans, were not engaged in criminal activities, they might well be utilized and placed under official training. The purpose was to get them prepared for " great enemies," so that they would not stir up disturbances. The Imperial Court showed a favorable disposition to this proposal. A decree was issued on May 1 ordering the Viceroy of Chihli and the Governor of Shantung to " consider it carefully from the standpoint of the local situations " and to report the actual facts to the Throne.[26]

On May 16 Viceroy Yü Lu submitted a memorial in reply. If the Viceroy was mild in language, he was unequivocal in opposition. His reasons were as follows: (1) Although peasants were permitted by law to study, in their leisure time, the art of fighting for the purpose of self-defense, roving vagabonds who practiced boxing and paraded on the streets with the purpose of reaping profit and fooling the people should be severely repressed. (2) The Boxers, who boasted of invulnerability against all weapons and stirred up strife between the people and converts, were working to enrich themselves. (3) They had been arrested by local officials and found wanting in any real abilities. (4) If these stupid people, whose skill was worthless and whose leaders were all bad elements, were organized into a militia, they could hardly be law-abiding, while the upright gentry would certainly refuse to take a lead in these organizations. [27]

On May 19 Governor Yüan Shih-k'ai replied with a similar opinion, but in much stronger words. The I Ho Ch'üan, he said,

[25] *Ch'ing Tê Tsung Shih Lu*, 461/7b.
[26] Yüan Shih-k'ai, *Yang Shou Yüan Tsou I Chi Yao*, 4/13.
[27] Yü's Memorial, K26/4/16, *Chih Tung Tien Ts'un*, Introduction /8.

had its origins in the White Lotus Sect. It was called the Boxer Society and had never been regarded as a village militia. It was led by bad elements; its activities were predatory in purpose; its behavior was heretical in character. Then answering pointedly the proposal, the Governor declared: " These Boxers, gathering people to roam on the streets and plundering at distances of several hundred miles, cannot be said to be defending themselves and their families; setting fire to houses, kidnaping people, and offering resistance to government troops, they cannot be said to have no criminal activities; plundering and killing the common people and stirring up disturbances, they cannot be said to be merely anti-Christian. Devoid of any skills and defeated repeatedly by government troops, how can they be prepared for great enemies? . . . The proposal of placing the Boxers under official training is absolutely not feasible." [28]

The opposition of Yü Lu and Yüan Shih-k'ai blocked the plan of organizing the Boxers, but the Imperial Court apparently was not convinced of the characterization of the Boxers in the two memorials, for, as shown in the following section, it was holding fast to the policy of pacification.

THE MISSION OF KANG AND CHAO

Upon receipt of the report that the Boxers had been attacking the railways, the foreign ministers bestirred themselves to action. On the evening of May 28, 1900, a meeting of the diplomats was called in which it was decided that legation guards should be brought to Peking without delay. The doyen of the diplomatic corps was authorized to inform the Tsungli Yamen of this decision and to request that transportation be supplied by the Chinese Government.[29] On the following day the Yamen replied, calling the attention of the diplomats to the fact that the Chinese Government had already sent troops to take the necessary action. It requested the foreign ministers to delay summoning the guards for a few days, by which time the measures of the government for the restoration of order would take effect. The foreign ministers,

[28] Yüan Shih-k'ai, op. cit., 4/13.   [29] China No. 4 (1900), p. 15.

however, insisted upon calling up the guards. On May 30 they called in a body upon the Tsungli Yamen and declared that should their request be refused the guards would come up without permission and in larger numbers. The following day the Yamen gave its consent, but with the condition that the number should not exceed thirty for each legation. This condition was, however, ignored by the Powers. The first detachment, which arrived at Peking on June 1 and 3, consisted of 75 Russians, 75 British, 75 French, 50 Americans, 40 Italians, and 25 Japanese.[30]

In the meantime the Chinese Government issued two decrees with regard to the Boxers. The decree of May 29 directed the military authorities to arrest the leaders of the Boxer societies and to disperse the followers. If they dared to resist, " they should be suppressed according to circumstances." The local authorities were not expected to attack the Boxers indiscriminately, for " among the villagers who practiced boxing, there are good and bad elements." [31] The decree issued the following day made the same distinction. Those Boxers who " stir up riots and intentionally create trouble " should be captured and punished severely. As to those who merely joined the Boxer societies, but " have no actual riotous activities," they should be earnestly admonished to disperse immediately.[32]

The selective policy was in accord with the position taken by the Imperial Court since April, 1899. With the growth of the movement, there must have been many who joined the cause simply because the antiforeign slogan appealed to them, and it might be unjust to treat them all alike. But the equivocal declaration of the Court assured the Boxers and confounded the troops. It was difficult to know who were the bad elements, and more difficult to attack them without injuring the good ones. The result was that the troops " looked on with folded arms " and the Boxers became more and more aggressive.[33]

[30] China No. 3 (1900), pp. 29-34; Foreign Relations of the United States, 1900 (Washington· Government Printing Office, 1902), p. 190.
[31] Decree, K26/5/2, Ch'ing Tê Tsung Shih Lu, 463/1a.   [32] Ibid., 463/2b.
[33] From Shêng, K26/5/3, Chih Tung Tien Ts'un, 3/17; from Shêng, K26/5/5, ibid., 3/39; from the two Ssŭ, K26/5/4, ibid., 3/28.

In the meantime, an accident occurred which complicated the situation. On May 31 a party of French and Belgian railway engineers sailed from Paotingfu to Tientsin and met with the Boxers twenty miles from Tientsin. In the fight which ensued four of the Europeans were killed and several wounded. A group of twenty-five Cossacks were dispatched to the countryside to rescue the missing members of the European party. They came upon a large body of the Boxers, killed many of them, and returned with two of their men wounded.[34] The incident heightened the excitement of the Boxers, who were already in a frenzied condition.

On June 4 the Boxers set fire to the Huangts'un station of the Peking-Tientsin Railway. General Nieh Shih-ch'êng's troops promptly arrived, and a pitched battle was fought in which several hundred Boxers were killed.[35] On the 6th it was reported that railway communication between Peking and Tientsin was interrupted.[36] The day before the Boxers at Chochou had attacked the Kaopeitien station and destroyed the Peiho Bridge of the Paotingfu Railway,[37] setting fire to more than ten villages south of Paoting.[38]

At this stage there was a strong demand from the provincial officials that the Boxers be suppressed by force. Chang Chih-tung, Viceroy at Hankow, telegraphed Peking that " the Boxer bandits " who " resist government troops, kill military officers, stir up riots at the gate of the capital, and destroy the railroads built by the country " must be executed in accordance with law. These people, he said, " are staging a rebellion on the pretext of anti-Christianity." [39] Shêng Hsüan-huai, Director of Railways and Telegraphs, also urged that the Boxers be suppressed so as to save the railways from destruction and the country from foreign intervention.[40] The responsible officials in Chihli were of the same

---

[34] *China No. 4* (1900), p. 3; *Chih Tung Tien Ts'un,* 4/2.

[35] *Chih Tung Tien Ts'un,* 4/3-4. [36] Shêng's telegram, K26/5/10, *ibid.,* 4/19.

[37] Two Ssü's telegram, K26/5/10, *ibid.,* 4/17.

[38] Shêng's telegram, K26/5/11, *ibid.,* 4/21.

[39] To Tsungli Yamen and Jung Lu, K26/5/4, Chang Chih-tung, *op. cit.,* 160/2.

[40] To Tsungli Yamen, K26/5/9, Shêng Hsüan-huai, *Yü Chai Ts'un Kao Ch'u K'an,* 21/19.

opinion.[41]   On June 2, Yü Lu, hitherto moderate toward the Boxers, telegraphed to the Tsungli Yamen: " Now the bandits have increased to such a number that they can no longer be dispersed by words or notices.   Unless a strong force is assembled to give them punishment, the fire will become a conflagration." [42]

In spite of these warnings, the Imperial Court refused to use forcible measures.   When General Nieh fought the Boxers and killed many of them along the Tientsin-Peking railroad, he was strongly reproved.   On June 5 he received from Jung Lu, the commander-in-chief, a telegram which read as follows:

The uniforms of your troops make them look like foreigners, and the ignorant villagers may mistake them for foreign troops.   The Boxers are the children of China.   You should earnestly explain to them and make every effort to disperse them.[43]

It may be safely presumed that Jung Lu was directed by the Throne to send this telegram.   There is evidence that Jung Lu stood for suppression at this stage.   In a telegram to Shêng Hsüan-huai on June 2, he wrote:

As regards the Lukouch'iao-Paoting Railway, I have received telegrams from General Nieh, saying that he has dispatched troops to protect every section of the railway.   I have ordered General Sun Wan-lin to deploy his troops near Ch'anghsintien and attack the Boxers when necessary.   I have also instructed General Nieh to repair immediately to Paoting to coordinate the operations in the center.   In short, to forestall conflicts with the foreign Powers, we must hasten to purge the metropolitan area of the Boxers.   This is an important step.   I have already memorialized the Throne on this.[44]

But he was immediately stopped by the Throne, which issued the following decree on June 3:

Near the metropolitan area, the Boxers have gathered people and stirred up riots and also destroyed the railways.   It has been repeatedly ordered that troops be sent there for protection and control.   Although there are good and bad elements among the Boxers, they are after all children of the Court. . . .   The Grand Secretary must not act impetuously and

[41] Two Ssü's telegram, K26/5/4, *Chih Tung Tien Ts'un*, 3/28.
[42] To Tsungli Yamen, K26/5/6, *ibid.*, 3/44.
[43] From Nieh, K26/5/9, *ibid.*, 4/11; from Jung Lu, K26/5/10, *ibid.*, 4/14.
[44] Jung to Shêng, K26/5/6, Shêng Hsüan-huai, *op. cit.*, 35/19.

dispatch troops to attack them and incite conflicts. This is very important.[45]

On June 6 there appeared a long decree which read as follows:

Recently many churches have been established in the various provinces. As the converts become numerous, there are bad elements mingling with them. . . . These bandits, under the name of Christians, oppress the common people and domineer in the villages. . . .

As to the Boxer societies, they were forbidden in the time of Emperor Chia Ch'ing. Recently, because they practice the art for self-defense and for the protection of their rural communities and have not created any trouble, the local officials are ordered by Imperial decrees to control the situation in a proper way. They are not to care whether people join the Society or not, but only to consider if they are bandits. Any one who stirs up riots should be severely punished. Whether they are Christians or common people, they are equally the sons of the country and receive the same kind of treatment from the Court. . . .

Now the Boxers, who make use of the anti-Christian feeling, have organized societies, and the bad characters among them have destroyed churches and railways which are the property of the State. Yesterday we appointed the Grand Councillor Chao Shu-ch'iao to propagate the Imperial message, to advise the Boxers that they should obey the decree and all disperse and live peacefully in their vocations. If there are seditious elements who stir up disturbances, the societies should surrender the ringleaders to be punished in accordance with the law. . . . After this proclamation, if they refuse to reform themselves, the Grand Secretary Jung Lu should order Generals Tung Fu-hsiang, Sung Ch'ing, and Ma Yü-k'un to proceed to exterminate them. It is important, however, to distinguish between leaders and followers and to disperse the followers. . . .[46]

The decree was a compromise between appeasement and suppression. Appeasement was to be tried first, and if it failed, suppression would follow. The threat of suppression was probably due to the efforts of Jung Lu,[47] who hastened to telegraph Shêng Hsüan-huai that if the Boxers did not disperse, " they will be exterminated without hesitation."[48] This interpretation by Jung Lu, however, was not justified. A close examination of the decree of June 6 will show that it was intended to be an admonition

[45] Decree, K26/5/7, Ch'ing Tê Tsung Shih Lu, 463/4a.   [46] Ibid., 463/5a.
[47] Yeh Ch'ang-ch'ih, Yüan Tu Lu Jih Chi Ch'ao, 8/26.
[48] Jung to Shêng, K26/5/10, Shêng Hsüan-huai, op. cit., 35/20.

rather than an ultimatum. It placed greater emphasis on appeasement than suppression. It was significant that among the generals
named in the decree to carry out the extermination of the Boxers
in case of their disobedience, General Nieh, who had been bitterly
fighting the Boxers, was left out. Chao Shu-ch'iao did not seem
to have any positive opinion about the Boxers. However, he was
not a man of forceful character, and since he had good connections with the reactionaries, it is understandable if he did not speak
out his own thoughts.[49] He was accompanied by Ho Nai-ying,
who by virtue of his pro-Boxer suggestions had just been promoted to be Vice-President of the Censorate.[50] But the reactionaries still seemed dissatisfied with the arrangement. As if to make
sure that the Boxers would not be mishandled, Kang I, the arch
reactionary, was given the same mission immediately after the
departure of Chao and Ho. The decree, which ordered Kang I
" earnestly " to instruct the Boxers to disperse, concluded with the
following declaration: " As to the troops dispatched to the area,
they are expected to get rid of the bad elements and protect the
good people. If, disregarding morale and discipline, they harass
the localities on any pretext, it is ordered that Kang I should make
an investigation and have them court-martialed." [51]

On June 7, Chao and Ho arrived at Chochou and ordered the
government troops to cease any operations.[52] Then came Kang I,
who immediately summoned the Boxer leaders. It was reported
that the Boxers presented three demands: (1) withdrawal of
General Nieh's troops; (2) punishment of the magistrates of
Hsinch'êng and Laishui; and (3) attack upon the foreigners under
the leadership of General Tung Fu-hsiang.[53] On June 8, Kang I
ordered General Nieh's troops to withdraw from Kaopeitien. The

---

[49] T'ang Yen, *Kêng Tzŭ Hsi Hsing Chi Shih*, 4; *Hsi Hsün Ta Shih Chi*, Introduction
/11; see also Hu Ssŭ-ching, *Lu Pei Chi*, 1/4; *Hsi Hsün Hui Luan Shih Mo Chi*,
2/129; 3/187.

After ordering the military commanders not to attack the Boxers pending Imperial
decision and putting up notice that the Boxers should disperse, Chao returned to Peking
on June 8, when the mission was taken over by Kang I. See Ai Shêng, *Ch'üan Fei
Chi Lüeh*, in Chien Po-tsan and others (eds.), *I Ho T'uan*, IV, 455-56; Yang Mu-shih,
Kêng Tzŭ Chiao Fei Tien Wên Lu, in Chien Po-tsan and others, *op. cit.*, IV, 347-48.

[50] Yeh Ch'ang-ch'i, *op. cit.*, 8/2b.   [51] *Ch'ing Tê Tsung Shih Lu*, 463/6b.

[52] *Chih Tung Tien Ts'un*, 4/32.   [53] Chang Chih-tung, *op. cit.*, 180/18a.

following day he reprimanded the magistrates of Hsinch'êng and Laishui. The commander at Kaopeitien protested vigorously against the withdrawal as the action would endanger the position of his troops.[54] He also appealed to Viceroy Yü Lu, his superior commander,[55] but all to no avail: the order of the Imperial Commissioner stood, and the troops were accordingly withdrawn to Paoting, while the troops at Laishui were similarly withdrawn to Tientsin.[56]

Instead of being dispersed, the Boxers thus won a victory without shedding blood. The tide turned so much that it was the Boxers who now ruled. When the magistrate of Hsinch'êng went to see Kang I at Chochou, they had him arrested and set him free only after " earnest persuasion " by the Imperial Commissioner.[57]

That Kang I was responsible for the encouragement of the Boxers was beyond doubt. However, the assertion that the Imperial Court decided to utilize the Boxers and called them into the capital after the return and personal report of Kang I [58] is not accurate. Kang I left Chochou for Peking about the midnight of June 14.[59] He probably did not arrive at Peking before June 16.[60] The day before, a decree was issued ordering him to return at once.[61] By that time the reactionaries had taken a firm grip on the government in Peking, and were energetically preparing for war. On June 10 Prince Tuan and Ch'i Hsiu, together with two others, were appointed to the Tsungli Yamen, with Prince Tuan succeeding Prince Ch'ing as President.[62] Three days later a decree

---

[54] *Chih Tung Tien Ts'un*, 4/41.   [55] *Ibid.*   [56] *Ibid.*, 4/49.
[57] From Colonel Hsing, K26/5/19, *ibid.*, 4/52.
[58] Hu Ssǔ-ching, *op. cit.*, 1/4; *Hsi Hsün Ta Shih Chi*, Introduction/11; Li Ti, *Ch'üan Huo Chi*, 1/25.
[59] From Colonel Hsing, K26/5/19, *Chih Tung Tien Ts'un*, 4/52.
[60] According to *Ch'ing Shih Kao*, Kang I did not come back to Peking until after the " declaration of war," which was made on June 21 (" Lieh Chuan," No. 25). According to Yün Yü-ting, however, Kang I, who had " just returned to the capital," attended the Imperial Council of June 20 (Yün Yü-ting, *op. cit.*). In the decree of June 16, which was issued after the meeting of the Imperial Council held the same day, Kang I's name was among those who had attended the meeting (*Ch'ing Tê Tsung Shih Lu*, 464/7). It is possible that the names therein were based upon the list of persons who were summoned but might not actually be present.
[61] *Ch'ing Tê Tsung Shih Lu*, 464/4b.
[62] *Ibid.*, 463/9a. Ch'i Hsiu had told an official that very soon " the foreigners in

was issued to Viceroy Yü Lu and Generals Nieh and Lo, ordering them to resist any further landing of foreign troops and to stop the Allied expedition under Admiral Sir Edward Seymour.[63] The same day the Boxers entered the capital in force,[64] and a reign of lawlessness set in.[65] It was apparent that before the return of Kang I the Court had decided to utilize the Boxers, although it was quite possible that the Imperial Commissioner contributed to the decision by reports sent from Chochou.

IMPERIAL AUDIENCES AND WAR

On June 9, on the strength of rumors that the Imperial Government had determined to exterminate all foreigners in Peking, the British Minister, without consulting other diplomats, dispatched an urgent telegram to Admiral Sir Edward Seymour of the British naval force that unless arrangements were made for the immediate dispatch of reinforcements to Peking, they might come too late. Later, as other ministers took a more favorable view of the situation, he countermanded his earlier request. But by the evening of that day the British Minister, having received some alarming news, telegraphed to the British Consul at Tientsin, and simultaneously to Admiral Seymour, for an immediate advance on Peking.[66] Upon receipt of the telegram, the British Consul called a meeting of consuls and naval commandants for that night, and next morning at 9 A.M. an international force of some 1,500 men left Tientsin by train. On June 11 they met the Boxers near Langfang, halfway from Tientsin to Peking, and killed about fifty. Two days later they were attacked by a large body of Boxers and the expedition was blocked from further advance.[67]

The Seymour expedition immediately aroused the people along the Peking-Tientsin Railway. Within a few hours after the first detachment of the international force left Tientsin, the telegraph line between Tientsin and Peking was cut. As the news traveled

---

Peking and the interior will be all driven out or exterminated by the patriotic people."
Yüan Ch'ang, op. cit., I.

[63] Grand Council to Yü Lu, K26/5/17, Chih Tung Tien Ts'un, Introduction /14.
[64] China No. 4 (1900), p. 20.   [65] Ibid.
[66] China No. 4 (1900), p. 6.   [67] China No. 3 (1900), pp. 45, 53.

toward Peking, frantic riots broke out. On the night of June 10 the British Summer Legation in the Western Hill was burnt. On the 11th Mr. Sugiyama, Chancellor of the Japanese Legation, was killed at the main gate of the southern city. During the afternoon of the 13th a large force of Boxers entered Peking. By nightfall, some of the churches and chapels in the East City were in flames, as well as many of the houses occupied by foreigners, and great numbers of Chinese converts were massacred. On the night of the 14th, there were several attacks on the guards of the legations.[68] The news that the Boxers had succeeded in balking the international force must have encouraged the bands and rallied the population.

Upon receipt of the news that an international force was heading toward Peking, the Chinese Government took a serious view of the situation. On June 11 and 12, members of the Tsungli Yamen called on the British Minister to urge strongly that the reinforcements should not advance.[69] This being of no avail, the Chinese Government prepared for war. On June 13 the Imperial Court issued the following significant decree:

We have received a report from Yü Lu saying that more than one thousand foreign troops will come to Peking by train. Now that the bandits have stirred up disturbances around the metropolitan area, we are handling a difficult situation. The legation guards that have arrived at Peking numbered more than a thousand and should be sufficient for protection. If the foreign detachments still come one after another, the consequences would be unthinkable. Let Yü Lu order the whole army under Nieh Shih-ch'êng back to the railway area near Tientsin to guard the strategical points there. If again there are foreign troops attempting to go up north by train, it is Yü Lu's responsibility to stop them. Let Nieh Shih-ch'êng prepare his troops for any emergency. As for the defense of the Taku forts, let Lo Jung-kuang be on the alert for any surprise. If foreign troops enter the metropolitan area, Yü Lu, Nieh Shih-ch'êng, and Lo Jung-kuang will certainly be held responsible.[70]

Two days later Yüan Shih-k'ai was ordered to speed to Peking with his troops. If he could not come because of the strategic importance of Kiaochow, he should select a competent general to bring the troops to Peking.[71]

[68] China No. 4 (1900), p 21.   [69] Ibid.
[70] Grand Council to Yü Lu, K26/5/17, Chih Tung Tien T'sun, Introduction/14.
[71] Decree, K26/5/19, Ch'ing Tê Tsung Shih Lu, 404/4b.

On June 16 at noon, the first Imperial Council was summoned
to deliberate on the situation. It was attended by all the Manchu
princes, dukes, nobles, and high officials of the boards and ministries. The Empress Dowager asked what should be the policy toward the situation now that riots had broken out in the capital
and a foreign force was heading toward the city. Some minister
suggested that the Boxers should be driven out of the city, but he
was immediately shouted down by Prince Tuan. When Yüan
Ch'ang, a minister of the Tsungli Yamen, spoke of the unreliabil-
ity of the Boxers, who, he said, were rebels rather than patriots
and whose invulnerability was merely a fiction, he was interrupted
by the Empress Dowager: " If we cannot rely upon the supernatural formulas, can we not rely upon the heart of the people?
China is weak; the only thing we can depend upon is the heart of
the people. If we lose it, how can we maintain our country? "
At last it was ordered that Na T'ung and Hsü Ching-ch'èng
should proceed to the front to dissuade the foreign force from advancing any farther, and that the Boxers should be pacified.[72]
After the audience, a decree was issued ordering the recruitment
of the " young and strong " Boxers into the army.[73] The same
day Viceroy Yü Lu and Generals Nieh and Lo were again ordered
to resist any further reinforcements by the Powers and to stop the
foreign troops from entering Peking. They were given discre-

---

[72] These Imperial audiences are described in several Chinese works: Yün Yü-ting,
Ch'ung Ling Ch'uan Hsin Lu; Yeh Ch'ang-ch'i, *Yüan Tu Lu Jih Chi Ch'ao*, 8/29;
Hu Ssŭ-ching, *Lu Pei Chi*, 1/6; Li Ti, *Ch'üan Huo Chi*, 1/28; and Lo Tun-yung,
Kêng Tzŭ Kuo Pien Chi. An account was also printed in the *North China Daily News*,
August 8, 1900, under the title of " Experiences of a Refugee at Peking on the Journey
South." The various versions are far from being the same, but there is agreement on
some important points, such as the domination of the Imperial Council by the re-
actionary party under the leadership of Prince Tuan, the inclination toward war of the
Empress Dowager, and the conciliatory attitude of the Emperor. The present account
is based upon Yün Yü-ting. Yün had been a Sub-Chancellor of the Hanlin Academy
and a recorder of the Court. In 1903 he was appointed Chief Editor in the Bureau of
National History. He attended the Imperial Council in those crucial days. His
Ch'ung Ling Ch'uan Hsin Lu was published in 1911.

[73] *Ch'ing Tê Tsung Shih Lu*, 464/7. Some words in this decree, as printed in the
facsimile edition, are in different handwriting from the rest of the text. It is possible
that the words were changed with the purpose of eliminating evidence detrimental to
the Court.

tionary power to deal with the situation.[74] Similar instructions were sent to General Tsêng Ch'i at Mukden,[75] and General Ma Yü-k'un was ordered to speed to Peking with his troops at once.[76]

The following afternoon the Imperial Council was summoned again and the Empress Dowager announced that she had just received from the Powers a demand covering four points: (1) a special place to be assigned to the Emperor for residence; (2) all revenues to be collected by the foreign ministers; (3) all military affairs to be committed to their hands. The fourth point was not mentioned. She then made the following statement: " Now they [the Powers] have started the aggression, and the extinction of our nation is imminent. If we just fold our arms and yield to them, I would have no face to see our ancestors after death. If we must perish, why not fight to the death? " Finally Hsü Yung-i, Li Shan, and Lien Yüan were ordered to go to the legations and inform the foreign ministers that, if they really wanted to start hostilities, they could haul down their flags and leave China.[77] That day a decree was sent to the authorities of the various provinces, ordering them to send troops to Peking.[78] The troops stationed in the Hsüchow-Huai River area were ordered to speed to the capital.[79]

According to Yün Yü-ting, the " Demand of Four Points " was communicated to Jung Lu at midnight, June 16, by an official by the name of Lo. The message was reported to the Empress Dowager the next morning.[80] It is believed that the " Demand " was fabricated by Prince Tuan in an attempt to infuriate the Empress Dowager and goad her into declaring war.[81] The fourth point, which the Empress Dowager omitted to mention in the Imperial Council, was " to restore the rule to the Emperor." The members of the Tsungli Yamen, through which all communications from

[74] *Chung Jih Shih Liao*, 53/15-16.
[75] *Ch'ing Tê Tsung Shih Lu*, 464/8a.
[76] *Ibid.*, 464/7a.
[77] Yün Yü-ting, *op. cit.*
[78] *Chung Jih Shih Liao*, 53/16a.
[79] *Ch'ing Tê Tsung Shih Lu*, 464/9a.
[80] Yün Yü-ting, *op. cit.*
[81] Ch'ên Kung-lu, *Chung Kuo Chin Tai Shih* (A Modern History of China [Shanghai: Commercial Press, 1935]), p. 514.

the foreign ministers should have gone, must have been skeptical of the matter and anxious to find out the real situation. The British Minister, Sir Claude MacDonald, had the following to report on the interview between himself and the three Chinese ministers on June 18: " Li Shan, who made a very favorable impression on me, asked several questions as to the object of our reinforcements and kept calling his colleagues' attention to the reasonableness of my attitude. I said that so far from our troops coming up with any hostile intentions towards the Chinese Government, their presence would be of material assistance in preserving order, and so preventing incidents which would have serious consequences both for the Government and for the Dynasty itself, in whose interests therefore their arrival should be welcomed." [82]   The manner in which the Chinese tried to find out the real situation was subtle, but they were apparently satisfied with the answer of the British Minister, who did not mention any " four points." The refusal of the British Minister to stop the international force did not, however, help the Chinese ministers who were inclined to peaceful settlement. On the same day Hsü T'ung and Ch'ung I were appointed to confer with Prince Ch'ing, Prince Tuan, and the Grand Councillors, on military affairs.[83] It is significant that such an uncompromisingly antiforeign minister as Hsü T'ung was appointed to take part in the military conferences.[84]

The policy of the Imperial Government since the Seymour expedition may be said to have been laid down in the decree issued to Yü Lu and Generals Nieh and Lo on June 13. There it was expressly ordered that resistance must be offered to any further foreign reinforcements, and that efforts must be made to stop the international force that was under way. The government considered the legation guards sufficient to protect the foreign ministers; a force of more than one thousand under Admiral Seymour was to the government a menace to Peking and the palace. The decree ordering resistance against the foreign troops was reminis-

---

[82] *China No. 4 (1900)*, p. 22.   [83] *Chung Jih Shih Liao*, 53/16b.
[84] Hsü T'ung, the veteran Grand Secretary and now tutor of the Heir Apparent, hated everything foreign, so much so that he would not use the Legation Street entrance to his residence.

cent of the policy so successfully adopted by the government toward the Italians in May, 1899, when the Italian Minister demanded by ultimatum the cession of the Sanmen Bay. After the issuance of the decree, the government energetically prepared for war. The movement of troops, the orders for resistance, and the organization of military conferences put the metropolitan area virtually on a war basis. The Imperial Council was repeatedly summoned in order to rally the ministers to the policy of the Imperial Court rather than to hear their advice. The policy as expressed by the Empress Dowager was explicit on two points: (1) to go to war if war was necessary to maintain China; and (2) to utilize the Boxers in case of war. But the Imperial Government had no intention of starting a war, and so the door of diplomacy was left open. The attack on Taku, however, settled the issue.

On June 19 the Imperial Court received the memorial sent out by Viceroy Yü Lu from Tientsin on the 17th.[85] The memorial, which reported the ultimatum presented by the Allied admirals for the surrender of the Taku forts, did not yet mention the actual hostilities which had broken out on the 17th around 2 A.M. The Imperial Court, however, assumed that hostilities had been started by the Powers, for they knew that the commander of the fort, in carrying out the Imperial orders issued on June 13, would have offered resistance. They therefore decided to break off diplomatic relations, and Hsü Ching-ch'êng was ordered to tell the foreign ministers to leave Peking within twenty-four hours.[86]

On June 21 the Imperial Court received another memorial from Yü Lu reporting hostilities both in Taku and in Tientsin. The report gave a somewhat encouraging picture of the first three days of fighting. It spoke of two foreign warships hit by the Taku fort, the repulse of the Allied troops in Tientsin, and the organization and cooperation of the Boxers.[87] It was on the basis of this report that, on the same day, an Imperial edict was issued declaring war against the Powers.

[85] *Chung Jih Shih Liao*, 53/16-17.
[86] Yün Yü-ting, *op. cit.*; *China No. 4 (1900)*, p. 22.
[87] *Chung Jih Shih Liao*, 53/18-19.

4

Peace amidst War

As THE BOXER MOVEMENT SPREAD rapidly toward Peking, the provinces in the southeast felt concerned. On June 3, as the Boxers attacked the railways and cut the telegraph lines, Shêng Hsüan-huai, Director of Railways and Telegraphs, sent a telegram to Li Hung-chang, then Viceroy of Kwangtung and Kwangsi, suggesting that he should memorialize the Throne. " The Grand Councillors Jung Lu and Wang Wên-shao understand the situation well, but they need the support of the provincial authorities in order to break the erroneous views and to convince the supreme authority." [1] Li replied that those people who had been opposed to railways must now feel pleased with the situation, and that he did not think officials out in the provinces could do anything. [2] As the situation deteriorated, Liu K'un-i, Viceroy at Nanking, [3] and Wang Chih-ch'un, Governor of Anhui, telegraphed to Li on June 13 and June 14 respectively, suggesting that he should do something to save the situation. " The words of an important person will carry weight," urged the Governor of Anhui, " and I hope you will immediately memorialize the Throne." [4] But Li was not moved. " The Imperial Court has decided on appeasement," he replied; " it is futile to memorialize. . . . Jung Lu has under his command several tens of thousands of troops; there is no reason that he should do nothing and let those petty fellows control the situation." [5] Unable to obtain the assistance of Li Hung-chang, Liu K'un-i approached Chang Chih-tung, Viceroy at Hankow, and on June 14 they sent a joint memorial to Peking

[1] From Shêng, K26/5/7, Li Hung-chang, Li Wên Chung Kung Ch'üan Chi, " Tien Kao," 22/18.
[2] To Shêng, K26/5/8, ibid., 22/18.　　　[3] From Liu, K26/5/7, ibid., 22/20.
[4] From Wang, K26/5/18, ibid., 22/20.　　　[5] To Wang, K26/5/18, ibid., 22/20.

urging that the Boxers should be "suppressed first and pacified afterwards," otherwise the armies of the various Powers would come to suppress them. "Never can heretical formulae resist enemies," they added, "nor can rebels protect the country. If the foreign troops penetrate deep and act violently, if bandits of the secret societies rise in the various provinces, the situation would become hopeless." [6] At the same time, the two viceroys separately sent telegrams to Jung Lu, urging him to suppress the Boxers so as to forestall the military intervention of the Powers. "Since the dawn of history," said Chang, "there has been no case where one country can fight all Powers." [7] They both emphasized that His Excellency was the most important minister in the Court, upon whom now rested the sole responsibility of saving the country.[8] Because of the interruption of telegraph communication, these telegrams did not arrive in Peking until war between China and the Powers had broken out.

After war had begun, the first problem confronting the southeastern provinces was what position they should take toward the war. As soon as hostilities broke out at Taku, but before the declaration of war, Shêng Hsüan-huai had suggested to Li Hung-chang that "hostilities had been started without orders from the Throne, and therefore peace should not be considered broken." [9] Li replied: "The Powers claim that fire was first opened from Taku. How can we make that assertion?" [10] Yet he telegraphed to the Chinese ministers abroad that "fighting at Taku was not ordered by the Throne," and asked them so to inform the foreign governments and to request a truce so that the case could be settled by negotiation.[11] After war was declared by the Imperial edict of June 21, the viceroys in the south faced a new situation. Ordinarily an edict must be obeyed, at least in form; for disobedience would incur severe punishment. But the viceroys firmly believed

---

[6] Chang Chih-tung, *Chang Wên Hsiang Kung Ch'üan Chi*, 160/7b-8b.
[7] Chang to Jung, K26/5/20, *ibid.*, 160/9-10.
[8] Liu to Chang, K26/5/22, *ibid.*, 160/13-14.
[9] Shêng to Li, K26/5/24, Shêng Hsüan-huai, *Yü Chai Ts'un Kao Ch'u K'an*, 35/33.
[10] Li to Shêng, K26/5/25, Li Hung-chang, *op. cit.*, "Tien Kao," 22/28/a.
[11] Shêng Hsüan-huai, *op. cit.*, 36/6.

that war with all the Powers was utterly futile, and that, in order
to leave the door of peace open, the southeastern provinces should
by no means be involved in the hostilities. So it was decided that
the declaration of war should be ignored. It so happened that in
a decree issued on June 20 it was ordered that the various viceroys
" should be united together to protect their territories." [12] It was
the intention of the Court that the viceroys should cooperate with
each other to defend the territories against foreign attacks, but the
phrase was immediately seized by Chang Chih-tung as giving
power to the viceroys to decide how to save the territories under
their jurisdiction from peril. He therefore suggested to his colleagues that they make use of that power and continue to protect
the foreigners by suppressing the seditious societies. Liu K'un-i
agreed, adding that the edict that declared war should be kept
from the public.[13] The idea was promptly supported by Li Hung-
chang, who telegraphed that he would not recognize the edict, but
would regard it as being issued without proper authorization from
the Throne.[14] Yüan Shih-k'ai, Governor of Shantung, also joined
in.[15] The decision was a bold and wise one, for it not only saved
the southern and eastern provinces from the devastation of war
but also made the war look like something beyond the control of
the Throne, thus leaving the door for peace open and incidentally
strengthening the position of the southern viceroys in the future
negotiations.

The second problem which worried Liu K'un-i and Chang Chih-
tung was the attitude of Li Ping-hêng, the Imperial Inspector of
the Yangtze Naval Forces. Li Ping-hêng was a man of strong
antiforeign sentiment who had been dismissed from the governorship of Shantung in 1898 under the pressure of the German Minister when two German priests were murdered in that province.
Upon receipt of the news that hostilities had started at Taku, he
left on June 22 for the Kiangyin fort near Shanghai and declared
that foreign warships would be fired upon if they sailed near the

12 *Ch'ing Tê Tsung Shih Lu*, 464/12a.
13 Liu to Chang, K26/5/28, Chang Chih-tung, *op. cit.*, 160/39b.
14 Li to Shêng, K26/5/9, Li Hung-chang, *op. cit.*, " Tien Kao," 22/40.
15 Shêng Hsüan-huai, *op. cit.*, 36/8.

fort.[16] Both Liu K'un-i and Chang Chih-tung were greatly disturbed, for the action of Li Ping-hêng might well frustrate their policy of conciliating the Powers. Liu immediately telegraphed Li Ping-hêng, urging him to come to Nanking for conference, and at the same time confidentially ordered the commanding officers along the coast " not to act rashly." [17] As the Imperial Inspector did not reply but planned to block the river mouth with mines, Liu became anxious. He sent an official down to persuade Li Ping-hêng and at the same time suggested to Chang Chih-tung that they both memorialize the Throne to stop the Imperial Inspector, since it was not stated in the decree relative to Li's appointment that the Imperial Inspector should also take charge of the defense of the Yangtze, " which duty clearly falls within the jurisdictions of the Viceroys at Nanking and Hankow." [18] Chang, however, preferred to try his power of persuasion first. On June 25 he sent a long telegram to Li Ping-hêng in which he stressed the advantages of peace in the southeast:

While disturbances are now breaking out in the north, it is learned that the British intend to maintain their business in the southeast and positively will not occupy any territory lest their business should be destroyed. . . . Now that the British are concerned with their Yangtze business, we may just as well accommodate them, for it is not to our advantage to break the peace. If the several provinces in the southeast are kept from war, we can support the capital and reassure the people of the five provinces in the north. ·Even if the Empress Dowager and the Emperor move to the west, there will still be ground for action. On the other hand, if the southeast collapses, the north will be helpless. Should in the future the Powers show any intention of gobbling up China, we will then play the last stake and do our utmost. But now it is inopportune. . . .[19]

The determination of Liu and Chang deterred the Imperial Inspector from impetuous actions until he left for Peking on June 30.[20] Although the Yangtze viceroys ignored the war as far as the

---

[16] Shêng to Liu and Chang, K26/5/26, *ibid.*, 36/3.
[17] Liu to Shêng, K26/5/27, *ibid.*, 36/4.
[18] From Liu, K26/5/28, Chang Chih-tung, *op. cit.*, 160/39a.
[19] To Li, K26/5/29, *ibid.*, 160/39b.
[20] Shêng to Prince Ch'ing and Jung Lu, K26/6/7, Shêng Hsüan-huai, *op. cit.*, 36/37; Li Ping-hêng, *Li Chung Chieh Kung Tsou I*, 16/28.

southeast was concerned, they sent troops to Peking in response to
the call of the Imperial Court. Upon receipt of the decree of
June 17, Chang Chih-tung maintained that "loyalty of a minister" required the dispatch of some troops. He calculated, however, that before the troops reached Peking the military situation
there might have been settled, and that the troops could then
come back.[21]   Altogether he sent 5,000 men from Hunan and
Hupeh.[22]   When Lu Ch'uan-lin, Governor of Kiangsu, was summoned to the capital, he brought with him a force of 1,500.[23] The
consuls in Shanghai protested, but the Governor maintained that
he had to have some troops for self-protection in the long journey.
He was supported by Liu K'un-i, who pointed out that such a small
number of troops could not be for reinforcement purposes.[24]

PEACE IN THE SOUTHEAST

To keep the provinces of the southeast out of war, it was necessary to have an understanding with the Powers.   On June 24
Shêng Hsüan-huai telegraphed Li Hung-chang, Liu K'un-i, and
Chang Chih-tung that, in order to save the southeast from war,
it was necessary to act before receipt of any decree that might
prejudice the situation.   The viceroys at Nanking and Hankow
should immediately instruct the *taotai* at Shanghai to negotiate
with the foreign consuls there for an agreement providing that
the foreign settlement in Shanghai should be protected by the
Powers and the interior of the Yangtze Valley by the two viceroys.
Such an arrangement, while effectively protecting the life and
property of the inhabitants, would prevent conflicts between
China and the Powers in the area.[25]   The suggestion was promptly
accepted by the two viceroys.   Yü Lien-yüan, the *taotai* at Shanghai, was accordingly instructed to approach the foreign consuls

---

[21] To Yü and Hsi, K26/5/7, Chang Chih-tung, *op. cit.*, 160/30a.
[22] To Jung Lu, K26/6/5, *ibid.*, 80/26.
[23] From Liu, K26/6/6, Shêng Hsüan-huai, *op. cit.*, 36/34.
[24] From Lu, K26/6/7, *ibid.*, 36/37; To Chang, K26/6/5, *ibid.*, 32/29.
[25] Shêng to Li, Liu, and Chang, K26/5/28, Shêng Hsüan-huai, *op. cit.*, 36/5. For
the origin of Shêng's idea, see Hsi-yin, "Kêng Tzŭ Ch'üan Huo Tung Nan Hu Pao Chih
Chi Shih," in *Jên Wên Yüeh K'an*, Vol. II (1931), No. 7.

there, while Shêng Hsüan-huai was requested to advise the *taotai*.[26]
On June 26 Yü Lien-yüan and Shêng Hsüan-huai met the foreign
consuls in Shanghai and presented to them a draft of nine articles.
The following are the important points:

Article 2. The duty of protecting Shanghai shall be entrusted to the
treaty Powers.

Article 3. In the region of the Yangtze Valley, the responsibility for
the maintenance of order shall pertain to the viceroys at Nanking and
Hankow.

Article 4. The foreign warships already stationed at the treaty ports
in the Yangtze shall be maintained as heretofore, but on condition of
their crews not being allowed to go ashore.

Article 5. The viceroys shall not be held responsible for the consequences of any disturbances which may be occasioned by the entrance of
foreign warships into the Yangtze, unless such entrance shall have been
sanctioned by them.

Article 6. No foreign warships shall pass near to or anchor in the
vicinity of the Woosung and Yangtze forts.

Article 7. Foreign warships shall not cruise or anchor near to any of
the Government powder-magazines.

Article 8. Foreigners and missionaries shall for the present refrain
from traveling in places in the interior where it might be difficult to
give them adequate protection.

Article 9. Any measures which the Powers may take for the defense
of Shanghai shall be conducted in the least obtrusive manner possible, so
as to avoid exciting the fears of the populace, some of whom might
otherwise avail themselves of the occasion to create disturbances which it
might not be easy to control.[27]

The consuls raised objection to Article 5, but agreed to discuss
the rest.[28] On June 27 they sent a memorandum to the *taotai*.
After acknowledging receipt of the assurance that the viceroys at
Hankow and Nanking would undertake to keep the peace and to
protect life and property in their provinces, they declared:

We desire you to inform their Excellencies that the Admirals of the
Allied fleets at Taku have made public Proclamation that they only fight
against Boxers and those who strive to prevent rescue of foreigners in

---

[26] Liu to Shêng, K26/5/29, Shêng Hsüan-huai, *op. cit.*, 36/5.
[27] *Tung Hua Hsü Lu*, 160/7; see *British Parliamentary Papers, China No. 1* (1901),
pp. 1-2.
[28] Shêng Hsüan-huai, *op. cit.*, 36/27.

danger at Peking and other places. We desire you to assure their Excellencies that our Governments had no intention, and now have no intention, either individually or collectively, to take any action or to land any force in the Yangtze Valley so long as their Excellencies are able to and do maintain rights of foreigners in their provinces provided for by the Treaties with the Government of China.[29]

Meanwhile Lo Fêng-luh, Chinese Minister at London, took up the matter with the British Foreign Secretary. On July 4 Lord Salisbury informed Lo that he "recognized fully the excellent spirit in which the proposals were devised." He pointed out, however, that they imposed on the British Government duties which properly belonged to the Chinese Government, and that they also involved the renunciation of treaty rights. He declared that the British Government "would gladly execute their provisions so far as it appeared to them expedient to do so, but that it was impossible for us to accept them as a contract which we were bound to execute, and each case must be judged on its merits." [30]

The Nine Articles were therefore not signed, but the Powers agreed that the Yangtze provinces should be neutralized.[31] Count von Bülow, the German Chancellor, thought the scheme a useful one; for it would "separate the two viceroys, who have a real influence, from the actual government in Peking," and at the same time "build a barrier against the ambitions that might lead to the partition of China." [32]

Other provinces in the south were invited by the Yangtze viceroys to join in the plan of keeping out of the war. Li Hung-chang, as early as June 26, gave his support and promised that he would do his best to maintain peace in Kwangtung and Kwangsi and to frustrate any designs of the seditious societies.[33] The Viceroy of Fukien replied that he had notified the foreign consuls that he would undertake to maintain peace and order in his

29 China No. 1 (1901), p. 12.   30 Ibid., p. 11.
31 Chang Chih-tung, op. cit., 161/3b; Shêng Hsüan-huai, op. cit., 36/32.
32 Die Grosse Politik der Europäischen Kabinette, 1871-1914: Sammlung der Diplomatischen Akten des Auswärtigen Amtes (Berlin, 1924), XVI, 200.
33 Li Hung-chang, op. cit., "Tien Kao," 22/43.

province.[34] Governor Yüan Shih-k'ai of Shantung adopted precautionary measures. He increased his force of troops to protect the treaty ports and sent the foreigners in the interior to Chefoo under military escort for greater protection.[35]

To ensure that peace would not be disturbed, the authorities of the southeastern provinces suppressed the Imperial edict that declared war and also the edict that ordered the organization of the Boxers.[36] On July 3 the Viceroy at Nanking issued a proclamation declaring that the existing hostilities between China and the foreign Powers were " beyond the expectation of the Imperial Court." The foreigners in his provinces were to be effectively protected " not only because China and other countries all have people living abroad, but also because natural reason, human sentiment, and cultural conceptions require protection of them." [37]

VICEROYS SEEK TO SAVE THE SITUATION

With regard to the general situation, the viceroys believed that war with all the Powers was utterly futile, and that to save the situation it was necessary that the Boxers be suppressed, the foreign ministers be saved, and diplomatic relations be maintained. To them the crux of the situation lay in the Imperial Court, which had to be won over from the reactionaries, who would ruin the country. Diplomatic maneuvers were, of course, not neglected, and the possibility that Japan might help was explored. The following are the measures adopted or contemplated by the viceroys in the early stages of the war.

(1) *Memorials to the Throne.* As early as June 20, a joint memorial was telegraphed to Peking through Paoting and Shanhaikwan, urging strongly that the Boxers be suppressed by force, for " no government since the beginning of history can rule a country with rebels who violate laws and kill people, nor can a country preserve itself when it fights six to seven Powers at a time and for no good reason." The Court was advised to notify the

---

[34] Hsü to Shêng, K26/6/6, Shêng Hsüan-huai, *op. cit.*, 36/34.
[35] Yüan to Shêng, K26/6/11, *ibid.*, 37/4.
[36] *Chung Jih Shih Liao*, 33/20.
[37] Chang Chih-tung, *op. cit.*, 161/4.

legations immediately that China had no intention of breaking the peace, and that Li Hung-chang, then Viceroy at Canton, had been appointed to negotiate with the Powers.[38]

The memorial was sent in the name of eight viceroys and governors of the Yangtze provinces, among whom were Li Ping-hêng, Liu K'un-i, Chang Chih-tung, and Lu Ch'uan-lin. Actually the memorial was drafted by Chang Chih-tung and was sent before Li Ping-hêng and Lu Ch'uan-lin were notified.[39]

Five days later another memorial was sent by Chang Chih-tung and Liu K'un-i, calling the attention of the Throne to the critical situation. "From the military point of view, it is impossible for one country to fight all the Powers: the result for China will inevitably be defeat. From the political point of view, the Powers can never yield to one country; they will fight on until they are victorious." The Imperial Court was urged not to recall the Chinese ministers from the foreign capitals; otherwise it would mean that China was resolved on war, and in that case it would be difficult to restore peace.[40]

(2) *Advice to Chinese ministers abroad.* To maintain diplomatic relations with the Powers and thus keep the door of peace open, it was imperative that the Chinese ministers abroad should not return home. On June 27 Li Hung-chang telegraphed the Chinese ministers in the various foreign capitals, suggesting that they might well stay on so long as the foreign governments accorded them hospitality.[41] On June 30 Chang Chih-tung also telegraphed them, suggesting that, since the instructions of the Tsungli Yamen granted them discretionary powers concerning their movements, they should stay on in the foreign capitals and thus avoid diplomatic rupture.[42] The Chinese ministers found no difficulty in accepting the viceroys' advice, for except in Germany, where there was considerable tension for some time after the murder of the German Minister at Peking,[43] the other Powers main-

[38] *Ibid.,* 80/22-3.   [39] *Ibid.,* 160/23.
[40] *Ibid.,* 80/24-26; *Chung Jih Shih Liao,* 53/26.
[41] Li Hung-chang, *op. cit.,* " Tien Kao," 23/3.
[42] Chang Chih-tung, *op. cit.,* 161/6b.
[43] Li Hung-chang, *op. cit.,* " Tien Kao," 23/39.

tained full courtesy toward the Chinese envoys. Indeed the Chinese Minister at St. Petersburg reported that the Russian Government seemed to be more cordial than before.[44]

(3) *Payment of foreign debts.* Early in July a decree was issued ordering the viceroys to stop payments on foreign loans. Chang Chih-tung suggested that the payments might be temporarily suspended if an understanding could be obtained with the foreign consuls.[45] Li Hung-chang, however, maintained that the payments should be continued and that the viceroys should jointly memorialize the Throne to explain the situation; for if word should spread that they were stopping payment, the bond markets in the foreign countries would be upset, which in turn would further complicate China's relations with the Powers.[46] This opinion was supported by Shêng Hsüan-huai, who pointed out that the monthly payment of these debts amounted to only 1,100,000 taels and that the Yangtze provinces could well afford to pay for two months, at the end of which time the crisis might well have been settled.[47] The decision was accordingly made, and on July 16 a joint memorial signed by twelve viceroys and governors was submitted to Peking, explaining the necessity for payment. The argument ran as follows:

If we stopped payment, the bond-holders would be frightened and would press their governments to occupy our customs and disturb the provinces along the Yangtze and the coast. . . . Then war would be spread everywhere, and the seditious elements in the interior would take the opportunity to stir up disturbances. With aggression from outside and disturbances within, the whole country would be in turmoil. Imports and exports would be cut off, and revenues from the customs and the *likin* would be reduced to nothing. This would seriously affect the defense preparations of the provinces outside Peking.[48]

The Court was convinced and on July 19 gave its approval to the recommendation of the viceroys.[49]

(4) *Rescue of the foreign ministers.* On July 5 the British

[44] *Ibid.*, 23/10.
[45] Shêng Hsüan-huai, *op. cit.*, 37/5.
[46] *Ibid.*, 37/6.   [47] *Ibid.*, 37/7.
[48] Yüan Shih-k'ai, *Yang Shou Yüan Tsou I Chi Yao*, 5/11.
[49] *Ch'ing Tê Tsung Shih Lu*, 465/17a.

Government served notice that the government at Peking would be " held personally guilty if the members of the European Legations and other foreigners in Peking suffer injury." [50]   On July 8 the French Government sent a similar note to the Chinese Minister at Paris.[51]   Upon receipt of these reports, the viceroys bestirred themselves to action.   It was the opinion of Chang Chih-tung that a joint telegram should be sent by the viceroys to Jung Lu, asking him to save the foreign ministers at all costs.   The British and French notes could be forwarded to Jung Lu, who would decide how much of the contents should be reported to the Throne. Chang feared that if they were forwarded directly to the Tsungli Yamen, they might never reach the Throne, and if they did, they might " incur the anger " of the Empress Dowager.[52]   But Li Hung-chang thought otherwise: " To save the foreign ministers is a matter of great importance.   The telegrams of Ministers Lü, Lo, and Yü should be forwarded to the Tsungli Yamen, who will memorialize the Throne.   The Yamen will not dare to suppress the reports, and we should not care whether the action will incur any anger." [53]   Finally the communications of Britain and France were forwarded to the Tsungli Yamen by Li Hung-chang,[54] and on July 14 a joint memorial was sent to Peking by the viceroys. It was pointed out that, if the foreign ministers suffered any injury, the Powers would use their military power to the utmost and would consider China beyond the pale of international law. If the Boxers were allowed to kill the foreign ministers, " the calamities would be unthinkable."   It was urged that the Imperial Court should expressly issue an edict assigning loyal officials and well-disciplined troops to protect the legations or ordering General Sung Ch'ing's army to take charge of their protection.   Only when the Powers knew that it was the Boxers who were attacking the legations, while the intention of Their Majesties was to save the foreign ministers, would a *rapprochement* be possible.[55]

[50] *China No. 1* (1901), p. 4.   [51] Shêng Hsüan-huai, *op. cit.*, 37/7.
[52] Chang Chih-tung, *op. cit.*, 162/1-2.
[53] From Li, K26/6/17, *ibid.*, 162/2b.
[54] Li Hung-chang, *op. cit.*, " Tien Kao," 23/21.
[55] Chang Chih-tung, *op. cit.*, 80/29.

(5) *Chang Chih-tung and Japan.* The connections which Chang maintained with the Japanese statesmen and his attitude toward Japan had far-reaching implications in the later development of China's diplomatic maneuvers. His early moves in this direction deserve attention. On June 2 Marquis Ito, who, though holding no responsible position at that time, had considerable influence with the Japanese Government in his capacity as elder statesman, called on the Chinese Minister at Tokyo and inquired what suggestions Viceroy Chang would have with regard to the existing crisis.[56] Not sure what the Japanese statesman really wanted of him and conscious of his limited power with regard to foreign affairs under the Imperial regime, Chang hesitated to go into details. He replied through the Chinese Minister and presented three points, which he hoped the foreign Powers could accept: (1) not to attack Peking, so that the rebellion could be suppressed by China; (2) not to " scare " Their Majesties, so that the people of the country would not be upset; and (3) not to advance their troops beyond Tientsin, so that Li Hung-chang could go up north to negotiate. " Japan," he added, " has common interests with China and common sentiments, because both peoples are of the same race and of the same continent. I am sure Japan will be able to understand China's internal disturbances and to help in settling China's external troubles. Japan's policy toward China should be different from that of other Powers." [57]

The requests made by Chang were of high importance and in some points involved the policy of other Powers. Ito, therefore, informed the Chinese Minister at Tokyo that he would reply some time later.[58] It was apparently Chang's desire to counterbalance other Powers with the weight of Japan. His thoughts were more frankly expressed in a telegram which he sent to Li Hung-chang on July 3. Upon receipt of the report that the Boxers were attacking the Chinese Eastern Railway in Manchuria, Chang thought that this disturbance might provide a welcome diversion. The

---

[56] *Ibid.*, 161/24b.
[57] Chang to Minister Li, K26/6/10 and K26/6/11, Shêng Hsüan-huai, *op. cit.*, 37/4; Chang Chih-tung, *op. cit.*, 161/24a, 29.
[58] From Li, K26/6/20, Chang Chih-tung, *op. cit.*, 161/29b.

Russians might take advantage of the crisis to occupy the territory there, thereby diverting troops from Tientsin, which they were now attacking. But Japan, he reasoned, could not afford to see the Russian ambitions realized; neither would Britain look on idly. So Japan would withdraw her main force, and Britain a small force, to checkmate Russia. Thus " the crisis would be shifted to Manchuria and the attack on Tientsin slowed down. The conflict between Russia and Japan might result in a change in the international situation and help resolve our crisis." [59] Chang's idea, however, was rejected by Li Hung-chang, who promptly replied that the crisis would not be shifted from Peking to Manchuria, for under the common purpose of rescuing the foreign ministers the Powers would be united in pushing toward the capital. Moreover, the Russians were aiming only at protecting the railways and did not seem to be occupying Chinese territory.[60] But Chang was not so easily convinced. On July 9 he asked his representative in Tokyo to give him information regarding possible Russo-Japanese conflicts in the Manchurian area.[61]

(6) *Plot for a coup d'état.* In the decree of June 26 it was declared that " the Boxers are found everywhere, from the abodes of soldiers and common people to the mansions of princes and dukes," and that " to suppress them by force would lead to calamities right near us." [62] It was therefore believed that it was not the free will of the Empress Dowager to use the Boxers against the foreigners, but that she must have been forced to do so under duress. To extricate her from the dangerous situation, Shêng Hsüan-huai proposed, as early as June 28, that Yüan Shih-k'ai should lead his new army from Shantung, march to Peking through Paoting, purge the Imperial Court of the undesirable elements, and protect the Empress Dowager and the Emperor. " Among the viceroys and governors, " said Shêng in the telegram, " your army is the strongest. It may not be strong enough to resist the foreign aggression, but it is more than sufficient to sup-

[59] From Chang, K26/6/7, Li Hung-chang, *op. cit.*, " Tien Kao," 23/14.
[60] To Chang, K26/6/7, *ibid.*, 23/15.
[61] To Ch'ien, K26/6/13, Chang Chih-tung, *op. cit.*, 161/32.
[62] *Ch'ing Tê Tsung Shih Lu*, 464/15a.

press the internal disturbances." [63]   Thus Yüan was again remembered at a time when a *coup d'état* was thought necessary. But once again the shrewd politician refused. He replied the following day: " The critical illness is undergoing a change; better not hurry with medicine." [64]   Shêng telegraphed back: " If we do not hurry with medicine for this critical illness, Their Majesties may move to the west. Then they will be more under the control of the usurpers." [65]   But Yüan was not moved. " It is an internal disease," he telegraphed, " and it has to be treated internally." [66]   To this Shêng could only reply: " It is hopeless to treat it internally." [67]

Five days later the matter was taken up again on the suggestion of the Japanese Foreign Minister, who asked if Yüan Shih-k'ai could march his troops to Peking to rescue the foreign ministers. The message was sent to Li Hung-chang, who forwarded it to Yüan. [68]   But Yüan consistently declined: " If I lead my troops to save the foreign ministers at Peking without Imperial orders, I am afraid that on the way I shall be defeated. This I really cannot do." [69]

(7) *Appeal to Jung Lu.* As Yüan Shih-k'ai refused to act, the viceroys turned to Jung Lu, the commander-in-chief of the northern armies, whose liberal attitude toward the situation was confirmed by a recent telegram to the southern viceroys. This telegram, which Jung Lu sent from Paoting on June 26, reached Chang Chih-tung about June 29. In view of the controversy over Jung Lu's attitude toward the war, it may be pertinent to quote the document at length:

If one weak country fights more than ten powerful countries, danger and ruin will follow at once. Moreover, when two countries are at war, it has been customary from far antiquity not to injure the envoys. The founding of the dynasty by our forefathers was an arduous task; how can it now be lightly thrown away by believing in the heretical brigands? It requires no particular sagacity to know all this. I have argued

---

[63] To Yüan, K26/6/2, Shêng Hsüan-huai, *op. cit.*, 36/20, 36/18.
[64] From Yüan, K26/6/3, *ibid.*, 36/24.   [65] To Yüan, K26/6/4, *ibid.*, 36/25.
[66] From Yüan, K26/6/5, *ibid.*, 36/30.
[67] To Yüan, K26/6/5, *ibid.*, 36/30.
[68] To Yüan, K26/6/10, Li Hung-chang, *op. cit.*, " Tien Kao," 23/19.
[69] From Yüan, K26/6/11, *ibid.*, 23/20.

with all my efforts, but without in the least succeeding in saving the
situation. Later I was ill and could not move; still during my leave I
submitted seven memorials. Then in spite of my illness, I memorialized
in person, but all to no avail. As you may have heard, all the princes,
peilê, and ministers, when they reported to the Throne, had but one
word on their lips. You must have heard of this, and so I need not
dwell on it. Moreover, half of the entourage of Their Majesties and the
princes belong to the Boxer societies, as do the majority of Manchu and
Chinese troops. They swarm in the streets of the capital like locusts,
several tens of thousands of them, and it is extremely difficult to reestab-
lish order. Even though there is the wisdom of Their Majesties, it is
hard to turn the majority. If Heaven decrees it, what can we do? . . .
Prince Ch'ing and Wang Wên-shao are of the same mind as myself, but
they again could not do much. Death I do not mind, but the guilt I
shall bear for all ages! Heaven alone can testify to my heart. What a
grief! . . .[70]

Assured of Jung Lu's liberal attitude toward the crisis and believing in his difficulty in meeting with the situation, the viceroys
considered that Their Majesties were under the undue influence
of the reactionaries and that, to save the situation, outside assistance was necessary. But before the provincial authorities could
do anything about the reactionaries and Boxers in Peking, they
must first have orders from the Throne. It was for this reason
that Shêng Hsüan-huai telegraphed Jung Lu on July 1: " You are
like the heart, while the provincial officials are like arms and legs.
In the present crisis, if there is anything which it is inconvenient
to say expressly in the Imperial decrees, you can telegraph secretly
to the viceroys at Nanking, Hankow, and Canton, so that they
can act accordingly." [71] On July 17 a joint telegram was sent to
Jung Lu and Prince Ch'ing by Li Hung-chang, Liu K'un-i, and
Chang Chih-tung. After pointing out the discrepancies between
the various decrees—some of which were conciliatory, while others
ordered that " the word peace should be swept from the hearts "
of the officials—the three viceroys called attention to the grave
danger that threatened if no proper action was taken before the
arrival of all the Allied forces. " Unless Your Excellency and

---

[70] Chang Chih-tung, *op. cit.*, 161/5-6; Shêng Hsüan-huai, *op. cit.*, 37/21; Li Hung-
chang, *op. cit.*, " Tien Kao," 23/10. *Peilê* are princes of the second rank.
[71] Shêng Hsüan-huai, *op. cit.*, 36/27.

Prince Ch'ing report in person to Their Majesties and request a secret decree, the ministers outside the capital can do nothing." [72] But no secret decree came, and consequently the viceroys could do nothing about the reactionaries in Peking.

THE ROLE OF SHÊNG HSÜAN-HUAI

In keeping the southern provinces from war, and thus saving more than half of China from military devastation and at the same time preserving a basis for peace negotiations, the policy makers concerned had done a great service to their country. But while credit is justly given to Viceroys Liu K'un-i and Chang Chih-tung, the contributions of another official have not been sufficiently noted, namely, Shêng Hsüan-huai, Director of Railways and Telegraphs and of the China Merchants Steam Navigation Company, who at that time held the rank of Assistant Secretary of the Ministry of Justice, and thus in the official hierarchy was junior to the viceroys of the Yangtze provinces. The first to manage the new enterprises of the empire, Shêng was destined to play an eminent role in China's foreign affairs. He had been recommended by Li Hung-chang as being "learned and capable and able to see the great issues in diplomatic negotiations." [73] He was regarded not only as the protégé but also as the "business agent" of Li Hung-chang. There is no doubt that he amassed a great fortune for himself. [74] But whatever reputation he might have had with regard to the management of finance, his resourceful mind was a motivating force in many of the measures taken by the southern viceroys. Thus it was he who first suggested to Li Hung-chang that fighting at Taku should not be regarded as war, inasmuch as it was started without orders from the Throne. [75] And it was he who recommended to Viceroys Liu K'un-i and Chang Chih-tung that the Imperial edict declaring war should be ignored and suppressed. [76] Then when he heard of Li Ping-hêng's

[72] *Ibid.*, 37/23.
[73] Shêng Hsüan-huai, *op. cit.*, Introduction /biography.
[74] Han-pin-tu-i-chê, *Chang Wên Hsiang Mo Fu Chi Wên*, 1/25; Hu Ssŭ-ching, *Kuo Wên Pi Ch'êng*, 1/18.
[75] To Li, K26/5/24, Shêng Hsüan-huai, *op. cit.*, 35/30.   [76] *Ibid.*, 36/32.

intention to fire upon foreign warships if they sailed near the
Kiangyin fort, he immediately telegraphed the two Yangtze viceroys so that precautionary measures could be taken to forestall any
impetuous actions of the Imperial Inspector.[77] When Liu K'un-i
received the decree ordering a moratorium on foreign debts, he
was confronted with the dilemma of disobeying the Throne or
creating new international complications. He was helped out of
his difficulty by Shêng, who proposed concrete ways of solving the
problem. Again and again it was Shêng who urged Yüan Shih-
k'ai and Jung Lu to take extraordinary actions to save the trouble-
some situation. As Director of Telegraphs, he was able to receive
the earliest reports from the various parts of China as well as from
the rest of the world. Stationed in Shanghai, he had close con-
tacts with the foreigners and was able to sense their feelings. Thus
he was in a position to make suggestions at the earliest moment to
meet the constantly changing situation. He was to contribute
more in the later development of the crisis. Thanks to the publication of his manuscripts [78] in 1939, it is possible to know that
many of the important measures during the period were initiated
by this bold and brilliant official.

[77] Ibid., 36/3.
[78] Yü Chai Ts'un Kao Ch'u K'an.

5

Peace Unrealized

THE REIGN OF THE BOXERS

SINCE THE REPORT of the Seymour expedition, the Imperial Court had been inclined to use the Boxers against the foreigners. Still, with regard to the burning and pillaging in the capital, decree after decree was issued directing that the ringleaders should be arrested and the followers dispersed.[1] It is true that these decrees were not carried out, but they showed that the liberals were exerting some moderating influence. After June 19, the day when the report of the Allied ultimatum to the Taku commander was received, a new era began for the Boxers. On that day the Court ordered Yü Lu to organize the Boxers immediately so as to strengthen the resistance.[2] Two days later, upon receipt of the report from Yü Lu that initial " victories " had been won in Tientsin through the joint effort of the troops and the Boxers, the Court was elated. In the decree to Yü Lu issued the same day, the Court commended the patriotism of the Boxers and attributed the success to the assistance of the ancestors and the blessing of the gods.[3] Simultaneously, a decree was issued to the viceroys and governors of the various provinces, ordering them to organize the Boxers to resist the foreign aggressors.[4] The following day formal organization of the Boxers in Peking was proclaimed. Prince Chuang and Kang I were appointed to command the Boxers, while Ying Nien and Tsai Lan were ordered to assist them.[5] The same day Kang I was issued 20,000 piculs of rice to be distributed to

[1] Decree, K26/6/17, K26/5/18, Ch'ing Tê Tsung Shih Lu, 464/1b, 2b, 4a, 5a.
[2] Decree, K26/5/23, ibid., 464/11a.
[3] Chung Jih Shih Liao, 53/19-20.
[4] Ibid., 53/20a.
[5] Pao Shih-chieh (ed.), Ch'üan Shih Shang Yü, in Chien Po-tsan, I Ho T'uan, Vol. IV; Hsi Hsün Hui Luan Shih Mo Chi, Introduction; Ching Chin Ch'üan Fei Chi Lüeh, Part I, 1/7.

the Boxers.[6]   On June 25 the Boxers, along with other armies in the capital, were awarded 100,000 taels.[7]

With these rewards and encouragements the Boxers, who had always been disorderly and undisciplined, became even more violent and reckless, making Peking a veritable pandemonium. There were some 30,000 Boxers under the command of Prince Chuang and Kang I, while over 1,400 bands were registered with Prince Tuan, each claiming from 100 to 300 men.[8]   Each band had its own leader and each leader made his own laws.   In fact, anyone wearing something red could claim to be a Boxer, and any Boxer seemed to be invested with authority to kill, burn, and plunder at will.   Notables such as Grand Secretary Sun Chia-nai, Grand Secretary Hsü T'ung, himself a supporter of the Boxers, Hanlin Chancellor I Ku, and Vice-President of the Censorate Tsêng Kuang-luan were subjected to pillage and in some cases personal violence.   Ch'ên Hsüeh-fên, Vice-President of the Board of Civil Service, was roughly handled in his office.   The newly appointed Governor of Kweichow, Têng Hsiao-ch'ih, was dragged from his sedan chair, forced to kneel down, and robbed of all his clothes. The Sub-Chancellor of the Hanlin Academy, Huang Ssŭ-yung, was sent to prison on a groundless accusation.[9]   As to how many of the lesser officials and the common people were pillaged, attacked, and killed, there are no statistics, but at one time the capital was so littered with dead bodies that the Imperial Court had to issue a decree ordering the commanders of the Peking Field Force to have them removed from the city.[10]   Soon the Boxers were joined by the soldiers in the depredations.   In one instance, a group of thirty-three attackers was captured, of whom eleven were found to be soldiers, while the remaining twenty-three were " pretenders." [11]   The officials of the various yamens were so frightened that

---

[6] *Ching Chin Chüan Fei Chi Lüeh*, Part I, 1/7.   [7] *Ibid.*, Part I, 1/8.
[8] Yüan to Chang, K26/6/2, Yüan Ch'ang, *Yüan Chung Chieh Kung Shou Cha, ts'ê* 1.
[9] Yün Yü-ting, *Ch'ung Ling Ch'uan Hsin Lu*; *Ching Chin Ch'üan Fei Chi Lüeh*, 5/5; *Ch'üan Fei Chi Shih*, 2/25, 6/12; *Hsi Hsün Hui Luan Shih Mo Chi*, 2/137; Hu Ssŭ-ching, *Lu Pei Chi*, 2/2.
[10] Decree, K26/6/1, *Ch'ing Tê Tsung Shih Lu*, 465/2a.
[11] Decree, K25/5/26, *Ch'üan Fei Chi Shih*, Introduction.

a great many of them left the capital without even asking for leave.[12]

The predicament of the Chinese Christians and the foreigners was serious, and would have been fatal if they had failed to withstand the attacks upon the Northern Roman Catholic Cathedral and the Legation Quarter, to which they had moved. There is no doubt that the attack on the legations was authorized by the Imperial Court, for not only the Boxers but also government troops participated. The following decree issued to the Grand Councillors on June 23 is interesting:

The work [shih] now undertaken by Tung Fu-hsiang should be completed as soon as possible, so that troops can be spared and sent to Tientsin for defense.[13]

It was unusual that the Court should use such vague language as " work now undertaken " in a decree to the ministers. Ordinarily it would at least name specifically the matter in question, if it did not spend a few words to explain its nature. The decree must have referred to the attack on the legations, for there was nothing else that would require such secretive wording and after the completion of which troops could be spared for the defense of Tientsin. The following memorial, submitted on July 7 by Li Cho-ying, a censor, was further evidence to the point:

When the Boxers first came, they claimed that they had supernatural power, that they were invulnerable to guns and swords, and that they were capable of burning the foreign houses and exterminating the foreigners as easily as turning over a hand. Now they are different: first they evade by artifice, then they retreat and make no advance. Only the army of Tung Fu-hsiang has attacked with all effort day and night.[14]

If the attack upon the legations had not been authorized by the Court, a memorial in such a vein could not have been submitted.

While it is evident that the attack upon the legations was authorized by the Imperial Court, it is not so clear why such an attack should have been made. The motives must have been complex, and possibly included the following:

[12] Ibid., 1/12; Yeh Ch'ang-ch'ih, Yüan Tu Lu Jih Chi Ch'ao, 8/37b.
[13] Decree, K26/5/27, Ch'ing Tê Tsung Shih Lu, 464/13b.
[14] Chung Jih Shih Liao, 53/40-41.

(1) *To give vent to hatred and anger.* The reactionaries hated the foreigners and so would seize every opportunity to take vengeance. Their feelings at that time were vividly expressed in the edict of June 25 declaring war against the Powers:

.... For the past thirty years [the foreigners] have taken advantage of our country's benevolence and generosity as well as our wholehearted conciliation to give free rein to their unscrupulous ambitions. They have oppressed our state, encroached upon our territory, trampled upon our people, and exacted our wealth. Every concession made by the Court has caused them day by day to rely more upon violence until they shrink from nothing. In small matters they oppress peaceful people; in large matters they insult what is divine and holy. All the people of our country are so full of anger and grievances that every one desires to take vengeance. . . .[15]

(2) *To stimulate the patriotism of the people.* In a joint memorial submitted on June 27 Grand Secretary Hsü T'ung and Grand Duke Ch'ung I said:

Though our troops are strong, their number is, after all, limited. It would be better if we could heed the intolerant sentiment of the people and make soldiers out of them all. We respectfully request that a decree be issued authorizing the people to exterminate any foreigner they see, no matter in what provinces or in what place. The grievances which the common people have suffered for several decades as a result of the aggression of the foreigners, the insults of the Christians, and the oppression of the prejudiced officials have had no way of redress. When they hear the Imperial authorization, they will feel exalted and zealous, grateful to the Throne, and impelled to give their service. Such popular support will prove invincible.[16]

(3) *To get rid of the menace within the capital.* Although only some 400 strong, the legation force was a formidable one to the Chinese. It held up a large Chinese force, and in the eyes of some officials constituted a constant menace to the capital. " If the foreign troops sally out during the night," wrote Chêng Ping-lin, a censor, on June 26, " one soldier would be as strong as one hundred, and one hundred as strong as one thousand. The consequences would be beyond description." He therefore suggested

---

[15] *Ching Chin Ch'üan Fei Chi Lüeh*, Part I, 1/5-6.
[16] *Chung Jih Shih Liao*, 53/24.

that tunnels be dug beneath the legations, so that the foreigners could be dynamited and " none will be left." [17]

(4) *To silence the witnesses.* It must have been within the thought of the reactionaries that if the foreigners in Peking were exterminated, the foreign Powers would be deprived of witnesses as to what actually was happening and who really was responsible. Thus Chêng Ping-lin wrote in a memorial submitted on July 5:

> The foreign troops in the legations still hold their position and wait for outside relief. It is requested that all the Wu Wei troops in the city be ordered speedily to dislodge them and kill them all, so that the mouths of the foreigners will be silenced. Later on we can put the blame upon the rebellious troops and rebellious people who went beyond our control. [18]

PEACE INCLINATIONS

After receiving the memorials of the southern viceroys dated June 20 and June 25, which urged that the Boxers be suppressed and peaceful relations with the Powers be maintained, [19] the Imperial Court became conciliatory toward the Powers. On June 29 a decree was issued to the Chinese ministers abroad, ordering them to explain to the various foreign offices the difficulties under which the Chinese Government was operating. China had no intention of making war on all countries, and least of all was it her purpose to rely upon the rebellious elements to battle the Powers. The Imperial Government would " strictly order the commanders to protect the legations to the best of their ability and to punish the rebels so far as circumstances permit." [20] Two days later another decree ordered that Chinese Christians, being also children of the state, should be pardoned for their past mistakes if they returned to the path of rectitude. " As hostilities have now broken out between China and the Powers," the decree added, " the missionaries should be sent back as soon as possible to their countries

---

[17] *Ibid.*, 53/21-22.
[18] *Ibid.*, 53/36b; see also Shêng Hsüan-huai, *Yü Chai Ts'un Kao Ch'u K'an*, 37/22.
[19] Chang Chih-tung, *Chang Wên Hsiang Kung Ch'üan Chi*, 80/22-23, 80/24-46.
[20] Decree, K26/6/3, *Ch'ing Tê Tsung Shih Lu*, 465/2b.

in order to avoid all inconveniences, but measures must be taken to give them protection on their way." [21]

However, on July 3, the very day an appeal was made by the Chinese Emperor to the rulers of Russia, England, and Japan, requesting their good offices for the peaceful settlement of the crisis,[22] a decree was issued to the authorities of the various provinces declaring that, " after war has broken out between China and the foreign countries, there is absolutely no possibility that we will immediately negotiate for peace." The generals, viceroys, and governors of the various provinces " must be united in effort and mind to save the general situation. It will be to your credit if you carefully guard your territory; it will be a crime if you sit idly and lose the chance. Accumulated credits will entitle you to high rewards; failure and loss will incur execution. The generals, viceroys, and governors must sweep the word ' peace ' from their hearts; they will then feel emboldened and strong." [23]

The discrepancy between this order and the foregoing decrees had been a source of concern to the viceroys of the south. They attributed it to the fact that the Empress Dowager was pressed upon by two forces: the reactionary and the liberal. The warlike decrees were issued upon the recommendation of the reactionary ministers.[24] That is generally true, but a close examination of the situation will show that this dual policy, though inconsistent in appearance, was not devoid of sense. The war, as the Imperial Court saw it, was forced upon China, and though it must be carried on with all energy, the door to peace should by no means be closed. But while the war was carried on, it was necessary that the country not be lax in its efforts to defeat the enemy. And the military situation at that time, as reported by Yü Lu, was not so hopeless as to warrant the laying down of arms.

On July 2 the Court received the report of Viceroy Yü Lu on the battle of Tientsin. The foreign artillery had hit the arsenal by Haikuangssŭ, burning many buildings, but the machinery, though damaged, could be repaired. The arsenal outside the

---

[21] Decree, K26/6/5, ibid., 465/5a.
[22] Chung Jih Shih Liao, 53/33-34.   [23] Ibid., 53/34b.
[24] See Shêng Hsüan-huai, op. cit., 37/12, 22, 20/21.

Eastern Gate had also been attacked, and one part of it was occupied by foreign troops, but the munition plants remained intact. The army under General Ma Yü-k'un had just arrived; the troops, the Viceroy said, " will be ordered to collaborate with the Boxers and drive the foreigners out." [25]   On July 4 Yü Lu sent in another memorial which reached Peking on July 6. The army under General Ma, he said, had repulsed the foreign troops, killed more than 100, and taken back the railway station. General Nieh's army had repulsed attacks from the Ch'ênchiakou Bridge and recovered Naok'ou. Plans were made, he added, to dislodge the enemy from the Eastern Arsenal; after that the foreign forces in Tzŭchulin and Laolungt'ou would be exterminated.[26]

In a memorial dated July 10, Yü Lu reported several victories by the Chinese army from July 6 to July 8.[27]   Actually the situation was not so encouraging as the Viceroy described. On July 9 General Nieh was killed in battle at Palit'ai, south of Tientsin.[28]

The death of General Nieh was a great loss to the Chinese army. The General had distinguished himself in the Sino-Japanese War of 1894-95, and since then had been considered one of the best generals in China. His troops, clad in uniforms of European style, had been trained along Western lines. The Boxers hated him and his troops, not only because of these Western attributes, but also because his army had fought and killed many Boxers along the Peking-Tientsin Railway in the beginning of June. Among the generals, he had been the most vehement in demanding the suppression of the Boxers by force. In spite of instructions from Peking not to use extreme measures,[29] the General had persisted in his policy. On June 6 he had telegraphed Yü Lu that the situation was so critical that nothing short of forcible suppression could settle the matter. " It is my duty to protect the railway," he stated. " I am now leading my army to attack them along the railway. After the crisis is resolved, I shall not evade whatever blame may be laid upon me." [30]   On June 9 he had telegraphed

[25] *Ibid.*, 53/32-33.   [26] *Ibid.*, 53/37-38.
[27] *Ibid.*, 53/44.   [28] *Ibid.*, 53/45.
[29] *Chih Tung Tien Ts'un*, 4/11, 4/14.   [30] *Ibid.*, 4/17.

again: "The Boxers intend to attack my army from the rear. Having no time to wait for a decree, I have directed my cavalry and infantry forces to attack and stop them and then proceed to suppress them all so as to save the general situation." [31]

It was because of his strong action against the Boxers that as soon as hostilities broke out at Taku his troops were harassed by the Boxers. His failure to stop the advance of the Allied forces gave his enemies a good pretext for impeaching him. On the day when he was killed in battle, a decree was issued dismissing him from his office but retaining him in service so that he could redeem his honor. If he failed again, the Imperial order declared, he would be court-martialed.[32]

The General may have heard of the Court's unfavorable attitude toward him. He fought desperately and exposed himself to the fire of the Allied troops. He was hit by an artillery shell. Upon receipt of the report of his death, the Imperial Court issued on July 11 an edict restoring to him his official rank but speaking disparagingly of his "Western drill." [33] It was not until March 7, 1902, that he was vindicated by Yüan Shih-k'ai, his comrade-in-arms, who sent in a memorial pointing out his contributions to the country. The Court gave its approval and the posthumous honors due his rank were conferred upon him.[34]

After the death of General Nieh, the Allied forces advanced rapidly. On July 13 they took Tientsin; the Chinese forces first retreated to Peich'ang and then to Yangts'un. The Boxers were the first to flee. Thus reported Yü Lu and General Sung Ch'ing:

In response to the Imperial decree, we pacified the Boxer leaders Chang Tê-ch'êng and Ts'ao Fu-t'ien and requested their assistance, but the Boxers were too wild to be trained. On the pretext of enmity against the Christians they pillaged everywhere but never had any intention of fighting the foreign troops. . . . Before the battle of July 13 we had requested their collaboration, but pretending either that the time was not opportune or that the date was not felicitous, they declined time and again. Then as the army was engaging the enemy, mines suddenly ex-

31 *Ibid.*, Introduction /12.
32 Decree, K26/6/13, *Chung Jih Shih Liao*, 53/43a.
33 Decree, K26/6/15, *Ch'ing Tê Tsung Shih Lu*, 465/12a.
34 Yüan Shih-k'ai, *Yang Shou Yüan Tsou I Chi Yao*, 14/5.

ploded on all sides, rocking the earth and shattering everything within tens of miles; by that time the Boxers had all vanished. . . . The so-called leaders have not shown up for many days; they could not be found and there is no way to reorganize the Boxers.[35]

Yet only a month earlier, immediately after hostilities broke out at Taku, Yü Lu had reported that he had organized 30,000 Boxers, whose leaders' patriotism was " manifest in their faces." [36]

With the loss of Tientsin, the Imperial Court had to reshape its policy. Meanwhile the Court received the joint memorial, dated July 14, from the thirteen southern viceroys and governors, requesting (1) protection of the foreign merchants and missionaries; (2) an Imperial letter to Germany, expressing regret for the death of Baron von Ketteler, and also Imperial letters to the United States and France, as these countries had been neglected when letters had been sent to Russia, Britain, and Japan; (3) an order to the Prefect of Shunt'ienfu and the Viceroy of Chihli to list the losses sustained by the foreigners on account of the Boxer disturbances, so that grants could be made by the Imperial Government as compensation; and (4) an express decree to the Viceroy of Chihli and the military officials that any riots on the part of the rebellious " bandits " or troops should be suppressed by force.[37] Then there arrived the warnings served by the Powers that the Imperial Government would be held responsible for any injury suffered by the foreigners in the legations.[38] About the same time the Japanese Government declared that, if the Chinese Government could effectively suppress the Boxers and protect the foreign ministers, the rest could be easily settled.[39]

Because of the military situation and because of these internal and external factors, the Imperial Court tended toward conciliation. On July 17 the Court issued an edict embodying all the recommendations made by the viceroys in their joint memorandum

---

[35] Memorial by Yü and Sung, K26/6/28, *Chung Jih Shih Liao*, 55/1-2.

[36] Memorial by Yü Lu, K26/5/24, *ibid.*, 53/18-29.

[37] Yüan Shih-k'ai, *op. cit.*, 5/8. Baron Clemens von Ketteler, German Minister at Peking, was shot in his sedan chair by a Chinese soldier on June 20.

[38] The reports from the Chinese ministers at London and Paris were forwarded to Peking by Li Hung-chang on July 7 and 8 respectively. Li Hung-chang, *Li Wén Chung Kung Ch'üan Chi*, " Tien Kao," 23/21.

[39] From Li, K26/6/19 (July 15, 1900), Shêng Hsüan-huai, *op. cit.*, 37/19.

of July 14.[40]   On the same day Imperial letters were sent to the
United States, France, and Germany, requesting them to help
China out of its existing difficulties.[41]   The next day a decree was
issued to Li Hung-chang, ordering the senior minister to inform
the foreign countries that their ministers at Peking were all well
and that the foreign governments need not be worried about their
safety.[42]

On July 14, the day after the fall of Tientsin, the Tsungli
Yamen sent a memorandum to the legations, saying that since there
were so many Boxers on the road to Tientsin, misadventure might
occur if, in accordance with previous agreement, the Chinese Government were to escort the foreign ministers out of the capital.
It was requested therefore that the foreign ministers and their
families, together with their staffs, leave the legations and temporarily stay in the Tsungli Yamen, pending further arrangements
for their return home.[43]   The foreign ministers, however, had no
confidence in the Tsungli Yamen, and replied that they " do not
understand why they should be safer in the Yamen than in the
Legations." [44]   On July 16 the Yamen wrote again.   It explained
that if all ministers should collect at the Tsungli Yamen, there
would be a concentration of force for the protection of a single
place.   But since the proposal was not acceptable to the foreign
envoys, China would increase the number of troops and strictly
restrain the Boxers, preventing them from again opening fire on or
attacking the legations.   " China will continue to exert all her
efforts to keep order and give protection in accordance with general
law." [45]   The Chinese Government then ordered a suspension of
hostilities which lasted about twelve days.[46]   To show their good
will, the Tsungli Yamen sent to the legations on July 20 four cart-
loads of vegetables and four of watermelons.[47]

[40] Ch'ing Tê Tsung Shih Lu, 465/15a.
[41] Chung Jih Shih Liao, 54/18.
[42] Ch'ing Tê Tsung Shih Lu, 465/16b.   [43] Chung Jih Shih Liao, 53/34.
[44] British Parliamentary Papers, China No. 4 (1900), p. 38.
[45] Chung Jih Shih Liao, 54/11; China No. 4 (1900), p. 38.
[46] China No. 4 (1900), p. 30.
[47] On July 26 the Yamen sent a further supply of melons and vegetables and also
some rice and 1,000 pounds of flour. Ibid., pp. 30, 33.

Having failed to persuade the foreign ministers to move to the Yamen, the Chinese Government proposed to escort them to Tientsin. On July 19 the Yamen wrote the legations: " After much consideration, our only course is again to request Your Excellencies temporarily to retire to Tientsin. The Throne will not fail to provide protection. It will dispatch the forces of Sung Ch'ing and Sun Wan-lin to give you effective escort and to guarantee your safety." [48] The foreign ministers again refused, asking the Yamen to explain " why, if the Chinese Government cannot insure the protection of the foreign Envoys in Peking, they feel confident of their power to do so outside the City, on the way to Tientsin." [49]

On July 25 the Yamen explained:

Being in the city is permanent, being on the road is temporary. If all the foreign ministers are willing to retire temporarily, we should propose the route to T'ungchou and thence by boat down the stream direct to Tientsin, which could be reached in only two days. No matter what difficulties there might be, an adequate force would be sent, half by water to form a close escort, half by road to keep all safe for a distance on both banks. Since it would be for a limited time, it is possible to guarantee that there would be no mischance. It is otherwise with a permanent residence in Peking where it is impossible to foretell when a disaster may occur. No matter whether by day or by night, a single hour or a single moment's laxness may leave no time for guarding against a sudden danger.[50]

The proposal ended there. Because of the foreign ministers' lack of confidence, the Chinese effort to deliver them from the dangerous spot was thwarted. The intention of the Imperial Government at this time was sincere. The proposal was made as a result of the urgent request of the southern viceroys, the warnings of the foreign governments, and the deterioration of the military situation. Both viceroys and the foreign governments insisted that the solution of the crisis depended upon the safety of the foreign ministers. It was for the purpose of resolving the situation that the Imperial Government suspended hostilities, supplied the legations with large quantities of food, and made efforts to escort the foreign ministers

48 *Chung Jih Shih Liao*, 54/22b.   49 *China No. 4* (1900), p. 42.
50 *Chung Jih Shih Liao*, 54/32a; *China No. 4* (1900), p. 44.

to Tientsin. The effort failed, and soon circumstances reversed the
conciliatory trend.

" VICTORY BEFORE PEACE "

The trend was reversed upon the arrival of Li Ping-hêng at
Peking. Li was highly patriotic and passionately antiforeign. He
had distinguished himself in the Sino-French War of 1885, when,
in charge of military supplies, he had kept the Chinese army from
suffering any shortage of food and thus had contributed greatly to
the Chinese victory at Liangshan.[51]   In 1895, when China was to
sign the peace treaty with Japan, Li, then Governor of Shantung,
had vehemently opposed the treaty. " The Powers," he wrote in a
memorial, " are watching with a tiger's voracity. . . . Their moves
will depend upon how we conclude the war with Japan." He
would rather have used the money demanded by Japan as indemnity to rearm and reorganize the Chinese army. " If the generals, viceroys, and governors are strictly ordered to fight to the
death," he declared, " the Japanese will collapse within half a
year." [52]   Li Ping-hêng hated everything that had foreign origins.
" Li Hung-chang has long taken up the Western enterprises, but
where is the promised power and prosperity? " he demanded.[53]
He was opposed to railroads, paper currency, mining, post offices,
and modern schools.[54]   He was removed from his Shantung governorship under the pressure of the German Government in 1898
when two German missionaries were killed in his province. But he
was soon appointed to other important offices. In November,
1899, when he was appointed Imperial Inspector of the Yangtze
Naval Forces, he at first declined on the ground that he was not
good in handling foreign affairs and that the Yangtze Valley was
a center of international intrigues.[55]   But Li Ping-hêng was known
for his efficiency, integrity, and strong will. " After twenty-five
years of public service, attaining as high as governorship," he once
wrote, " what I have accumulated is a debt of 20,000 taels, but

[51] *Ch'ing Shih Kao*, " Lieh Chuan," No. 254.
[52] Memorial, K21/4/1, Li Ping-hêng, *Li Chung Chieh Kung Tsou I*, 8/13.
[53] Memorial, K21/9/6, *ibid.*, 10/3.
[54] Memorial, K21/9/16, *ibid.*, 11/1a.
[55] Memorial, K25/10/20, *ibid.*, 16/19.

not a single month's food. After the victory of Liangshan, I recommended 6,000 persons, but not a single relative or favorite friend."[56]

On June 26, 1900, upon receipt of the Imperial decree that the various provinces should at once send troops to Peking to await orders, Li Ping-hêng immediately offered his services. In a joint memorial submitted together with the Viceroy at Nanking and the Governor of Kiangsu, Li requested that the two armies of Chang Ch'un-fa and Ch'ên Tsê-lin, which were moving from the Hsüchow and Huai River area, be placed under his command.[57] The Imperial Court was eager to secure his services. On June 24 a decree was issued ordering him to proceed to Peking at once. The decree was received on June 29 and Li Ping-hêng hastened on his journey.[58] On July 6, when he reached Shantung, he received the second decree ordering him to expedite his journey.[59] The following day he received another decree directing him to double his speed by traveling day and night.[60]

On July 26 Li Ping-hêng arrived at Peking. He met Hsü T'ung and Kang I and was greatly encouraged by the two reactionaries.[61] In the audience with the Empress Dowager his theme was, " Only when one can fight can one negotiate for peace." [62] The Empress Dowager was apparently pleased, as a decree was promptly issued conferring upon him the rare honor of riding within the Forbidden City and using a sedan chair borne by two persons in the Winter Palace.[63] Another decree appointed him Deputy Commander of the Northern Armies and placed under his command the four armies of Chang Ch'un-fa, Ch'ên Tsê-lin, Wan Pên-hua, and Hsia Hsin-yu.[64]

The positive policy of Li Ping-hêng at once heightened the spirit of the Imperial Court and the reactionaries. The Boxers were naturally encouraged. On July 27 Prince Ch'ing wrote to the

[56] Biography, ibid., 1/4b.
[57] Memorial, K26/5/3, ibid., 16/27.
[58] Ibid., 16/28.
[59] Chung Jih Shih Liao, 54/6.
[60] Ibid.
[61] Yün Yü-ting, Ch'ung Ling Ch'uan Hsin Lu.
[62] Ibid. See also Hu Ssŭ-ching, Lu Pei Chi, 2/16; Li Hung-chang, op. cit., " Tien Kao," 24/24.
[63] Decree, K26/7/1, Ch'ing Tê Tsung Shih Lu, 466/19.
[64] Ibid.

southern viceroys: "The Boxers in and out of the capital daily increase. It is true, as said in your letter, that they should be suppressed so as to deprive the foreigners of their pretext. But the responsibility is too great for my humble abilities, and as the power is exercised by the Court, I really dare not make any request." [65]

That was indeed not the time for a minister to make any proposal against the Boxers. On July 28 Hsü Ching-ch'êng, ex-Minister to Russia, and Yüan Ch'ang, Minister of the Tsungli Yamen, were executed by Imperial order. [66] Two weeks later, Hsü Yung-i, President of the Board of War, Lien Yüan, Sub-Chancellor of the Grand Secretariat, and Li Shan, President of the Board of Finance, were also executed. [67] For some time even the life of Grand Councillor Wang Wên-shao was in danger. [68] The situation was so confused that Yüan Shih-k'ai telegraphed Shêng Hsüan-huai on August 2: "It is hopeless; better say less." [69]

The reason for the execution of the five ministers has been a subject of controversy, [70] particularly in the case of Yüan Ch'ang and Hsü Ching-ch'êng. In the case of these two it has been suggested that their death was due to three memorials which circulated widely after the fall of Peking; they were allegedly drafted by Yüan Ch'ang and submitted jointly with Hsü Ching-ch'êng. The first of these memorials, dated June 18, recommended that Jung Lu be ordered to suppress the Boxers by force; the second, dated July 12, urged that the foreign ministers at Peking be protected; the third, dated July 22, requested that the reactionary leaders Hsü T'ung, Kang I, Ch'i Hsiu, Chao Shu-ch'iao, Yü Lu, Yü Hsien, and Tung Fu-hsiang, who "had brought calamities to the country and the people," all be executed. [71]

---

[65] Shêng Hsüan-huai, op. cit., 38/21.

[66] Ching Chin Ch'üan Fei Chi Lüeh, Part I, 1/12.

[67] Decree, K26/7/17, Ch'ing Tê Tsung Shih Lu, 467/1b.

[68] Yün Yü-ting, op. cit.; Hsi Hsün Ta Shih Chi, Introduction /15.

[69] Shêng Hsüan-huai, op. cit., 38/23. For a story about Prince Tuan plotting to kill Yüan Shih-k'ai, see Wang Hsiao-yin, "Hua Hsü Man Lu," in Jên Wên Yüeh K'an, Vol. IV (1923), No. 6.

[70] See Ch'êng Ming-chou, "The So-called 'Diary of Ching Shan,'" in Yen Ching Hsüeh Pao, June, 1940.

[71] The "three memorials" appeared in many Chinese works, notably the following: Yüan Ch'ang Hsing Lüeh, in Chuan Chi Hsing Shu Hui Chi; Hsü Wên Su Kung I

The Imperial Court later emphatically denied that it had ever received these three memorials. In a telegram to Prince Ch'ing and Li Hung-chang on February 12, 1901, the Court declared: " The five ministers were punished because of repeated impeachments against them . . . not because of their opposition to the violation of international law. There were no memorials submitted by them on the subject." [72] On March 2 another Imperial decree was issued to Ch'ing and Li: " As the five ministers did not submit any memorials opposing the attack on the legations, there is no way to copy them. Recently the press has often carried sensational rumors. It is quite possible that the foreign countries become suspicious on seeing these private fabrications. But it is easy to tell the difference between private fabrications and official documents. The actual causes for punishing the five ministers were the false accusations by the reactionary leaders." [73]

The denial of the Imperial Court was substantiated by Chang Shên, editor of the official history of the Ch'ing Dynasty, who thoroughly searched the archives of the Grand Council, the Grand Secretariat, and the Memorials Office and found none of the supposed memorials.[74] Yüan Ch'ang was not given to recklessness. As his son testified, he was a man of prudence.[75] The third memorial, which has been asserted to be the immediate cause of his death, requested the execution of seven powerful officials: one Grand Secretary, three Grand Councillors, one viceroy, one governor and one general—all in the favor of the Empress Dowager. No man of practical statesmanship would submit such a reckless memorial, and Yüan Ch'ang was reputed to be a practical and cautious man.[76]

The causes of the execution are not far to be found. It was a time when the reactionaries had just decided to continue the war

Kao, 3/1-9; Ch'ing Chi Wai Chiao Shih Liao, 143/8-14. For an English translation, see Foreign Relations of the United States, 1901, Appendix (Washington: Government Printing Office, 1902), pp. 75 ff.

[72] Hsi Hsün Ta Shih Chi, 4/38a.   [73] Ch'ing Tê Tsung Shih Lu, 478/14b.
[74] Chang Shên, I Shan Wên Ts'un, 3/18.
[75] Note by Yüan Yung-sou, in Yüan Ch'ang, Yüan Chung Chieh Kung Shou Cha, ts'ê 2.
[76] Postscripts by Wu Yü-shêng and K'ang Yu-wei, ibid., ts'ê 2.

with renewed vigor. To solidify their position and to silence those who advocated peaceful settlement, they resorted to terrorism. The five executed ministers were regarded as friendly to the foreign Powers and hostile to the Boxers. Yüan Ch'ang had been emphatic in his opposition to the Boxers: he had been outspoken in condemning them in the Imperial Council summoned by the Empress Dowager on the eve of war. Hsü Ching-ch'êng had held that the Boxers should be suppressed and that the foreign ministers should be protected. He was the minister whom the Emperor had asked in the Imperial Council of June 19 to negotiate "in a better way" with the foreign ministers.[77] Hsü Yung-i had suggested to Prince Ch'ing that he take care of the dead body of Baron von Ketteler. He had maintained that the Boxers should not be tolerated and that China could not fight all the Powers.[78] Li Shan had pointed out that the Boxers were not invulnerable to weapons,[79] and he had the misfortune of living near the Northern Roman Catholic Cathedral, thus giving rise to the story that he had tendered assistance to it through an underground channel.[80] As to Lien Yüan, he had argued with Ch'ung I before the Throne that, while the support of the people was useful, the support of the bandits was futile. Since China had been unable to defeat Japan, how could she hope to defeat eight Powers? [81] Hsü Yung-i, Li Shan, and Lien Yüan were appointed in the Imperial Council of June 17 to inform the foreign ministers that, if they wanted to break the peace, they could haul down their flags and leave China. The Empress Dowager was at that time furious with the so-called Four-Point Demand of the Powers and was ready for war.[82] On June 18 the three ministers, accompanied by Hsü Ching-ch'êng, called on the British Minister, Sir Claude MacDonald. Instead of informing MacDonald of the Empress Dowager's instructions, however, they told him that "they had come by Imperial order to express the regret of the Throne at recent disturbances, and to convey the assurance

[77] Yün Yü-ting, op. cit.
[78] Ch'ing Shih Kao, " Lieh Chuan," No. 253.   [79] Ibid.
[80] Yün Yü-ting, op. cit.
[81] Ch'ing Shih Kao, " Lieh Chuan," No. 253.   [82] See Yün Yü-ting, op. cit.

that quiet would now be restored." [83]   Li Shan, in particular, " made a very favorable impression " on the British Minister.   He " kept calling his colleagues' attention to the reasonableness of my attitude," reported Sir Claude MacDonald, " [and] was emphatic in his promises to place matters before the Empress Dowager in their true light." [84]   It was not unnatural that the reactionaries who were intent on war should have hated the four ministers, who must have reported that the British Minister had said nothing of the " Four-Point Demand," but had declared that far from having any hostile intentions toward the Chinese Government, the foreign reinforcements would be of material assistance in preserving order and so work for the good of the Ch'ing Dynasty.

Thus it was because they opposed the Boxers and the war that the five ministers incurred the anger of the reactionaries.   The reasons given in the Imperial decree ordering their decapitation, though vague in terms, were not far from the truth.   Hsü Ching-ch'êng and Yüan Ch'ang, declared the decree of July 29, " had been repeatedly denounced as being of bad reputation and as keeping private ideas in their handling of foreign affairs.   When they were summoned to Imperial audiences, they allowed themselves to make wild proposals and to disturb the government by their evil discourse.   Their words, which created dissensions, were intolerable. They really have committed the crime of gross disrespect. . . ." [85] Similar explanations were given in the decree condemning the other three ministers to death. [86]

THE FALL OF PEKING

On August 6 Li Ping-hêng left Peking and at noon on the 7th arrived at Mat'ou.   There he received the report that Peich'ang had been lost and that the army under General Sung Ch'ing was retreating to Ts'aits'un. [87]   In the early morning of the 6th the Allies had attacked Yangts'un and defeated the Chinese army, whereupon Viceroy Yü Lu had committed suicide. [88]   On the 9th, two

[83] MacDonald to Salisbury, Sept. 20, 1900, *China No. 4* (1900), p. 22.   [84] *Ibid.*
[85] Decree, K26/7/4, *Ching Chin Ch'üan Fei Chi Lüeh*, Part I, 1/12.
[86] Decree, K26/7/17, *Ch'ing Tê Tsung Shih Lu*, 167/1b.
[87] *Chung Jih Shih Liao*, 55/21.   [88] *Ibid.*, 55/22.

of the armies under Li Ping-hêng met the Allies near Hosiwu and were quickly defeated. The next day Li planned to join with the forces of Ma Yü-k'un and make a stand, but before he had time to concentrate his forces, the Allies launched their attack and took Hosiwu. The Chinese forces retreated to Mat'ou, only to give it up the following day. The situation was reported by Li Ping-hêng on August 11:

I have retreated from Ma'tou to Changchiawan. For the past few days I have seen several tens of thousands of troops jamming all the roads. They fled as soon as they heard of the arrival of the enemy; they did not give battle at all. As they passed the villages and towns, they set fire and plundered, so much so that there was nothing left for the armies under my command to purchase, with the result that men and horses were hungry and exhausted. From youth to old age, I have experienced many wars, but never saw things like these. . . . Unless we restore discipline and execute the retreating generals and escaping troops, there will be no place where we can stand. But I am unable to do this because of lack of authority. . . . The troops under Chang Ch'un-fa are brave, but they are newly recruited and so easily break when they suffer defeat. Ch'ên Tsê-lin is crafty and knows nothing about war. Hsia Hsin-yu and Wan Pên-hua are capable commanders, but they have too few troops at their disposal. . . . As all the armies are taking to flight, the situation is getting out of control. There is no time to regroup and deploy. But I will do my utmost to collect the fleeing troops and fight to the death, so as to repay the kindness of Your Majesties and to do the smallest part of a minister's duty.[89]

The same day, as the Chinese forces collapsed before the attack of the Allies at T'ungchou, Li took his life.[90]

As the military situation deteriorated, the Imperial Court made a last effort for peace. In a decree issued on August 11, it declared that Li Hung-chang had been appointed plenipotentiary to negotiate with the Powers, and that telegrams had been sent to the foreign governments asking for a truce. General Sung Ch'ing was ordered to notify the foreign commanders at the front of the above decree and to negotiate with them for a truce.[91] The following day, upon receipt of Li Ping-hêng's report that Hosiwu had

[89] Li's memorial, K26/7/17, *Chung Jih Shih Liao*, 55/27; Li Ping-hêng, *op. cit.*, 16/29.
[90] *Ch'ing Tê Tsung Shih Lu*, 468/15b.   [91] *Ibid.*, 467/2a.

fallen, the Tsungli Yamen was ordered by the Empress Dowager to send some members to the legations to negotiate for a truce.[92] The Yamen wrote to the British Minister, proposing a call from its ministers so that a preliminary suspension of hostilities could be arranged.[93] The British Minister replied that the Chinese representatives would be received at 11 o'clock the next morning.[94] But the Yamen ministers were afraid that they would be detained in the legations, and so on August 13 they informed the British Minister that they " all have important official engagements " and could not come.[95] Thus the last chance of negotiating with the foreign ministers was lost.

As the northern armies suffered defeat after defeat, the southern viceroys became anxious for a truce. Upon the report that the Chinese armies were retreating to Ts'ai-ts'un, Li Hung-chang, newly appointed plenipotentiary to negotiate with the Powers, telegraphed on August 9 to the various Chinese ministers abroad, instructing them to approach the foreign offices for a truce. General Terauchi, Japanese Deputy Chief of Staff, suggested that at this stage the Chinese Government should appoint some important ministers who were respected by foreigners to go to the front and arrange with the high command of the Allied forces for the safe escort of the foreign ministers. The American Government also indicated that, if the Allied forces approached the capital, the Chinese Government might send representatives to negotiate with the Allied commanders. On the basis of these reports, Li sent a memorial on August 13 urging that the Court should at once order some Tsungli Yamen ministers to the front and suggesting that Sir Robert Hart be appointed to accompany them. Li also strongly advised against the Court's moving to the west.[96]

The memorial came too late: before it reached its destination the Allied troops had entered Peking, and the Imperial Court had fled

[92] *Chung Jih Shih Liao*, 55/28b. [93] *Ibid.*, 55/28b.
[94] *China No. 4* (1900), p. 36.
[95] Jung Lu's memorial, K26/8/7, *Chung Jih Shih Liao*, 56/15; *Hsi Hsün Ta Shih Chi*, Introduction /16.
[96] Li's memorial, K26/7/19, received, K26/8/12, *Hsi Hsün Ta Shih Chi*, 1/31.

westward.[97]   There was also no reply from General Sung Ch'ing to the decree of August 11 ordering him to negotiate for a truce at the front.   Apparently the decree also came too late, for after the defeat in T'ungchou the Chinese armies collapsed so rapidly that there was practically no time for any negotiations.

The Allied forces entered Peking in the afternoon of August 14 and relieved the legations from the siege which had lasted nearly eight weeks.   It was considered a miracle that some 500 defenders could withstand the attack of thousands of troops and Boxers.[98] " There were occasions," wrote Arthur H. Smith, who was in the Legation Quarter during the siege, " as on the day when the gathering at the British Legation took place, when it would have been easy by a strong, swift movement on the part of the numerous Chinese troops to have annihilated the whole body of foreigners, and without serious risk to the attackers, but the opportunity was not seized." [99]   B. L. Putnam Weale (B. Lenox Simpson) also wrote: " Were Chinese commanders united in their purpose and their men faithful to them, a few determined rushes would pierce our loose formation." [100]   Why were the Chinese commanders not united in purpose and why did they not seize these opportunities and destroy the legations?   Sir Robert Hart offered the following explanation:

That somebody intervened for our semi-protection seems, however, probable.   Attacks were not made by such numbers as the Government had at its disposal—they were never pushed home, but always ceased just when we feared they would succeed—and, had the force round us really attacked with thoroughness and determination, we could not have held out a week, perhaps not even a day.   So the explanation gained credence that there was some kind of protection—that somebody, probably a wise

[97] Lord Salisbury also agreed that if the foreign envoys could be escorted outside the capital and received by the Allied liason officers holding white flags, the Allied forces would refrain from entering the city.   But the telegrams sent by the Chinese Minister in London were not received by Li Hung-chang until August 14 and 15 when the Allied forces had already entered the city.   Li Hung-chang, op. cit., "Tien Kao," 24/29, 32.

[98] Arthur H. Smith, China in Convulsion (New York: Fleming H. Revell, 1901), II, 508.

[99] Ibid., I, 317.

[100] B. L. Putnam Weale, Indiscreet Letters from Peking (New York: Dodd, Mead & Co., 1907), p. 242.

man who knew what the destruction of the Legations would cost the Empire and Dynasty, intervened between the issue of the order for our destruction and the execution of it, and so kept the soldiery playing with us as cats do with mice, the continued and seemingly heavy firing telling the Palace how fiercely we were attacked and how stubbornly we defended ourselves, while its curiously half-hearted character not only gave us the chance to live through it, but also gave any relief forces time to come and extricate us, and thus avert the national calamity which the Palace in its pride and conceit ignored, but which some one in authority in his wisdom foresaw and in his discretion sought how to push aside.[101]

If there was any one who could have intervened in this manner, it was Jung Lu, who alone had the military power to do so. As noted above, Jung Lu had been opposed to the Boxers and the war.[102] But Jung Lu was a shrewd man; he had no desire to risk his neck by opposing the reactionary party, which, under the leadership of Prince Tuan and Kang I, comprised almost all the Manchu princes and dukes as well as the majority of the Grand Councillors. Furthermore, the Empress Dowager was on their side. A minister had to obey Imperial orders, and there was no reason why Jung Lu should offend the Empress Dowager. Jung Lu's troops participated in the attack on the legations, but he realized that the foreign ministers had to be saved if a national calamity were to be averted.[103] As early as June 25, he ordered a "cease-fire" and attempted to communicate with the legations. The attempt failed as one of the men sent out by Jung Lu to deliver a dispatch was shot dead.[104] The position of Jung Lu may be seen from the following telegram sent by him to Liu K'un-i and Chang Chih-tung on July 9:

If we can save the foreign ministers, it will be good for the future. But after the death of the German Minister, the British Minister had Prince Su driven out of his palace and ordered thousands of Christian converts to live there. The various legations were united and daily fired their rifles and guns, killing innumerable officials and people. Four times they

---

[101] *These from the Land of Sinim* (London: Chapman & Hall, 1901), p. 40.

[102] See above, pp. 66-67.

[103] According to Liu K'un-i, Jung Lu had stopped Tung Fu-hsiang from using high explosive shells (from Liu, K26/ intercalary 8/27, Chang Chih-tung, *Chang Wên Hsiang Kung Ch'üan Chi*, 167/3b). Chang Chih-tung, too, maintained that Jung Lu had tried to restrain Tung Fu-hsiang (to Liu, K26/intercalary 8/27, *ibid.*, 167/3).

[104] *China No. 3 (1901)*, p. 7.

attacked the Tunghua Gate, but were repulsed by the troops of Tung
Fu-hsiang. They occupied the wall above the Chunghsing Terrace and
from there daily fired into the Imperial City, where the palace often received the bullets. It was therefore impossible for the Headquarters
Army and Tung Fu-hsiang's troops not to defend their positions and
make counterattacks. Meanwhile the Boxers stirred up more disturbances. I have tried to give protection and to bring about a reconcilia-
tion. I have put up notices allowing the Christian converts to redeem
themselves. On June 25 I had a notice written in big characters saying
that in accordance with the Imperial decree we will protect the legations,
that shooting is forbidden, and that we should communicate with each
other. [The legations] not only paid no attention, but [opened fire].
Recently there have been quite a few memorializing the Throne for the
protection of the foreign envoys, but the difficulty is that there is no
way to communicate with [the legations]. Under these circumstances
Their Majesties were also helpless. We can only do what is humanly
possible and await the mandate of Heaven. What would Your Excellencies advise me? [105]

In the arrangement for the truce and in the negotiations for the
escort of the foreign ministers to Tientsin in the middle of July,
Jung Lu played a leading role. When a Chinese Christian serving
as a messenger of the legations was captured, Jung Lu immediately
seized the opportunity and advised the Throne that attempts
should be made to communicate with the foreign envoys.[106] He
sent Wên Jui, a secretary of the Tsungli Yamen, to the legations
to explore possibilities of *rapprochement*.[107] The British Minister
noted the difference between the troops under Tung Fu-hsiang and
those under Jung Lu:

There were noteworthy differences, however, between the troops on
different sides of us, those to the north and west—all Kansuh men under
Tung Fu-hsiang—remaining sullen and suspicious. From other directions, and especially on the east, where Jung Lu's troops were posted, it
was possible to obtain supplies (small, but welcome) of eggs and vegetables, the sellers being smuggled through the Chinese soldiers' lines in spite
of the prohibition of their officers, and it was from this side that the
messengers came with all later letters. They declared, in fact, that they
could not get through the troops on our western side without being
shot.[108]

105 Chang Chih-tung, *op. cit.*, 162/23b.
106 From Yüan, K26/6/27, Shêng Hsüan-huai, *op. cit.*, 37/30.
107 *China No. 4 (1900)*, p. 31.   108 *China No. 4 (1900)*, p. 30.

The behavior of Jung Lu's troops displeased the reactionaries. On August 10, when it was reported that Tung Fu-hsiang's troops would be sent out of the capital and that Jung Lu's troops were to take their place, Prince Tsai Lien submitted the following memorial:

Since Tung Fu-hsiang attacked the legations he has made good progress, and the position of the foreigners has appeared untenable. But because of the truce, for two weeks he had no orders and so could not move. Both officials and people have regretted this. Now it is heard that he has been ordered by Imperial decree to dispatch his troops out of the capital and that the Wu Wei Headquarters troops [troops under the direct command of Jung Lu] are to take their place. The people in Peking feel alarmed and apprehensive. Yesterday so many inhabitants and shopkeepers went to urge Tung to stay that the streets were jammed. This shows how he had gained the heart of the people, who regard him as the Great Wall. The Wu Wei Headquarters troops are newly recruited and have no experience of war; they cannot be much relied upon. It is requested that an Imperial decree be issued, ordering all Kansu troops to remain and to collaborate in the work of defense and extermination, so that the heart of the people will be gratified and the general situation stabilized.[109]

[109] Memorial by Tsai Lien, K26/7/16, *Chung Jih Shih Liao*, 55/27a. The so-called Letter of Tung Fu-hsiang to Jung Lu, as found in *Hsi Hsün Hui Luan Shih Mo Chi*, 6/373, and quoted in *Ch'ing Shih Kao*, "Lieh Chuan," No. 242, and Li Chien-nung, *Chung Kuo Chin Pai Nien Chêng Chih Shih* (A Political History of China for the Past Hundred Years, Shanghai, 1947), II, 207, is not a reliable source. The charge in the letter that, in spite of his remonstrances, he was ordered by Jung Lu to attack the legations is contrary to the evidence shown in the above pages. As will be shown below, chap. VII, Jung Lu was persistently opposed to Tung's severe punishment which was demanded by the foreign ministers. There seems to be no reason why Tung should have written such a scathing letter to Jung Lu.

6

The Indispensable Diplomat

As THE ALLIED FORCES were fast approaching Peking, the Imperial Court decided to move to the west. On August 10 a decree was issued ordering Jung Lu, Hsü T'ung, Kang I, and Ch'ung I to remain in Peking to take charge of governmental affairs after the departure of the Court, which was to leave the following day.[1] The viceroys in the south heard of the plan, and on August 12 Li Hung-chang, over the protest of Chang Chih-tung, sent a memorial strongly advising against the move.[2] The memorial, however, did not reach the Court until after the fall of Peking.[3] Meanwhile, the Court postponed its departure. It was after the Allied force had entered Peking that the Empress Dowager and the Emperor left the city in the early morning of August 15.

Their Majesties left in a hurry and put on only simple clothes. There was no time to have the Imperial carts ready, so the Empress Dowager rode in the cart of Duke Lan, while the Emperor rode in that of Ying Nien, Commander of the Peking Field Force. The Empress and the Heir Apparent had to ride in a commoner's cart.[4]

The Imperial retinue was a small one. In addition to Duke Lan and Ying Nien, there were Na Yen-t'u, P'u Lun, Ting Ch'ang, Chih Chün, Chao Shu-ch'iao, and P'u Hsing. They went by way of the northwest Gate and stopped for a short while at the Summer Palace. Then they rode another twenty miles and arrived in the evening at Kuanshih, where they stayed overnight in a temple.[5]

The next day the Imperial carts rode out of Chüyungkuan and

---

[1] *Hsi Hsün Ta Shih Chi,* 1/1b.
[2] Chang Chih-tung, *Chang Wén Hsiang Kung Ch'üan Chi,* 163/43-51.
[3] The memorial did not reach the Court until September 5. *Hsi Hsün Ta Shih Chi,* 1/31-33.
[4] *Hsi Hsün Ta Shih Chi,* Introduction/15-16.　　　　　[5] *Ibid.,* 1/1a.

arrived at Ch'ataochên of the Huailai District in the evening. At Chüyungkuan, Prince Tuan caught up with the retinue.[6] At Ch'ataochên, Kang I, who had been ordered to remain in Peking, joined the Court. The Emperor, angry at Kang's violating the decree, ordered him back, but the Empress Dowager interceded and permitted him to stay.[7]

On August 17 the Imperial Court arrived at Huailai City and stayed there for three days. Here Their Majesties were received by the Magistrate, Wu Yung, and were furnished with better food and better clothing. For three days since leaving the palace, Their Majesties had suffered hardships: they had been hungry, tired, and without even a regular bed to sleep on. The great care which Wu Yung took in furnishing minimum comforts to the Empress Dowager immediately placed him in her favor.[8] On August 18

---

[6] *Ibid.*, Introduction/17a.   [7] *Ibid.*, Introduction/17, 1/1b.

[8] One of the widely quoted Chinese sources on the Imperial flight is *Kêng Tzŭ Hsi Shou Ts'ung T'an*, told by Wu Yung and transcribed by his friend Liu Chih-hsiang in 1927. The work was translated into English by Ida Pruitt under the title *The Flight of an Empress* (New Haven: Yale University Press, 1936). An examination of the account will reveal many inaccuracies. According to the account, the Imperial Court arrived at Huailai on August 18 (Wu Yung, *op. cit.*, 1/42); actually it arrived there on August 17 (*Ch'ing Tê Tsung Shih Lu*, 467/7-8). The assertion that on August 20 a decree was issued appointing Wu Yung Deputy-Director of Provisions (Wu Yung, *op. cit.*, 1/65a) was incorrect. Actually the decree of August 19 appointed only Ts'ên Ch'un-hsüan as the Director of Provisions, but no Deputy-Director was named (*Ch'ing Tê Tsung Shih Lu*, 467/10a). The day before, however, Yü Ch'i-yüan and Wu Yung were ordered to arrange with the local authorities for the supply of provisions to the accompanying troops (*ibid.*, 467/9a). The story that, at the suggestion of Chang Chih-tung, Wu Yung spoke to the Empress Dowager about the removal of the Heir Apparent is to be doubted. The account did not give the exact date of the interview with Chang in Hupeh, nor the date of his reporting to the Empress Dowager. It was stated, however, that he returned to Sian at the beginning of the 5th Moon and there obtained the support of Jung Lu, whose advice on the question he had requested (Wu Yung, *op. cit.*, 2/5-6). The impression given is that he reported to the Empress Dowager about that time. As a matter of fact, it was on November 24, 1901, that Chang Chih-tung wrote to Lu Ch'uan-lin, then Grand Councillor, informing him that the German Minister had come to Hupeh the preceding month and had expressed great displeasure against the Heir Apparent, whose father, Prince Tuan, had been chiefly responsible for the Boxer calamities. Lu was requested to report the opinion of the German Minister to the Throne "if chances permit" (Chang Chih-tung, *Chang Wên Hsiang Kung Ch'üan Chi*, 175/13b). It was apparently on the basis of this letter of Chang's that on November 30 an edict was issued removing the Heir Apparent (*Ch'ing Tê Tsung Shih Lu*, 488/12a).

The story that Wu Yung asked the Empress Dowager to redress the reputations of Hsü Yung-i, Hsü Ching-ch'êng, and Yüan Ch'ang is also to be doubted. First, the redress of the executed ministers' reputations was an international problem pressed by

Grand Councillor Wang Wên-shao arrived at Huailai with the seal
of the Grand Council;[9] henceforth the Imperial Government

---

the Powers (see Li Hung-chang, *Li Wên Chung Kung Ch'üan Chi*, "Tien Kao,"
32/24b). It would have been unbecoming for a minor official like Wu Yung to speak
on such a subject before the Throne. Secondly, Wu Yung was not even clear about the
causes or the dates of the executions (see Wu Yung, *op. cit.*, 1/15a, 2/7-10). How
could one memorialize on such an important subject without knowing the basic facts?
Thirdly, according to Wu Yung, the Empress Dowager was furious when he mentioned the subject (*ibid.*, 2/6-7). Actually, the Court raised no objection to the
demands made by the foreign ministers relative to the redress. The Empress Dowager
was quoted by Wu Yung as saying that "Kang I and Chao Shu-ch'iao spoiled the
country; their death cannot cover their guilt" (*ibid.*, 2/13-14). As a matter of fact,
the Court insisted that Chao Shu-ch'iao was not guilty and that the severe punishment
demanded by the foreign ministers was unjust (*Ch'ing Tê Tsung Shih Lu*, 477/6b;
Chang Chih-tung, *op. cit.*, 170/37b).

There are other mistakes, particularly in those sections which Wu Yung said he heard
from others. An example of these is the statement that Kang I, although sent by the
Court to investigate the Boxers at Chochou, "actually did not go" (Wu Yung, *op. cit.*,
2/15a). In short, as a source on the Boxer crisis, Wu Yung's book must be used
with great caution.

[9] *Hsi Hsün Ta Shih Chi*, 1/3a. Another widely quoted Chinese source on the Imperial flight was the so-called *Wang Wên Shao Chia Shu* (Family Letter of Wang
Wên-shao). A careful examination of the account gives rise to doubt about its authenticity. There are inconsistencies in the "Letter" itself. For instance, it says that
the author stayed on duty in the palace on the night of August 14, but almost immediately it states that on August 15 at 7 A.M. he went to the palace in a small chair and
found that Their Majesties had left the city in the early morning (in Tso Shun-shêng,
Chung Kuo Chin Pai Nien Shih Tzŭ Liao Hsü Pien). In another version it is stated
that Wang went to the "city" on the morning of the 15th and there learned of the
departure of Their Majesties (in *Hsi Hsün Hui Luan Shih Mo Chi*, book 3; also *Ching
Chin Ch'üan Fei Chi Lüeh*, book 6). But if he stayed overnight in the palace, how
could he have missed the news of the Imperial departure, and why did he have to learn
of it in the "city" the following day?

Again, in one place, the "Letter" says that all Wang's drivers had fled and that
therefore he had to leave all his carts, horses, and other belongings with a family inside
the city. But, in another place, it states that, in order to save his carts and horses from
being seized by the fleeing soldiers, Wang had them taken out of the city by his
servants, and he and his son went on foot to join them outside the West Gate (*Ching
Chin Ch'üan Fei Chi Lüeh*, book 6; also Tso Shun-shêng, *op. cit.*).

There seems also a discrepancy of fact. According to the "Letter," in the last
audience held about the midnight of the 14th, only Kang I, Chao Shu-ch'iao, and the
author were present, and the Empress Dowager said: "You three must accompany us."
As a matter of fact, Kang I was ordered on August 10 to remain in Peking with Jung
Lu, Hsü T'ung, and Ch'ung I to take charge of governmental affairs after the Court's
departure, and that order still stood. It is not likely therefore that the Empress Dowager
ordered Kang I to accompany Their Majesties. Had the Empress Dowager so commanded, it would hardly have been appropriate for the Emperor to order Kang I back
to Peking upon seeing him in Ch'ataochên on August 16. And why did Kang I not
accompany Their Majesties, if he had been ordered to go with them?

The several versions of the account vary considerably; there seems to have been much
editing and rewriting. It is difficult to see how such an important and responsible

began to function regularly. There were several problems that required its immediate attention. First was the procurement of supplies, particularly food for the troops that escorted the Imperial Court. On August 17 Magistrate Wu Yung had been ordered to put up whatever money he could collect for the food of the hungry soldiers.[10] On the 19th Ts'ên Ch'un-hsüan, Deputy-Governor of Kansu, was appointed Director of Provisions.[11] The districts nearby were ordered to send all available money to the Court, and the various provinces were directed to deliver all possible revenues.[12] Secondly, the Imperial Court had to maintain some kind of order amidst the confusion and turmoil created by the disorderly conduct of the accompanying troops. The roads were crowded with defeated soldiers, who pillaged and plundered as they retreated from the front. The situation was so much out of control that the Court had to detail some reliable troops at Nank'ou and Chüyungkuan and order them to stop by force the entry of any wandering soldiers.[13] Thirdly, while General Tung Fu-hsiang was ordered to deploy his troops at Huolu between Chihli and Shansi, and Governor Yü Hsien to guard Kukuan,[14] the Imperial Court at the same time looked for diplomatic solutions. On August 19 a decree was issued to Jung Lu, Hsü T'ung, and Ch'ung I, who were supposed to remain in Peking, to renew the truce negotiations with the British Minister.[15] The same day Li Hung-chang was directed to make every effort to establish relations with the foreign governments with a view to resolving the situation.[16]

On August 23 the Imperial Court decided to move to Shensi. The governor of the province was ordered to prepare the temporary palace at Sian.[17] The Court left Hsüanfa on August 25 and arrived at Tat'ung, Shansi, on the 30th. After staying there

---

minister as Wang Wên-shao should have let a "family letter" about the Imperial flight be published in the newspapers.

[10] *Hsi Hsün Ta Shih Chi,* 1/1b.

[11] *Ch'ing Tê Tsung Shih Lu,* 467/10a.

[12] *Hsi Hsün Ta Shih Chi,* 1/1-2, 4, 6.

[13] *Ibid.,* 1/3.

[14] *Ibid.,* 1/1-2.

[15] *Ibid.,* 1/3-4.

[16] *Ch'ing Tê Tsung Shih Lu,* 467/10b.

[17] *Ibid.,* 467/18a.

for four days, it started again and arrived at T'aiyüan on September 10. There it stayed until October 1, when it left for the province of Shensi. After nearly a month of traveling, it reached Sian on October 26.

THE DIPLOMAT TARRIES

For thirty years Li Hung-chang had been the leading statesman of China. Since his appointment as Viceroy of Chihli in 1870, the burden of China's diplomacy, military defense, and internal reconstruction had largely lain upon his shoulders. The interruption came in 1895, when the defeat of China in the war with Japan caused his dismissal from the important post of Viceroy of Chihli. He was, however, appointed a member of the Tsungli Yamen and still took an active part in the negotiations with foreign countries. When in October, 1898, he was sent to Shantung to survey the Yellow River, and then in December, 1899, at the age of 76, he was appointed Viceroy of Kwangtung and Kwangsi, it looked as if he were receding from the political center to pass the rest of his life in Canton. But it was not his fate to wind up his career in any such uneventful way.

On June 18, when war seemed imminent, the Imperial Court ordered Li Hung-chang to repair to Peking at once.[18] Upon receipt of the decree, Li planned to leave. He asked Shêng Hsüan-huai in Shanghai to send a ship to Canton immediately so that he could sail straight to Taku.[19] On June 19, after the fall of Taku, he still planned to land at Chinwangtao and take a train to Peking.[20] Two days later he began to change his mind. He telegraphed Shêng Hsüan-huai that the railroad service between Shanhaikwan and Tientsin might have been interrupted. As the people in Canton urged him to stay, said Li, he thought he might as well await further instructions from the Throne.[21] Actually what troubled him was the predominant influence of the Boxers and the possible removal of the Court to Sian.[22] Then he planned

---

[18] Shêng Hsüan-huai, *Yü Chai Ts'un Kao Ch'u K'an*, 35/29.   [19] *Ibid.*
[20] Li Hung-chang, *Li Wên Chung Kung Ch'üan Chi*, "Tien Kao," 22/25-6.
[21] To Shêng, K26/5/25, *ibid.*, 22/27.
[22] From Li, K26/5/25, *ibid.*, 22/27; Shêng Hsüan-huai, *op. cit.*, 35/31.

to go to Shanghai and to wait there for Imperial instructions.[23]
But as his proposal for the protection of the legations and the re-
straint of Tung Fu-hsiang's troops received no Imperial response,
he felt the futility of even this move.[24]   Meanwhile telegrams
from various quarters urged him to go up to the north.   The
Viceroy at Nanking, the Viceroy of Fukien, the General of Szechuan, the Minister to Japan, and his protégé Shêng Hsüan-huai
were all of the opinion that he alone could save the situation, and
that the sooner he went north, the better for the Throne and for
China.[25]   But Li was unmoved.   " If Prince Ch'ing and Jung Lu
could do nothing," he wrote to Liu K'un-i, " how could I?   Very
soon the Allied forces will come near the city; I imagine it would
take a pitched battle or two to clarify the issue." [26]

As the military situation deteriorated, the Court became anxious
to have the assistance of the veteran statesman.   On July 3 a decree
was issued ordering Li to obey the former decree and repair to
Peking " without a moment's delay." [27]   Three days later he was
ordered again to start at once, to take the land route if it was
inconvenient to come by boat.[28]   On July 8 Li was appointed
Viceroy of Chihli and Minister of Trade for the Northern Ports,[29]
a post he had held from 1870 to 1895.   Thereafter telegram after
telegram was sent to the Viceroy, ordering him to depart at once.[30]

Under this pressure Li sailed from Canton on July 17 and arrived at Shanghai on the 21st.[31]   There he received a telegram from
Yüan Shih-k'ai saying that Peking was determined on war and
that the foreign ministers were in grave danger.[32]   Another official
telegraphed from Têchou, reporting the fall of Tientsin and the
danger of the military situation.   He also urged Li not to leave for
the north so as to " preserve your life for the country." [33]   There-

---

[23] From Li, K26/5/25, Shêng Hsüan-huai, op. cit., 35/31.
[24] To Shêng, K26/5/26, Li Hung-chang, op. cit., " Tien Kao," 22/31; to Yüan, K26/5/26, ibid., 22/33; to Po Hsing, K26/5/27, ibid., 22/35.
[25] Li Hung-chang, op. cit., " Tien Kao," 22/27, 32, 34, 37; Shêng Hsüan-huai, op. cit., 35/29, 30.
[26] To Liu, K26/6/5, Li Hung-chang, op. cit., " Tien Kao," 23/11b.
[27] Ch'ing Tê Tsung Shih Lu, 465/6b.   [28] Ibid., 465/9b.
[29] Ibid., 465/10a.   [30] Ibid.
[31] Li Hung-chang, op. cit., " Tien Kao," 23/48.
[32] From Yüan, K26/6/26, ibid., 23/50.   [33] Ibid., 23/51.

upon Li decided to remain in Shanghai. He told Shêng Hsüan-huai that the reactionaries had not yet awakened from their dreams, nor vented all their anger. It was difficult to arrange for a truce, and without the authority to negotiate it was useless to go up to Tientsin.[34]

Taking the hint from Li Hung-chang, the southern viceroys memorialized the Throne on July 24, requesting that Li be appointed plenipotentiary to negotiate with the Powers.[35] In the meantime Li tried to find out the intention of the Powers. First he wanted to know whether the Powers considered themselves at war with China. The Taku forts, he notified the foreign governments, had opened fire on the Allied naval forces without orders from the Imperial Court. His mission to Peking would be useless if it were considered that a state of war existed.[36] To this inquiry Li obtained a satisfactory answer. The foreign governments took the view that they were not in a state of war with China.[37]

Li then attempted to arrange a truce in the north. At this early stage he paid special attention to the United States, for he considered Germany and Russia " pernicious and brutal." [38] But here Li Hung-chang was not so successful. The Japanese Foreign Secretary declined to tender good offices; the Russian Government demanded effective protection of the Russian subjects; [39] Lord Salisbury advised that Li should wait in Shanghai until the foreign ministers were safely escorted to Tientsin; [40] and the American Government declared that it would be glad to offer its good offices if other Powers so agreed.[41]

Without any assurance that the situation could be resolved, Li Hung-chang determined to remain in Shanghai. It was manifest that the solution of the crisis lay in the protection of the foreign

34 Shêng Hsüan-huai, op. cit., 37/29.
35 Ibid., 21/21.
36 Salisbury to Scott, June 22, 1900, British Parliamentary Papers, China No. 3 (1900), p. 69.
37 China No. 3 (1900), pp. 70, 71, 73-74.
38 To Liu, K26/7/4, Shêng Hsüan-huai, op. cit., 38/1.
39 To Yüan, K26/7/5, Li Hung-chang, op. cit., " Tien Kao," 24/11.
40 To Yüan, K26/6/29, ibid., 23/53.
41 Yüan Shih-k'ai, Yang Shou Yüan Tsou I Chi Yao, 6/1.

ministers, and that to dissuade the international force from advancing toward Peking it was necessary that the Boxers be suppressed. On July 28 Yüan Shih-k'ai proposed that a joint memorial be submitted along these lines.[42] Chang Chih-tung, however, had other ideas. He felt that the Imperial Court might not dare to suppress the Boxers at this stage for fear the latter might launch a rebellion right in the capital, or might not want to take action because of the powerful influence of the reactionary party. He therefore suggested that the viceroys should send a memorial asking for a secret decree authorizing them to march their troops to Peking. The Boxers could thus be suppressed, and the Court could pretend not to know of the action of the viceroys and thus save itself from the wrath of the reactionaries. Chang also thought it advisable to wait until the Court had received the note of the French Government which declared that Prince Tuan and others would be held responsible for any injury suffered by the foreign ministers. "If the Court becomes angry, the situation will be hopeless; if it becomes worried, the situation can be saved." [43] Chang's proposal was regarded by Liu K'un-i as improper and dangerous. It was improper to memorialize the Throne for a secret decree; it was dangerous if the Court did not agree to the proposal.[44] Li Hung-chang, on the other hand, considered the situation too critical to wait any longer. He dictated to Shêng Hsüan-huai a joint memorial consisting of four points: (1) To issue an express decree directing Jung Lu to appoint some high officers to escort the foreign envoys to Tientsin. If the foreign ministers were unwilling to leave the legations for fear of danger, the troops that were attacking the legations should be withdrawn. (2) To issue an express decree ordering the various provinces to protect the foreign merchants and missionaries in accordance with the decree of July 17. (3) To issue an express decree ordering the various provinces to exterminate the bandits and rebellious elements who stirred up disturbances. (4) To issue an express decree ordering relief for the poor so that the Boxer followers could

---

[42] Li Hung-chang, *op. cit.*, " Tien kao," 24/4a.
[43] From Chang, K26/7/4, *ibid.*, 24/6.   [44] From Liu, K26/7/5, *ibid.*, 24/8b.

return home.[45]   Chang Chih-tung still demurred.   He maintained that an understanding should first be secured from the foreign governments that they would suspend hostilities when the Boxers were suppressed.[46]   Yüan Shih-k'ai also wanted to moderate some of the expressions in the memorial.[47]   But Li Hung-chang was determined.   He telegraphed Yüan Shih-k'ai to forward the memorial " without a moment's delay and without changing a single word.   You can state that the memorial was drafted by Li Hung-chang." [48]   He also telegraphed to Liu K'un-i and Chang Chih-tung: " In time of emergency, there is no time for hesitation." [49]

At that time the Court had decided to continue the war with vigor, and the reactionaries were relentlessly hunting down the liberal ministers.   Still the joint memorial was not without effect. On August 2 a decree was issued ordering Jung Lu to select some high officials to escort the foreign envoys out of Peking.   Another decree was issued the same day ordering the protection of the foreign merchants and missionaries.[50]   But the execution of Hsü Ching-ch'êng and Yüan Ch'ang was apparently a shock to Li Hung-chang.   He canceled the trip of one of his staff members, who had been scheduled to take a Japanese warship to Peking to converse with Prince Ch'ing with a view to convincing the Empress Dowager of the necessity of escorting the foreign ministers out of Peking.   At the same time he submitted a request to the Throne for a sick leave of twenty days.[51]   The Imperial Court rejected Li's request.[52]   On August 7 Li Hung-chang was appointed plenipotentiary to negotiate with the Powers.[53]

After the fall of Peking, Li Hung-chang was looked upon as the only person who could save the country.   On August 18 Liu K'un-i telegraphed Li: " The safety or peril of the ancestral temple depends upon Your Excellency.   If you do not go to Peking, no negotiations can be held.   Not only will the situation not be re-

---

[45] Joint Memorial, K26/7/4 (July 29, 1900), Shêng Hsüan-huai, *op. cit.*, 21/23.
[46] From Chang, K26/7/5, Li Hung-chang, *op. cit.*, " Tien Kao," 24/9b.
[47] Shêng Hsüan-huai, *op. cit.*, 38/17; Li Hung-chang, *op. cit.*, " Tien Kao," 24/11.
[48] To Yüan, K26/7/4, Li Hung-chang, *op. cit.*, " Tien Kao," 24/7.
[49] *Ibid.*, 24/10a.   [50] *Ibid.*, 24/19a.
[51] To Chang, K26/7/10, Shêng Hsüan-huai, *op. cit.*, 38/24.
[52] Decree, K26/7/14, *Ch'ing Tê Tsung Shih Lu*, 466/17b.
[53] Decree, K26/7/13, *ibid.*, 466/10b.

solved, but it is feared that the Powers may change their minds. What would the situation be if the Court had to flee thousands of miles? " [54] Liu was afraid that the Powers would change their intention of not harming the Imperial persons and that they would pursue the Imperial Court. Li Hung-chang, however, thought the Allied force would not pursue far and that, as no government remained in Peking, it was difficult to start any negotiations. But he would request the foreign governments to appoint their plenipotentiaries and would go up north if they agreed to do so.[55]

Meanwhile the Imperial Court, defeated and in flight, looked to Li Hung-chang as the only person who could help. On August 19, when the Court was in the Huailai District, a decree was issued ordering Li immediately to approach the foreign governments for peace negotiations. " The minister has been well known for his loyalty and respected by the foreigners. Now that the country has come to such a situation, how he should exert himself! " [56] On August 24 Li was given powers of discretion; he was " not to be controlled " by the Court in the negotiations.[57] Three days later Li was ordered to take a boat to Peking without delay, and Sir Robert Hart was instructed to arrange passage for him.[58] But Li Hung-chang took his time.

WAS LI JUSTIFIED?

The delay of Li Hung-chang in proceeding to the north has been subject to severe criticism. Never had a minister been so much urged to come, and never had a minister delayed so long. On June 18 he was first ordered to repair to Peking, but it was three months later that he arrived at Tientsin. During that period the Court had sent him twelve decrees ordering him to start without delay. The language used was unusually indulgent and in some instances near solicitation. For instance, the Court said in one decree: " Upon the journey of the Grand Secretary will de-

---

54 Li Hung-chang, *op. cit.*, " Tien Kao," 24/38-39.

55 To Liu, K26/7/24, *ibid.*, 24/38b.

56 *Ch'ing Tê Tsung Shih Lu*, 467/10b; received K26/8/8, Li Hung-chang, *op. cit.*, " Tien Kao," 25/23a.

57 *Ch'ing Tê Tsung Shih Lu*, 467/19a; received K26/8/14, Li Hung-chang, *op. cit.*, " Tien Kao," 25/47b.

58 *Ibid.*, 26/1a.

pend not only the country's safety or danger but also its existence or extinction. There is no other person that can reverse our perilous position. We earnestly hope that he will exert himself in spite of difficulties." [59]

But while all looked to him to save the country and while Tientsin and Peking fell to the international force, Li Hung-chang remained unmoved. Was he not disloyal and unpatriotic? [60] It is believed by some historians that had he gone up to Peking earlier, the crisis might have been alleviated.[61] An examination of the existing situation will show that Li was not unjustified in his delay.

In the first place, there was no assurance that, if he arrived at Peking earlier, he could swing the Imperial Court to his policy. The reactionary elements were dominant throughout the crisis, and although there were times when the Court seemed to listen to the advice of the southern viceroys, it did not shake off the reactionaries. The solution of the crisis lay in the protection of the foreign envoys. Li and other viceroys had memorialized again and again for the relief of the legations, but the legations remained under siege until the last day. Li had asked for the suppression of the Boxers, but the Boxers were all-powerful in Peking. As he said, he had not even a battalion under his command; he might well become an object of persecution.[62] If Jung Lu, the confidant of the Empress Dowager and the commander-in-chief of the northern armies, could do nothing, how much could a minister do who had not been in power since the conclusion of the Sino-Japanese War in 1895?

Secondly, there was no assurance that he could arrange a truce with the Powers by going north. Before the fall of Peking the foreign governments had insisted that a truce could be arranged only after the foreign ministers had been safely escorted out of Peking. Li Hung-chang had recommended that, if the foreign ministers refused to leave the legations, the attacking troops should

---

[59] Decree, K26/8/15, *ibid.*, 26/13a.
[60] To Viceroy Liu, K26, Chang Chien, *Chang Chi Tzŭ Chiu Lu*, 1/23b.
[61] Ch'ên Kung-lu, *Chung Kuo Chin Tai Shih* (A Modern History of China [Shanghai: Commercial Press, 1935]), p. 529.
[62] Li's Memorial, received K26/8/2, *Ch'ing Chi Wai Chiao Shih Liao*, 144/5-7. A Hanlin official impeached Li Hung-chang and recommended his execution (Entry K26/6/14, Yeh Ch'ang-ch'ih, *Yüan Tu Lu Jih Chi Ch'ao*, 8/36b-37a).

be withdrawn. The advice had not been taken by the Court. After the fall of Peking and the relief of the legations, Li Hung-chang communicated with the Powers, requesting the cessation of hostilities.[63] The replies he received were far from encouraging. The American Government replied that it " is ready to welcome any overtures for a truce, and invite the other Powers to join when security is established in the Chinese capital, and the Chinese Government shows its ability and willingness to make, on its part, an effective suspension of hostilities there and elsewhere in China." [64] The Japanese Foreign Minister replied that Japan had approached other Powers for a truce, but that except for the United States, no one had replied.[65] The German Government declared that it could not recognize Li Hung-chang as the plenipotentiary, for " the appointment was made by Prince Tuan." [66] When the new German Minister, Dr. Mumm, arrived in Shanghai, he refused to have anything to do with Li Hung-chang.[67] The British newspapers in Shanghai stigmatized Li as pro-Russian and even a supporter of Prince Tuan. The British consuls indicated British disinclination to negotiate with Li and declared that when the time for settlement arrived, the advice of the viceroys at Nanking and Hankow would be asked for.[68] The British attitude annoyed Li Hung-chang so much that he telegraphed to Lo Fêng-luh, Chinese Minister to Britain:

After vigorous persuasion by Minister Yang, Russia has agreed to withdraw her troops to Tientsin and to request the other Powers to take simi-

---

63 To Chinese Ministers Abroad, K26/7/25, Li Hung-chang, op. cit., " Tien Kao," 24/39a.
64 China No. 1 (1901), p. 105.
65 To Liu and Chang, K26/7/30, Shêng Hsüan-huai, op. cit., 39/30.
66 Chang Chih-tung, op. cit., 164/36a.
67 Ibid., 165/19b. The German Emperor even contemplated the capture of Li Hung-chang if he sailed to the north in a merchantman. See Die Grosse Politik der Europäischen Kabinette, 1871-1914: Sammlung der Diplomatischen Akten des Auswärtigen Amtes (Berlin, 1924), XVI, 123-24.
68 Shêng Hsüan-huai, op. cit., 39/29, 40/17; China No. 1 (1901), pp. 101, 104. In reply, the two viceroys expressed their gratitude and the hope that the British Government could invite the other Powers to negotiate with Li Hung-chang (Shêng Hsüan-huai, op. cit., 40/17; Chang Chih-tung, op. cit., 164/27-28). In a conference with Grand Secretary K'un Kang and others immediately after the fall of Peking, Sir Robert Hart told the Chinese officials that whether Li Hung-chang came or not, it did not matter. But Prince Ch'ing, " respected by all Powers," should come at once (Chung Jih Shih Liao, 56/2).

lar action. You have stayed long in England and have good connections with the Foreign Office, why is it that you do nothing? The British, influenced by the rumors of the foreign merchants, have called me pro-Tuan and pro-Russian. You should tell them the truth. Now they do not recognize my status as plenipotentiary and refuse to open negotiations. England has had good relations with China, why has she come to this? Think of your duties and reply plainly.[69]

Of all the Powers, only Russia gave an encouraging answer. The Russian Government informed the Chinese Minister at St. Petersburg that Russia would withdraw her troops, minister, and people to Tientsin. Count Witte was particularly intent on showing his friendship to China. He advised the Chinese Government immediately to appoint plenipotentiaries to open negotiations, for after the arrival of the German Supreme Commander there would be great difficulties.[70] It was on the basis of this advice that Li Hung-chang memorialized the Throne on September 2 to the effect that Prince Ch'ing and Jung Lu should be ordered to go back at once to Peking, and that he would sail for the north as soon as the Court approved this proposal.[71] On September 11, when it was learned that Prince Ch'ing had been ordered to return to Peking, Li decided to sail for Tientsin on the 14th " in spite of the distrust of Britain and Germany." [72]

As early as August 12, the Russian Consul in Shanghai had confidentially informed Li Hung-chang that the Russian Government had ordered a large ship for his journey to the north.[73] On September 12 Li still planned to take a Russian warship to Tientsin, but at the last moment he changed his plan to avoid " suspicions," and took a Chinese ship which sailed on September 16. The Russian Government agreed to give him protection.[74] He arrived at Taku on the 18th and proceeded to Tientsin the following morning.[75]

---

[69] To Lo, K26/8/10, Li Hung-chang, op. cit., " Tien Kao," 25/34b.
[70] From Yang, K26/7/21, from Yang, K26/7/29, Chung Jih Shih Liao, 56/20.
[71] Memorial by Li, K26/8/9, ibid., 56/17-18.
[72] Li Hung-chang, op. cit., " Tien Kao," 26/11b.
[73] Shêng Hsüan-huai, op. cit., 39/5.
[74] Memorial, K26/intercalary 8/8, Li Hung-chang, op. cit., " Tien Kao," 80/6.
[75] To Shêng, K26/8/25, ibid., 26/23a.

7

Peace Negotiations

PRELIMINARY MANEUVERS

WHEN LI HUNG-CHANG ARRIVED at Tientsin the first problem that confronted him was how to open negotiations with the Powers. Circumstances forced him to rely once again upon the aid of Russia. The arrogance of Germany and the disdain of Britain gave him little choice. The American Government was conciliatory, but America did not as yet play an active part in international politics. Japan, uneasy about Russian designs, chose to be friendly to China, but Japan did not seem to be in a position to sway the decisions of the European cabinets. To Russia, therefore, Li Hung-chang looked for support. Not that Li particularly liked Russia. He had written to Hsü Ying-k'uei, Viceroy of Fukien, that all Powers had the same attitude toward China, and that no country was particularly close in its relationship with China.[1] He had thought Russia as well as Germany " pernicious and brutal." [2] But faced with the hostile attitude of Germany and Britain, he gradually leaned toward Russia. The Russian leaders, on the other hand, eagerly seized the opportunity to oblige Li Hung-chang. They declared they would withdraw their troops to Tientsin and that they had no territorial ambitions in northeast China.[3] They advised the Chinese Government to suppress the Boxers and punish the reactionary ministers before the arrival of the German Field Marshal Waldersee.[4] They offered protection to Li Hung-chang in his journey to the north [5] and professed friend-

[1] To Hsü, K26/8/1, Li Hung-chang, Li Wên Chung Kung Ch'üan Chi, " Tien Kao," 25/3a.
[2] To Liu, K26/7/4, Shêng Hsüan-huai, Yü Chai Ts'un Kao Ch'u K'an, 38/1.
[3] Memorial by Li, K26/8/9, Chung Jih Shih Liao, 56/17-18.
[4] From Yang, K26/7/21, ibid., 56/20.
[5] Li Hung-chang, op. cit., " Tien Kao," 80/6.

ship for the Imperial Government.[6] In two telegrams to Li Hung-
chang, Count Witte expressed his confidence in Li and hoped that
" His Excellency would trust in Russia's support in the future." [7]
Count Lamsdorff, the Russian Foreign Minister, also assured Yang
Ju, Chinese Minister at St. Petersburg, that when negotiations were
opened in Peking, Russia would set an example of moderation so
that the other Powers would not make extreme demands.[8] The
extraordinary good will of Russia surprised Yang Ju, and he observed that, properly managed, it could be turned to great advantage for China.[9] Even Chang Chih-tung conceded that the solution of the crisis lay in the mediation of Russia, although he added
that Japan could also be of assistance.[10]

The early moves of Li Hung-chang after the fall of Peking
were mainly based upon the suggestions of the Russian Government, which had taken the initiative in sounding out the other
Powers about their intentions. The prerequisite for opening negotiations, the Russian Government informed the Chinese Minister
at St. Petersburg, was the return of·the Imperial Court to Peking.
As it was, the Powers would consider China without a government.[11] Furthermore, the return of the Imperial Court would expedite the negotiations, for then it would not be necessary for the
Chinese plenipotentiaries to communicate back and forth with the
Court far away from Peking.[12]

On September 21 Li Hung-chang submitted a memorial,
strongly urging the return of the Imperial Court. He listed three
main reasons: (1) The purpose of the Powers in requesting the
return of the Court was not to place it under their control but
rather to facilitate the negotiations, since the Chinese plenipotentiaries could conveniently obtain Imperial instructions if the Court

[6] From Yang, K26/7/5, *Ch'ing Chi Wai Chiao Shih Liao*, 144/1.
[7] From Yang, K26/7/29, *Chung Jih Shih Liao*, 56/20.
[8] From Yang, K26/8/23, Shêng Hsüan-huai, *op. cit.*, 41/16.
[9] Yang to Li, K26/8/23, *ibid.*, 41/16.
[10] From Chang, K26/8/16, *ibid.*, 40/27; Chang Chih-tung, *Chang Wên Hsiang Kung Ch'üan Chi*, 165/1a.
[11] To Tuan, K26/8/13, Li Hung-chang, *op. cit.*, " Tien Kao," 25/42b.
[12] To Tuan, K26/8/14, *ibid.*, 25/46a.

were stationed in Peking. (2) Owing to the delicate play of the balance of power, the foreign Powers were now rather interested in the preservation of China. To take advantage of this circumstance and to win over the foreign envoys, it was necessary for the Court to return to Peking. (3) In Peking there had been built a solid foundation for the capital. On the other hand, if the government moved to another province, it would have insurmountable difficulties with supplies. And if the Allied forces decided to cut off the various provision routes, the empire would disintegrate.[13]

Liu K'un-i, Viceroy at Nanking, at first had some doubt as to the wisdom of the Court's returning. He feared the Powers might seize Their Majesties and dictate the terms of peace. On the other hand, he was afraid that if the Court did not return, the Powers might refuse to open negotiations and the crisis could never be ended.[14] At last he decided that the viceroys should submit a joint memorial urging the Court to cancel the plan of moving to Sian.[15]

Chang Chih-tung had always been concerned about the safety of the Empress Dowager and the Emperor. On the eve of the fall of Peking, he was so excited over the possible harm that might come to Their Majesties in the Allied attack on the capital that he sent a note to the foreign consuls demanding that the foreign governments guarantee the personal safety of the Chinese rulers.[16] He had opposed Li Hung-chang's effort to stop the Court from moving to the west before the fall of Peking; and now, consistent in his concern over the Imperial safety, he opposed the Court's return. He argued that the conclusion of peace did not depend upon the return of the Imperial Court. If China were to accept the demands of the Powers, the latter would not care whether the Court returned or not. On the other hand, if the demands were not accepted, there would not be any settlement even though the Court returned to Peking. When Prince Ch'ing went back to Peking,

[13] Li's Memorial, received 26/intercalary 8/3, *Hsi Hsün Ta Shih Chi*, 2/15-17.

[14] From Liu, K26/8/21, Li Hung-chang, *op. cit.*, "Tien Kao," 26/21a.

[15] Memorial by Liu, etc., K26/intercalary 8/17 (received K26/intercalary 8/19), *Chung Jih Shih Liao*, 57/26.

[16] Chang to Li, K26/7/23, Chang Chih-tung, *op. cit.*, 164/26; see also Li Hung-chang, *op. cit.*, "Tien Kao," 24/35; Shêng Hsüan-huai, *op. cit.*, 39/16.

Chang pointed out, he was disarmed and guarded by foreign troops; when Li Hung-chang arrived in Tientsin, he was protected by foreigners and his subordinates were not allowed to put on official robes. " If Their Majesties returned to Peking, what would become of them? " [17]

But the arguments of Li Hung-chang and the viceroys were in fact unnecessary, for the Empress Dowager had her own calculations. First, as pointed out in the decree of October 13, Peking was under foreign occupation. It was divided into sectors, each of which was guarded by a foreign force. Neither the common people nor government officials had any freedom of movement between the sectors. How could the Imperial Court return under these circumstances? [18] Secondly, the Court was apparently afraid that, if it returned, some unacceptable demands would be forced upon it. The Japanese Government had informed the Chinese Minister at Tokyo that the Chinese ministers must be changed, and a new administration set up, before the Powers could agree to open negotiations.[19] It was also reported that the foreign envoys would demand the restoration of power to the Emperor.[20] " If the Powers really have peaceful intentions," continued the above-mentioned decree, " they should not infringe upon our sovereignty and demand what is impossible from us. After the peace agreement has been reached, the Court will at once issue a decree designating the date of return." [21]

THE IMPERIAL COURT AND THE GRAND COUNCIL

One of the reasons which prompted the viceroys to oppose the Imperial journey to the west, but which had not been mentioned in their memorial, was that the Court, as it moved farther into the interior, would be more and more under the control of the reactionaries who accompanied it.[22] This apprehension of the viceroys

---

[17] To Liu, etc., K26/intercalary 8/10, Chang Chih-tung, *op. cit.*, 166/12b.

[18] Decree, K26/intercalary 8/20, *Ch'ing Tê Tsung Shih Lu*, 471/7b.

[19] To Prince Ch'ing, K26/intercalary 8/1, Li Hung-chang, *op. cit.*, " Tien Kao," 27/1b.

[20] To Yang, K26/8/15, *ibid.*, 25/49a.

[21] Decree, K26/intercalary 8/20, *Ch'ing Tê Tsung Shih Lu*, 471/7b.

[22] From Shêng, K26/7/20, from Liu, K26/7/20, Chang Chih-tung, *op. cit.*, 163/28b.

was not unfounded. On August 31 Prince Tuan was appointed a Grand Councillor.[23] As Jung Lu had not joined the Court on its travels, the Grand Council now consisted entirely of reactionaries with the sole exception of Wang Wên-shao.

The policy of the reactionaries was twofold: to move the government to Sian and to continue the war. It was the strategy of Kang I to increase the troops of Tung Fu-hsiang, to send the army under Têng Tsêng-t'ung to the front, and to order the forces of Ma Yü-k'un and Ch'êng Wên-ping to defend T'ungkuan.[24] It was asserted by the reactionaries that the fall of Tientsin and Peking was due to military unpreparedness. Reorganized and reinforced, the Chinese army could still resist the Allied forces.[25]

It was for the purpose of counteracting the reactionary force that Liu K'un-i suggested to Li Hung-chang that some liberal elements be included in the government party. According to Liu's plan, Chang Chih-tung and K'uei Chün, Viceroy of Szechuan, should join the Grand Council, while Yang Ju, Chinese Minister to Russia, and Shêng Hsüan-huai should enter the Tsungli Yamen.[26] The plan, however, did not materialize. Shêng Hsüan-huai declined the offer on the ground that he was " too bold in assuming responsibilities " and that his opinions " may not fit in with the times." [27] As to Chang Chih-tung, he had as early as September 14 written a letter to Li Hung-chang begging the latter not to recommend him for " the important post." For two years, he said, his health had been getting worse and worse. He slept only an hour and a half during the night and only about an hour in the daytime. His mind was clear only four hours a day; for the rest of the time he was absent-minded and tired. After receiving fifty guests and speaking fifty sentences, he would find his tongue hard and dry and could not speak any more. In reading the papers he would feel dizzy after going through a few lines.

[23] Hsi Hsün Ta Shih Chi, 1/19a.
[24] Yüan's telegram forwarded by Shêng, K26/intercalary 8/6, Li Hung-chang, op. cit., " Tien Kao," 27/5b.
[25] Wang Shih-chieh's memorial submitted by Ying Nien, K26/8/29, Chung Jih Shih Liao, 57/8.
[26] To Li, K26/8/25, Shêng Hsüan-huai, op. cit., 41/22.
[27] Ibid.

His legs were too weak to walk, nor could he stand a sea journey.[28] Indeed, if his account was to be believed, he would have been a wreck physically as well as mentally. Actually his health was far from being so bad, and his mind was vigorous. It was not surprising if a viceroy did not desire transfer to the Grand Council. A viceroy was a king within his jurisdiction; a Grand Councillor had to attend to the pleasure or displeasure of Their Majesties. But perhaps what worried Chang Chih-tung was the complicated politics in the Imperial Court and the great difficulty of the international situation. He " will certainly be harmed " by the recalcitrant reactionaries, he declared. He begged " with thousands of kowtows " that he be spared.[29]

The attention of the viceroys was soon turned to Jung Lu, the Grand Councillor and the generalissimo of the northern armies. Before the flight of the Imperial Court, Jung Lu, together with Kang I, Hsü T'ung, and Ch'ung I, had been ordered to remain in Peking to take charge of the governmental affairs.[30] When Peking fell to the Allied forces, however, Jung Lu did not follow the decree; instead, he retreated to Paoting.[31] Then, in spite of a decree ordering him to stay in Paoting, he proceeded to Huolu and planned to join the Imperial Court.[32] The reason why Jung Lu tried to get away from Peking as far as possible was the hostile attitude of the foreign ministers toward him, for his troops had been among those attacking the legations.[33] In the meantime Li Hung-chang, upon the suggestion of the Japanese Government, had recommended to the Throne that Jung Lu be appointed a plenipotentiary for the peace negotiations.[34] The recommendation was approved by the Imperial Court, and Jung Lu was ordered on September 7 to return from Huolu to Paoting and await the word of Li Hung-chang.[35] Learning that the foreign ministers maintained a hostile attitude toward Jung Lu, Li Hung-chang thought

---

28 *Ibid.*, 41/12.   29 *Ibid.*   30 *Hsi Hsün Ta Shih Chi*, 1/1b.
31 Memorial by Jung Lu and Ch'ung I, K26/7/28, *Chung Jih Shih Liao*, 56/8b.
32 Jung Lu's Memorial, K26/8/13, *ibid.*, 56/25-26.
33 Shêng Hsüan-huai, *op. cit.*, 40/24.
34 Li's Memorial, K26/8/3, *Chung Jih Shih Liao*, 56/5.
35 Decree, K26/8/14, *Ch'ing Tê Tsung Shih Lu*, 468/17b.

it advisable to have Jung Lu join the Court so as to counterbalance the influence of the reactionaries.[36] As Shêng Hsüan-huai keenly observed, " the resolution of the situation lies in Shansi rather than Peking." [37] On October 2 Li Hung-chang memorialized the Throne, reporting the hostile attitude of the foreign ministers toward Jung Lu and requesting his recall to the Court.[38] The request was promptly granted, and Jung Lu was ordered to join the Grand Council.[39]

On November 11 Jung Lu arrived at Sian. By this time the pro-Boxer ministers had been dismissed from the Grand Council, which now consisted of three members: Wang Wên-shao, Lu Ch'uan-lin, and Jung Lu. Wang Wên-shao was a liberal. He had had unfavorable views of the Boxers and recently had advised against the move to Sian.[40] He was, however, a modest old man and not inclined to self-assertion.[41] Lu Ch'uan-lin, the former Governor of Kiangsu, had agreed with Li Ping-hêng, after the outbreak of hostilities at Taku, to stop by force any British warship from entering the Yangtze River.[42] He left for Peking with 1,500 troops in July, 1900, at the summons of the Court.[43] Before he reached Peking, the capital had fallen to the Allies. He joined the Court in Shansi and supported the policy of moving to Sian.[44] He was appointed to the Grand Council on September 25.[45] The leadership in the Grand Council was naturally assumed by Jung Lu, the senior minister and the confidant of the Empress Dowager. After the fall of Peking he realized that the only way to save the country was to suspend hostilities and negotiate for peace.[46] But

---

36 To Yüan, K26/8/16, to Shêng, K26/intercalary 8/7, Li Hung-chang, op. cit., 26/2b, 27/7b; Li to Jung, K26/8/17, Shêng Hsüan-huai, op. cit., 41/2.

37 To Wang, K26/8/28, Shêng Hsüan-huai, op. cit., 41/28. The Imperial Court was then in T'aiyüan, Shansi.

38 Li's Memorial, K26/intercalary 8/9, Hsi Hsün Ta Shih Chi, 2/29a.

39 Decree, K26/intercalary 8/13, Ch'ing Tê Tsung Shih Lu, 470/17b.

40 Li Hung-chang, op. cit., " Tien Kao," 27/11a, 28/2b.

41 Hu Ssŭ-ching, Lu Pei Chi, 3/11; Hsi Hsün Ta Shih Chi, Introduction/33b.

42 To Liu, K26/5/26, Chang Chih-tung, op. cit., 160/24.

43 Shêng Hsüan-huai, op. cit., 36/34, 36/37.

44 See Hsi Hsün Hui Luan Shih Mo Chi, 3/190; Ch'ing Tê Tsung Shih Lu, 469/16b; Hu Ssŭ-ching, op. cit., 4/18.

45 Ch'ing Tê Tsung Shih Lu, 470/2b.

46 From Yüan K26/8/13, Li Hung-chang, op. cit., " Tien Kao," 25/45b.

Jung Lu was different from the southern viceroys, who had had
nothing to do with the crisis and the war. Although he disagreed
with the reactionaries, he had participated in the war. As commander-in-chief of the northern armies he was responsible for the
defeat of the country; he could hardly view the situation arising
from the defeat as something that was entirely the fault of others.[47]
Nor, as a loyal minister of the Empress Dowager, could he con-
demn the policies adopted by Her Majesty. Consequently the
position he took was often that of a mediator, sometimes interced-
ing with the Empress Dowager, sometimes with Li Hung-chang
and the viceroys.

As to the Empress Dowager, she was sorry that such calamities
had been brought about. Tears would come to her eyes when she
discussed the situation with the ministers. It was reported that she
often got up in the middle of the night and sighed.[48] She softened
toward the Emperor, who was given more attention and was even
permitted to vent his anger once in a while upon the pro-Boxer
ministers.[49] But the Empress Dowager was not a person to surrender unconditionally. The decisions to move to Sian and to
increase the troops of Tung Fu-hsiang[50] were indications that the
Allies would be defied if their demands were unacceptable. Argument for continuation of war was not infrequently heard in Sian.
It was asserted, for instance, that the fall of Tientsin and Peking
was due to the betrayal of traitors, that the Allies could never
penetrate deep into the interior, and that if Tung Fu-hsiang's army
was augmented to 50,000, the Allied forces could be defeated.[51]
A Hanlin official denounced Chang Chih-tung, Liu K'un-i, and
Li Hung-chang for " currying favor with the barbarians " and
disobeying the orders of the Throne.[52] Hsia Chên-wu, a secretary
in the Board of Works, argued for a strong policy and continuation of the war if " the oppression of the foreign Powers went

[47] See his memorials immediately after the fall of Peking, in which he spoke of aveng-
ing the defeat and recovering the lost land (*Chung Jih Shih Liao*, 56/3, 7).
[48] From Governor Ts'ên, K26/9/18, Li Hung-chang, *op. cit.*, " Tien Kao," 28/30.
[49] From Governor Tuan Fang, K26/8/30, Shêng Hsüan-huai, *op. cit.*, 41/31.
[50] Jung Lu's Memorial, K26/intercalary 8/10, *Hsi Hsün Ta Shih Chi*, 2/25b.
[51] To Shêng, K26/10/30, Chang Chih-tung, *op. cit.*, 169/38.
[52] Memorial by Hsia Shou-t'ien, K26/11/12, *Chung Jih Shih Liao*, 59/35.

too far." [53]   He was so encouraged by the Empress Dowager [54] that he impeached Liu K'un-i, Chang Chih-tung, and even Wang Wên-shao. He was finally reproved by the Throne as "ignorant of the current affairs," but excused for "possessing a loyal heart." [55]   Such being the atmosphere in Sian, it was not surprising that the Chinese plenipotentiaries often had a hard time in persuading the Court to accept their recommendations.

THE PROBLEM OF PUNISHMENT

It was the insistence of the Powers that punishment of the pro-Boxer ministers must precede the opening of negotiations.[56]   In an attempt to fulfill this requirement of the Powers, Chang Chih-tung proposed on September 9 that General Tung Fu-hsiang be punished and that all blame be laid on him.[57]   Li Hung-chang, however, did not think that the foreign Powers would be satisfied with the punishment of Tung Fu-hsiang alone. He agreed with Yüan Shih-k'ai that a joint memorial be submitted to the Throne requesting the punishment of Kang I as well.[58]   Liu K'un-i believed that Prince Tuan, Kang I, and Chao Shu-ch'iao should be cashiered, and that a decree should be issued laying blame on these three.[59]   Chang Chih-tung, however, thought it improper for provincial officials to request punishment of the ministers, but that Li Hung-chang, as a plenipotentiary, could do so.[60]   Considering the situation too urgent for any delay, Li Hung-chang, on the eve of his sailing for Tientsin, drafted a memorial and, without obtaining the consent of his colleagues, sent it in the name of Liu K'un-i, Chang Chih-tung, Yüan Shih-k'ai, and himself. He requested that the following ministers be discharged pending punishment:

---

[53] Memorial by Hsia Chên-wu, K26/11/19, *ibid.*, 59/37.

[54] The Empress Dowager read one of Hsia's memorials, wept, and told him, "If all the ministers in the Court had been as patriotic and loyal as you, the nation would not have come to such a calamity" (*ibid.*).

[55] Decree, K26/11/28, *Ch'ing Tê Tsung Shih Lu*, 475/19b; see also Shêng Hsüan-huai, *op. cit.*, 49/29, 31, 32.

[56] Shêng Hsüan-huai, *op. cit.*, 41/4; Chang Chih-tung, *op. cit.*, 164/2, 165/2a.

[57] To Li, etc., K26/8/16, Chang Chih-tung, *op. cit.*, 165/2-3.

[58] To Liu and Chang, K26/8/18, Li Hung-chang, *op. cit.*, "Tien Kao," 26/12a.

[59] From Liu, K26/8/20, Shêng Hsüan-huai, *op. cit.*, 41/7.

[60] To Li, etc., K26/8/21, Chang Chih-tung, *op. cit.*, 165/11.

Prince Chuang, Kang I, and Ying Nien, the three commanders of the Boxers; Prince Tuan, the chief patron of the Boxers; and Chao Shu-ch'iao, who had made a spurious investigation of the Boxers. When this was done, stated Li, he would be able to approach the Powers on the opening of negotiations.[61]

On September 25, 1900, an edict was issued depriving Princes Chuang, I, Tsai Lien, and Tsai Ying of their titles of nobility. Prince Tuan was deprived of all his posts and handed over to the Clansmen's Court for the determination of further penalty. Duke Tsai Lan and Ying Nien were handed over to the boards concerned for punishment; Kang I and Chao Shu-ch'iao to the Court of Censors.[62] Three days later Yü Hsien, Governor of Shansi, was dismissed from his office.[63]

The punishment was at once considered too light by the foreign ministers at Peking.[64] Thereupon Li Hung-chang sent in another memorial on October 11 advising that the ministers be more severely punished so that the sovereignty of China would not be impaired by the Powers.[65] To this the Court replied that the Imperial decision on punishment was made upon the basis of impartiality and justice. Princes I, Tsai Lien, and Tsai Ying, it pointed out, had not been mentioned by Li and the Powers, and yet they were punished together with the others. All these princes would not be permitted to attend the Imperial Court. Further punishment of the others would be inflicted in accordance with the recommendations of the boards concerned.[66]

In the meantime, the Allied forces vigorously pushed westward toward Shansi.[67] On October 30 Li Hung-chang reported to the Throne that the foreign ministers demanded the execution of nine princes and ministers mentioned in the previous decree as well as Tung Fu-hsiang and Yü Hsien. He urged that the Imperial Court

---

[61] Memorial, K26/8/21, Li Hung-chang, *op. cit.*, "Tsou Kao," 80/5.
[62] *Ch'ing Tê Tsung Shih Lu*, 470/1b.
[63] Decree, 26/intercalary 8/5, *ibid.*, 470/7a.
[64] Li Hung-chang, *op. cit.*, "Tien Kao," 27/14.   [65] *Ibid.*, 28/1a.
[66] Decree, K26/intercalary 8/26, *Chung Jih Shih Liao*, 57/33a.
[67] Hsi Liang's Memorial, K26/9/3, *Hsi Hsün Ta Shih Chi*, 3/2, *Ch'ing Tê Tsung Shih Lu*, 472/3a; Li's Memorial, 26/9/5, *Hsi Hsün Ta Shih Chi*, 3/6; Decree, K26/9/7, *Ch'ing Tê Tsung Shih Lu*, 472/8b.

should act immediately and inflict the maximum penalty on the persons concerned so as to confront the foreign ministers with a *fait accompli*.[68] The Imperial Court found it difficult to follow the advice. It was afraid that after heavy punishment had been inflicted upon the princes and ministers the Powers would still not be satisfied. Anyway, the heaviest penalty for Yü Hsien was exile, the Court declared. As to Tung Fu-hsiang, he was a military commander; he obeyed orders and had no decision of his own. It was therefore difficult to inflict heavy penalty upon him. Nor was it expedient to deprive him of his command at the present juncture.[69]

To break the deadlock, Chang Chih-tung suggested to Liu K'un-i, Yüan Shih-k'ai, and Shêng Hsüan-huai that the assistance of Jung Lu, who was then on his way to Sian, should be invoked. A joint telegram was sent to Jung Lu, in which it was declared that, in order to save the Throne, the "guilty ministers" must be severely punished. If action was further delayed, the Allied forces would penetrate deep into the west and there might come some unacceptable demands. " To punish the guilty ministers is in the interest of Their Majesties; to punish Tung Fu-hsiang is in the interest of Your Excellency." Jung Lu was urged to persuade the Empress Dowager not to suffer because of prestige, nor to get into difficulty because of the ministers.[70]

On November 11 Jung Lu arrived in Sian. Two days later an edict was issued announcing the punishments for the ministers. Princes Tuan and Chuang were to be immured for life at Mukden. Princes I and Tsai Ying were to be handed to the Clansmen's Court for imprisonment. Prince Tsai Lien was to be confined to his house. Duke Tsai Lan was to be degraded one degree in rank and lose all his emoluments. Ying Nien was to be degraded two degrees in rank. Penalties against Kang I were waived because he had died of illness. Yü Hsien was to be banished for life to the most remote frontier for hard labor.[71] In a telegram to Prince Ch'ing

---

[68] To Shêng, 26/9/8, Li Hung-chang, *op. cit.*, " Tien Kao," 28/14a; to the Grand Council, K26/9/12, *ibid.*, 28/22a.

[69] Decree, K26/9/11 (November 2), *Ch'ing Tê Tsung Shih Lu*, 472/13a.

[70] From Yüan, K26/9/18, Shêng Hsüan-huai, *op. cit.*, 45/2.

[71] Decree, K26/9/22, *Ch'ing Tê Tsung Shih Lu*, 473/9a.

and Li Hung-chang, the Grand Councillors stated that the punishment of Tung Fu-hsiang was reserved for further consideration on account of his being in command of Imperial troops.[72]

The feelings of the Imperial Court on the matter may be seen from two letters written by Jung Lu. In the letter to Shêng Hsüan-huai, he began with the remark that after his earnest persuasion the Court had issued a decree inflicting heavy penalties upon the guilty princes and ministers. He then pointed out that the Allied forces had killed " six Chinese officials " in Paoting,[73] including the Acting Viceroy of Chihli, who offered no resistance whatsoever. " Tooth for tooth," said Jung Lu, the death of these officials should be sufficient for the wrong suffered by the Powers. The Imperial Court did not even protect the princes of the blood or the important ministers. They were either imprisoned for life or banished to the most distant frontier. The Powers ought to be willing to open negotiations, for although war was terrible for China, it was not altogether an advantage to the Powers. They had to station their troops overseas and to spend huge sums of money. Without peace their trade would be seriously affected. The Court indeed did not want war, Jung Lu declared, but there were still ignorant people and fierce partisans. If they were forced to extremes, the Chinese Government would not be able to control them, nor could the Powers easily guard against them.[74] In the letter to Prince Ch'ing and Li Hung-chang, Jung Lu maintained that even though no one was executed, those imprisoned for life or exiled to the distant frontier would never be pardoned—such punishment was not much different from death. This should satisfy the foreign Powers and start the peace negotiations. He had done his best, he wrote; and, to be fair to Their Majesties, they had undergone the utmost humiliations.[75]

---

[72] From Jung Lu, Wang Wên-shao, and Lu Ch'uan-lin, K26/9/22, Li Hung-chang, op. cit., " Tien Kao," 28/42.

[73] Actually five were arrested, but only three were executed. See Foreign Relations of the United States, 1901, Appendix (Washington: Government Printing Office, 1902), p. 47.

[74] Jung Lu to Shêng, K26/9/24 (received November 15), Shêng Hsüan-huai, op. cit., 45/23.

[75] Jung Lu to Prince Ch'ing and Li, K26/9/25 (received November 16), ibid., 45/26.

The high tone of Jung Lu immediately drew criticism from Li Hung-chang, who declared that Jung Lu's assumption of credit was " as sycophantic as it is disgusting." [76] For the time, however, attention of the plenipotentiaries and the viceroys was concentrated on having Tung Fu-hsiang punished.

Since Tung Fu-hsiang was regarded as the protégé of Jung Lu, pressure was brought to bear upon the latter. On November 20 Li Hung-chang and Prince Ch'ing telegraphed him that the foreign ministers considered Tung Fu-hsiang the most important of the guilty ministers, and that they suspected His Excellency of protecting him. The plenipotentiaries hoped His Excellency would be careful about the problem, so that the situation could be resolved.[77] On November 22 Liu K'un-i also wired Jung Lu, asserting that the negotiations were not opened because Tung Fu-hsiang was not punished. " As Tung has been your protégé, I hope you will soon arrange to satisfy the public." [78] But it was Yüan Shih-k'ai, formerly a lieutenant of Jung Lu, who was the most eager to give advice to his friend. In three telegrams Yüan pleaded with Jung Lu that he must deprive Tung Fu-hsiang of his command; otherwise His Excellency would not be excused by future generations. From the ancient times, he wrote in one telegram, no wise ruler or good premier " would love a single man against the public opinion of the nation, not to mention against the interests of the people." [79]

In the case of Tung Fu-hsiang, the Imperial Court had its difficulties. The Kansu general had under him 15,000 troops, and he was much liked by the Moslem people in Kansu and Shensi. His troops were stationed in Sian, and there were no other strong forces that could safely keep them under control. If a rebellion broke out as a result of extreme measures taken against this Moslem leader, it might lead, as the Court observed in a decree, to great

[76] To Shêng, etc., K26/10/2, Li Hung-chang, op. cit., " Tien Kao," 29/1b.
[77] To Jung Lu, K26/9/29, ibid., 28/50b.
[78] From Liu, K26/10/1, Chang Chih-tung, op. cit., 169/14b.
[79] From Yüan, K26/10/3, Shêng Hsüan-huai, op. cit., 46/5; from Yüan, K26/10/2, Chang Chih-tung, op. cit., 169/15; from Yüan, K26/10/2, Shêng Hsüan-huai, op. cit., 46/34.

calamities.[80]   The cautious attitude taken by the Court was sincere. As early as November 8 measures had been taken to get the Kansu troops out of Sian.   On that day Tung Fu-hsiang was ordered to dispatch his troops to T'ungkuan and the area between Shensi and Honan.[81]   Then on November 19 a decree was issued ordering Tung to decrease his troops by 2,500.[82]   Later, another 2,500 were cut.[83]   On November 30 the Court received a memorial from Li Hung-chang reporting that the envoys of ten Powers formally demanded the expulsion of Tung from Sian, and urging immediate action.[84]   Three days later a decree was issued depriving Tung of his official ranks but allowing him to remain in office.   He was ordered to go to Kansu at once.[85]

In the problem of punishment as well as in other problems, Li Hung-chang invariably showed courage in counseling the Throne. Although Prince Ch'ing was a plenipotentiary along with Li Hung-chang,[86] he preferred to let his colleague assume the leadership.   Thus it was upon Li's recommendation that Liu K'un-i and Chang Chih-tung had been ordered by the Imperial Court to confer with the plenipotentiaries on the problem of peace negotiations.[87]   The two viceroys contributed much in sounding out the opinions of the foreign governments, in suggesting policies and tactics, and in adding their weight to recommendations to the Throne.   But with regard to matters of serious consequence, it was Li Hung-chang who invariably took the responsibility of speaking the truth and who boldly advocated actions which the Court would not like.[88]   When the foreign ministers demanded the execution of eleven princes and ministers, Prince Ch'ing declined to join with Li in reporting it to the Throne.[89]   Liu K'un-i was bolder; he gave

---

[80] Decree, K26/9/25, *Hsi Hsün Ta Shih Chi*, 3/25.

[81] *Ch'ing Tê Tsung Shih Lu*, 473/28.   [82] *Ibid.*, 473/21b.

[83] Decree, K26/10/1, *ibid.*, 474/1a.

[84] To the Grand Council, K26/10/6, Li Hung-chang, *op. cit.*, " Tien Kao," 29/7a; *Chung Jih Shih Liao*, 59/6a.

[85] Decree, K26/10/12, *Ch'ing Tê Tsung Shih Lu*, 474/8.

[86] Decree, K26/intercalary 8/20, *Ch'ing Tê Tsung Shih Lu*, 471/9a.

[87] Decree, K26/8/7, Li Hung-chang, *op. cit.*, " Tien Kao," 26/23b.

[88] To Liu, etc., K26/9/10, Shêng Hsüan-huai, *op. cit.*, 44/18.

[89] To Liu, K26/9/11, Chang Chih-tung, *op. cit.*, 167/30a; see also Shêng Hsüan-huai, *op. cit.*, 44/18.

his support to Li Hung-chang.[90] Chang Chih-tung was always cautious, sometimes to the extent of timidity. When Shêng Hsüan-huai suggested that the two Yangtze viceroys should support Li Hung-chang in requesting severe punishment of the eleven princes and ministers, Chang Chih-tung positively refused: " Even Prince Ch'ing did not dare to join in. How can three Chinese ministers request the execution of many Manchu princes? "[91]

POLICIES OF THE POWERS

As indicated previously, Russian policy since the occupation of Peking had been one of professed friendship and good will toward China. Repeatedly the Russian Government offered its services to Li Hung-chang; repeatedly it assured the Chinese Government that it would set an example of conciliation in the peace negotiations.[92] Soon after the legations were relieved, Russia proposed that the Powers withdraw their toops to Tientsin.[93] Russia did not join in the advance of the Allied forces to Paoting and expressed disapproval of the Allied military excursions after the occupation of Peking.[94] The purpose of Russia was to ingratiate herself with China so that she could realize her ambitions in Manchuria.[95] For the time, it seemed that she was to succeed in winning the confidence of some Chinese statesmen. Yang Ju, Chinese Minister to Russia, was a little surprised at the Russian attitude,[96] but he reported with apparent pleasure the Russian assurances. " The relationship," he wired Li Hung-chang, " between myself and the Russian Emperor and ministers is based upon sincerity and faith."[97]

[90] See Shêng Hsüan-huai, op. cit., 41/12.
[91] To Liu, K26/9/11, Chang Chih-tung, op. cit., 167/30a. See also From Chang, K26/9/12, Shêng Hsüan-huai, op. cit., 44/23.
[92] Chung Jih Shih Liao, 56/17, 20, Shêng Hsüan-huai, op. cit., 40/27, 41/16; Foreign Relations of the United States, 1901 (Washington: Government Printing Office, 1902), p. 94. Besides offering protection and passage to Li Hung-chang, the Russian Government intervened when it heard that the Allied admirals would interdict Li from communicating with the Chinese authorities from Taku (Foreign Relations of the United States, 1901, Appendix, p. 17). It inquired if the American Government recognized the full powers of Li Hung-chang and Prince Ch'ing (ibid., p. 23).
[93] See British Parliamentary Papers, China No. 1 (1901), pp. 128, 130, 148-49, 172, 198, 199.
[94] From Yang, K20/10/7, Shêng Hsuan-huai, op. cit., 46/19.
[95] See below, chap. IX.
[96] Yang to Li, K26/8/23, Shêng Hsüan-huai, op. cit., 41/16.   [97] Ibid.

Count Witte, he wrote in another telegram, " is frank and sincere. The Russian Emperor believes in him . . . and this is a great opportunity." [98]   When the Russian troops advanced into Manchuria, Li Hung-chang declared that Russia did not have any territorial designs.[99]

In contradistinction to Russia's profession of good will, Germany stood for severity and intimidation. As soon as news of the commencement of hostilities at Taku reached Germany, the Kaiser spoke of a grand military action and the complete destruction of Peking.[100]   Foreign Secretary Count von Bülow, however, considered that the time was not yet ripe for Germany to act, and advised that Germany should wait until the conflict of interests between the Franco-Russian group and the Anglo-Japanese group developed further.[101]   But when the murder of Baron von Ketteler was confirmed, Bülow considered the situation changed. It was necessary, he said, " to show to the nation that those who direct state affairs know how to defend the prestige and honor of Germany with promptitude and energy." He thought of occupying Chefoo and attacking and seizing the Chinese navy in the Yangtze River, as these measures would help " increase the might of our nation in East Asia and show it not to be weak on the sea, particularly in the eyes of Japan and America." [102]   The plan did not materialize, apparently because order was well maintained in Shantung and the Yangtze Valley was soon neutralized. But the desire of the Kaiser to expand his influence in the Far East remained. To emphasize the military might of Germany, the Kaiser caused Field Marshal von Waldersee to be appointed commander-in-chief of the Allied forces.[103]   And to give the German general enough time to demonstrate the prowess of the German army, every effort was

[98] *Chung Jih Shih Liao,* 56/17-18.

[99] To Shêng, K26/intercalary 8/28, Li Hung-chang, *op. cit.,* " Tien Kao," 27/30a.

[100] William II to Bülow, June 19, 1900, *Die Grosse Politik der Europäischen Kabinette, 1871-1914: Sammlung der Diplomatischen Akten des Auswärtigen Amtes* (Berlin, 1924), XVI, 14 (cited hereafter as *Die Grosse Politik*).

[101] Bülow to William II, June 19, 1900, *Ibid.,* XVI, 15.

[102] Bülow to Minister of Foreign Affairs, July 3, 1900, *ibid.,* XVI, 32.

[103] See G. P. Gooch and Harold Temperley (eds.), *British Documents on the Origins of the War, 1898-1914* (London: His Majesty's Stationery Office, 1927), II, 5, 8.

made to stop Li Hung-chang from going to the north to start peace negotiations. A plan was made to capture the Chinese plenipotentiary during his voyage from Shanghai to Tientsin and to detain him as a prisoner of war in Tsingtao.[104] The plot was shelved only when it was feared that the capture would entail war with Russia.[105] But the German Government continued to place obstacles in the way of negotiations. The German Minister insisted that no negotiations would be opened before the severe punishment of the pro-Boxer ministers.[106] The arrogance of Count von Waldersee particularly hurt Chinese feelings. He took the I-luan Tien, the palace of the Empress Dowager, as his living quarters and refused to receive Li Hung-chang.[107] The violence of the German troops made the Chinese people detest and fear them more than any other foreign force.[108]

The British worked parallel with the Germans in the negotiations. The British Consul-General in Shanghai snubbed Li Hung-chang; the British Minister in Peking cooperated with his German colleague in demanding severe punishment of the pro-Boxer ministers.[109] Anxious to stop the Russian advance in north China, the British sought a close understanding with Germany.[110] Considering Li Hung-chang pro-Russian, the British diplomats attempted to check him by invoking the services of Chang Chih-tung and Liu K'un-i. The Chinese at first had hopes that Great Britain, in view of its widespread commercial interests in China, would be interested in restoring peace to the country.[111] They were soon

---

[104] Richthofen to Bülow, Sept. 9, 1900, *Die Grosse Politik*, XVI, 123-24.

[105] Bülow to Minister of Foreign Affairs, Sept. 10, 1900, *ibid.*, XVI, 125.

[106] To Li, etc., K26/8/16, Chang Chih-tung, *op. cit.*, 164/42a.

[107] Li Hung-chang, *op. cit.*, " Tien Kao," 27/11b, 28/24b, 28/29a.

[108] Beau to Delcassé, July 1, 1901, Ministère des affaires étrangères, *Documents diplomatiques français (1871-1914)* (Paris, 1930), 2nd Series, I, 365.

[109] To the Grand Council, K26/10/25, Li Hung-chang, *op. cit.*, " Tien Kao," 29/28a; see also *Foreign Relations of the United States*, 1901, Apendix, p. 71.

[110] The Anglo-German Agreement, signed on October 16, 1900, provided that " in case of another Power making use of the complications in China in order to obtain territorial advantages, the Contracting Parties would come to an understanding as to the steps to be taken to protect their own interests." John Van Antwerp MacMurray (ed.), *Treaties and Agreements with and concerning China* (New York: Oxford University Press, 1921), I, 203.

[111] To Liu and Chang, K26/8/3, Shêng Hsüan-huai, *op. cit.*, 29/40; from Liu, K26/

disappointed at the highhanded policy of the British in Paoting [112] and the stiff attitude of the British Minister.[113] "It is useless," telegraphed Sir Claude MacDonald, "to attempt serious negotiations with the Chinese Government until the Chinese military power is disheartened and completely crushed." [114] The policy of Britain drove Li Hung-chang more to the side of Russia.

The Japanese were apprehensive of Russian ambitions in northeast China, but, unlike Britain, they adopted the policy of cultivating the friendship of China. Throughout the crisis Japan assumed a conciliatory attitude. When the Allied forces were approaching Peking, the Japanese Government advised China to send delegates to the front to negotiate for a truce with the Allied commanders.[115] It offered protection to Li Hung-chang in his journey to the north [116] and agreed to withdraw part of its troops from Peking to Tientsin.[117] A Japanese source advised Chang Chih-tung that the Japanese Foreign Office did not consider the return of the Imperial Court to Peking a necessary condition for the opening of negotiations.[118] In regard to the severe penalty for the princes of the blood, the Japanese Foreign Secretary agreed to take up the matter with the other Powers with a view to its miti-

---

8/4, *ibid.*, 40/2; from Chang, K26/8/8, Li Hung-chang, *op. cit.*, "Tien Kao," 25/22a; from Liu, K26/8/8, Chang Chih-tung, *op. cit.*, 164/27.

112 The British commander in Paoting seized the provincial treasury and executed three Chinese officials, including the Acting Viceroy T'ing Yung. See Li Hung-chang, *op. cit.*, "Tien Kao," 28/19b, 28/31a, 28/34b.

113 *Ibid.*, 25/21b.

114 MacDonald to Salisbury, August 24, 1900, *China No. 1 (1901)*, p. 105.

115 Shêng Hsüan-huai, *op. cit.*, 39/3-4.

116 Li Hung-chang, *op. cit.*, "Tien Kao," 26/7a.

117 From Li, K26/8/16, Li Hung-chang, *op. cit.*, "Tien Kao," 26/4a. Marquis Ito, who had been ordered by the Japanese Emperor to assist the Japanese cabinet with regard to the Boxer crisis, recommended on August 22 to the Japanese Prime Minister and the Foreign Secretary that, as the purpose of relieving the legations had been achieved, Japan should be the first to propose the withdrawal of troops, so as to show that Japan did not have any ambitions and at the same time to gain the gratitude of China. The two ministers agreed. Probably owing to the unfavorable responses of Germany, Britain, and France, however, no action was taken. Ito was greatly displeased that Japan should have lost the opportunity of taking the leadership in the matter and that later she did not act in unison with Russia when the latter proposed to withdraw the Allied troops to Tientsin. "Notes by Ito," in Kaneko Kintaro, *Ito Hirobumi* (Tokyo, 1940), III, 438 ff.

118 From Chang K26/8/21, Li Hung-chang, *op. cit.*, "Tien Kao," 26/20a.

gation.[119]   He also told the Chinese Minister at Tokyo that the Japanese troops had not joined in the military operations beyond Peking.[120]   The Japanese military officials in Tokyo advised the Chinese Minister that the Chinese troops should withdraw from Paoting with their ammunition and supplies.[121]   The Japanese Foreign Secretary informed the Chinese Minister of the Allied demands before they were formally presented to the Chinese plenipotentiaries.[122]   Repeatedly the Japanese Government assured the Chinese officials that they would use their influence to moderate the demands of the Powers.[123]   The Japanese statesmen, knowing the pro-Russian inclinations of Li Hung-chang, were especially eager to gain the friendship of Chang Chih-tung and Liu K'un-i. Contact was kept with Chang through various channels, and Chang, too, had a representative in Tokyo.[124]   It was upon the suggestion of the Japanese Government that Chang Chih-tung and Liu K'un-i were ordered by the Imperial Court to assist in the negotiations by correspondence with Li Hung-chang and Prince Ch'ing.[125]   In October, 1900, the Japanese Foreign Office and Prince Ito again suggested that the two viceroys go to Peking and take part in the negotiations.[126]   As will be seen later, the conciliatory approach of the Japanese Government, particularly its efforts in winning the friendship of Chang Chih-tung and Liu K'un-i, bore fruit in China's resistance to the Russian demands in Manchuria.

France played a rather quiet part during the crisis and, in spite of her alliance with Russia, kept a somewhat independent position. As announced by Foreign Secretary Delcassé on July 3, 1900, " France has no interest in provoking or desiring the break-up of China. . . . France is certainly anxious for the maintenance of the

[119] See *Chung Jih Shih Liao*, 59/1b, 59/6.

[120] To the Grand Council, K26/10/2, Li Hung-chang, *op. cit.*, " Tien Kao," 29/1a.

[121] From Shêng, K26/intercalary 8/23, *ibid.*, 27/23a.

[122] From Shêng, K26/9/26, *ibid.*, 28/51a.

[123] Chang Chih-tung, *op. cit.*, 167/15b; 169/8a.   [124] Ch'ien Hsün.

[125] Li Hung-chang, *op. cit.*, " Tien Kao," 24/45a.

[126] To Li, K26/intercalary 8/16, to Liu, K26/intercalary 8/16, Chang Chih-tung, *op. cit.*, 166/32. The Japanese suggestion was not taken, for, as Chang pointed out, it was impossible for the two viceroys to leave the Yangtze Valley at that time (*ibid.*; also Liu, K26/intercalary 8/17, *ibid.*, 166/34b).

equilibrium in the Far East. She will see that it is not broken to her detriment, but she cherishes no secret designs." [127]   In the negotiations, however, M. Pichon, French Minister at Peking, although disavowing any thought of vengeance, usually voted for severity in the matter of penalty.[128]

The policy of the United States throughout the crisis was that of traditional friendship toward China. The American admiral had opposed the attack on the Taku forts, and in the bombardment which followed he had chosen to stand aside and take no part in the action.[129]   In the course of the negotiations the American Government invariably stood for moderation and showed a readiness to consider the proposals of the Chinese Government.[130] The American Government rejected the German demand that preceding the negotiations the pro-Boxer ministers be handed to the Allies for punishment.[131]   It objected to the ultimatum form in which the Allied demands were to be presented to China.[132]   As early as July 3, when the legations were still under siege, John Hay, the American Secretary of State, had sent a circular telegram to the Powers stating that the policy of the American Government was to bring about " permanent safety and peace to China " and to preserve " Chinese territorial and administrative entity." [133]   The American position was so helpful to China that M. Beau, French Minister to China during the later period of the negotiations, observed that the United States " appeared, in the proposals, to be inspired by the sole preoccupation to help, or affect to help, China

[127] Statement in the Chamber of Deputies, July 3, 1900, *Foreign Relations of the United States*, 1900 (Washington: Government Printing Office, 1902), pp. 312-13.

[128] See Pichon to Delcassé, Feb. 27, 1901, *Documents diplomatiques français (1871-1914)*, 2nd Series, I, 127.

[129] Paul H. Clements, *The Boxer Rebellion* ("Studies in History, Economics, and Public Law," Vol. LXVI, No. 3 [New York: Columbia University Press, 1915]), pp. 129-30.

[130] *Foreign Relations of the United States*, 1900, pp. 217, 218, 224, 322-23, 339-40; *ibid.*, 1901, Apendix, pp. 12, 50, 87, 95.

[131] Shêng Hsüan-huai, *op. cit.*, 41/18; *Foreign Relations of the United States*, 1900, p. 342.

[132] Li Hung-chang, *op. cit.*, "Tien Kao," 29/14b, 21a.

[133] *Foreign Relations of the United States*, 1900, p. 299.

to evade the responsibilities of whatever kind she has incurred in this adventure." [134]

THE JOINT NOTE

When Li Hung-chang arrived at Tientsin on September 19, 1900, he stayed there for some three weeks instead of proceeding at once to Peking. He saw the Russian Minister, Michael de Giers, who came down to Tientsin.[135] He soon found that the situation was not favorable for the opening of negotiations.[136] Germany had proposed on September 18 that the Powers should make it a condition preliminary to entering upon negotiations with the Chinese Government that the guilty leaders should be surrendered for punishment at the hands of the Powers.[137] To forestall the acceptance of the German proposal by the Powers, Li urged the Imperial Court to punish the offenders itself. The result was the decree of September 25 announcing the punishment of the five princes and the two Grand Councillors.[138] This anticipatory measure of the Chinese Government achieved its purpose; for while the diplomatic corps considered the penalties imposed not sufficiently severe, they declared that the list was a correct one, except that Tung Fu-hsiang and Yü Hsien were not included.[139] The German proposal was opposed by the United States and Russia;[140] it was dropped after the Chinese Government, in the decree of November 13, augmented the list of guilty ministers and increased their penalties.

In the meantime the attention of the Powers was drawn to the French proposals. On October 4 the French Government submitted the following six points to the Powers as a basis for negotiations with the Chinese Government:

1. Punishment of the principal culprits, to be designated by the representatives of the Powers at Peking.

[134] Beau to Delcassé, July 1, 1901, *Documents diplomatiques français (1871-1914)*, 2nd Series, I, 366.

[135] Li's Memorial, K26/intercalary 8/12, *Hsi Hsün Ta Shih Chi*, 2/29a.

[136] From Shêng, K26/intercalary 8/23, Chang Chih-tung, *op. cit.*, 166/17a.

[137] *Foreign Relations of the United States*, 1900, p. 34.

[138] *Ch'ing Tê Tsung Shih Lu*, 470/1b.   [139] *China No. 5* (1901), p. 22.

[140] *Foreign Relations of the United States*, 1900, pp. 341-42; *China No. 1* (1901), pp. 184, 197.

2. Maintenance of the prohibition of imports of arms.

3. Equitable indemnities for states, societies, and individuals.

4. Establishment of a permanent legation guard at Peking.

5. Dismantling of the forts at Taku.

6. Military occupation of two or three points on the road from Tientsin to Taku, which would thus be always open in the event of the legations' wishing to reach the sea, or for forces coming from the sea with the object of proceeding to the capital.[141]

The French proposals were accepted by the Powers as a basis for negotiations, and the diplomatic corps at Peking was assigned the task of formulating the demands to be presented to the Chinese plenipotentiaries. After many modifications and additions, the foreign envoys at last agreed on a Joint Note of eleven points to be presented to the Chinese Government. The document as handed over to the Chinese plenipotentiaries on December 24 consisted of twelve articles:

Art. 1. (a) Dispatch to Berlin of an Extraordinary Mission, headed by an Imperial Prince, to express the regrets of His Majesty the Emperor of China and the Chinese Government for the murder of his Excellency the late Baron Ketteler, German Minister.

(b) Erection on the place where the murder was committed of a commemorative monument suitable to the rank of the deceased, bearing an inscription in the Latin, German, and Chinese languages expressing the regret of the Emperor of China for the murder.

Art. 2. (a) The severest punishment in proportion to their crimes for the persons named in the Imperial Decree of the 25th September, 1900, and for those whom the Representatives of the Powers shall subsequently designate.

(b) Suspension of all official examinations for five years in all the towns where foreigners have been massacred or have been subjected to cruel treatment.

Art. 3. An honourable reparation shall be accorded by the Chinese Government to that of Japan for the murder of Mr. Sugiyama, Chancellor of the Japanese Legation.

Art. 4. An expiatory monument shall be erected by the Chinese Government in each of the foreign or international cemeteries which have been desecrated, and in which the graves have been destroyed.

Art. 5. Maintenance, under conditions to be settled between the

---

[141] *China No. 5 (1901)*, p. 5; *Foreign Relations of the United States*, 1901, Appendix, p. 27.

Powers, of the prohibition of the importation of arms, as well as material serving exclusively for the manufacture of arms and ammunition.

Art. 6. (a) An equitable indemnity to Governments, Societies, private individuals, as well as for Chinese who have suffered during the recent occurrences in their persons or property, in consequence of their being in the service of foreigners.

(b) China shall adopt financial measures acceptable to the Powers, for the purpose of guaranteeing the payment of the said indemnities and the service of the loans.

Art. 7. The right of maintaining, by each Power, a permanent guard for its Legation, and of placing the Legation quarter in a condition of defence. Chinese not to have the right of residing in that quarter.

Art. 8. The Taku and other forts, which might impede free communication between Peking and the coast, are to be razed.

Art. 9. Right of military occupation of certain points to be determined by agreement between the Powers in order to maintain communication between the capital and the sea.

Art. 10. (a) The Chinese Government shall cause to be posted up for two years in all the Sub-Prefectures an Imperial Decree embodying—

Perpetual prohibition under pain of death of being a member of an anti-foreign Society.

Enumeration of the penalties which shall have been inflicted on the guilty persons, including the suspension of all official examinations in the towns where foreigners were massacred or subjected to cruel treatment.

(b) An Imperial Edict shall be issued and published everywhere in the Empire, making all Viceroys, Governors, and provincial and local officials responsible for order within their jurisdictions; and whenever anti-foreign disturbances or any other Treaty infractions occur therein which are not forthwith suppressed and in regard to which the guilty persons are not punished, these officials shall be immediately recalled, without the possibility of being given new posts or of receiving fresh honours.

Art. 11. The Chinese Government will undertake to negotiate regarding amendments to the Treaties of Commerce and Navigation considered useful by the Powers, and also other subjects connected with commercial relations with the object of facilitating them.

Art. 12. The Chinese Government shall undertake to reform the office of foreign relations, and modify the Court ceremonial relative to the reception of foreign Representatives in the manner which the Powers shall indicate.[142]

Upon receipt of the Joint Note, the Imperial Court ordered the Grand Councillors to review carefully the demands and communi-

---

[142] *China No. 6* (*1901*), pp. 60-63; Li Hung-chang, *op. cit.*, " Tien Kao," 30/5a.

cate their views to the Chinese plenipotentiaries for reference.
Accordingly Jung Lu, Wang Wên-shao, and Lu Ch'uan-lin telegraphed Li Hung-chang the following observations:

Art. 2. Yü Hsien, guilty of cruel deeds, should be executed. But except for high treason, there is no such law as putting princes of the blood
to death. Suspension of examination should be confined to the individual districts where offenses against the foreigners have actually been
committed.

Art. 5. Materials prohibited for importation should be specifically
named and limited only to those exclusively used for war purposes.

Art. 6. A heavy indemnity has to be paid, but consideration should
be given to the financial capacity of China. Either the terms of payment should be liberal or the amount of indemnity should be decreased.

Art. 7. The number of legation guards should not be excessive, and
there should be regulations preventing them from creating trouble beyond the legations.

Art. 8. The guns and gunners of the Taku forts may be removed, but
the forts should remain so that China would not be helpless in case of
piracy.

Art. 9. The points for military occupation should be specified, and
the number of troops should be limited. The occupation forces should
not interfere with Chinese territory or Chinese travelers.

Art. 10. Local officials shall be heavily punished if, because of inadequate protection by them, foreigners suffer from anti-Christian disturbances or other Chinese-foreign disputes. But if because of conflicts
between the people and the converts the [foreign] missionaries or tour-
ists are injured, the punishment should vary according to actual situations, and the officials concerned should not, without discrimination, be
forever prohibited from holding office.

Art. 11. Treaties of commerce and navigation may be amended so
long as the rights and interests of China are not impaired.

Art. 12. The Court ceremonial may be modified if the dignity of the
nation is not impaired.[143]

On December 27 the Imperial Court received the memorial from
the Chinese plenipotentiaries urging the acceptance of the demands.
The attitude of the Powers, they pointed out, was categorical and
admitted of no argument. Unless the demands were accepted, the
Allied forces would not be withdrawn, and if the negotiations were

---

[143] From Jung Lu, etc., K26/11/4, *Chung Jih Shih Liao*, 59/25; received K26/11/6,
Li Hung-chang, *op. cit.*, "Tien Kao," 30/10.

broken, the existence of the nation would be in danger.[144]   The same day a decree was issued by the Imperial Court ordering the acceptance of " the general principles laid down in the Twelve Articles [i.e., the Joint Note]." As regards the details, the pleni-potentiaries were ordered to make utmost endeavors to secure attenuation and reduction on the basis of the observations made by the Grand Councillors.[145]

Among the provincial officials, Yüan Shih-k'ai considered the Joint Note acceptable, for he found there none of the conditions that had worried him, namely, (1) partition of China, (2) control of the salt administration, (3) seizing of industrial privileges, (4) control of the armed forces, and (5) restoration of power to the Emperor.[146]   Chang Chih-tung, however, considered some of the demands objectionable.   In the first place, Article 5 should be modified to prohibit only arms and ammunition for a certain num-ber of years.   The importation of machines and material for the manufacture of arms and ammunition should not be prohibited; otherwise China would be helpless in case of rebellion or banditry. Secondly, if Articles 7, 8, and 9 were accepted, China would have no forts on the coast and no troops on the road from the coast to Peking, while the foreign Powers would maintain more than 1,000 troops in the legations, 5,000 to 6,000 along the road from the coast to Peking, and about 3,000 in the warships around the ports. Confronted with such a strong foreign force, Peking would be extremely vulnerable.   If in the future disputes arose between China and some foreign Powers, China would find it hard to de-fend herself, while this weakness of China would tempt the Powers to further aggressions.   Foreign military installations between the coast and Peking must therefore be confined to the purpose of pro-tecting the legations, and must not be taken advantage of by some individual Power for war purposes.   Thirdly, before these military questions were settled, the Imperial Court should not return to Peking.   If the foreign ministers considered Sian too far for their

144 To the Grand Council, K26/11/3, Li Hung-chang, op. cit., " Tien Kao," 30/52.
145 Ibid., 30/12b.
146 From Yüan, K26/11/4, Shêng Hsüan-huai, op. cit., 48/4.

residence, a place convenient to both sides in the upper Yangtze Valley, some twenty or thirty miles from the coast but accessible only by small gunboats,[147] might be chosen as a temporary capital. Fourthly, the declaration in the preamble of the Joint Note that the attacks upon the legations were made by regular troops " who obeyed orders of the Court emanating from the Imperial Palace " carried dangerous insinuations. In conformity with the previous Imperial declarations that the attacks had not been intended by the Imperial Court, the above-quoted clause should be deleted.[148]

The suggestions of Chang Chih-tung were endorsed by the Imperial Court, and Li Hung-chang and Prince Ch'ing were ordered to give them careful consideration.[149] It was natural that Chang's proposal should appeal to the Empress Dowager, who had not the least intention of returning to Peking at that time. In the eyes of the Sian Government, Chang Chih-tung often understood its position better than Li Hung-chang, who seemed too ready to counsel acceptance of the foreign demands. The Court therefore thought of moving the negotiations from Peking to Shanghai, where Chang Chih-tung, together with Liu K'un-i and Shêng Hsüan-huai, might participate. On January 5, 1901, Lu Ch'uan-lin, a Grand Councillor, telegraphed Chang Chih-tung, inquiring if the Powers would agree to such a move. At first Chang Chih-tung considered that it might be better to have the negotiations carried on in Nanking, which is near Shanghai and not far from Hankow, so that they could all participate without much inconvenience.[150] On second thought, however, Chang gave up the idea. On January 7 he replied to Lu Ch'uan-lin that moving the negotiations to Shanghai would take time, while the Joint Note had to be acted upon soon. Moreover, the Powers might not agree to negotiate in Shanghai, and action of this kind would have a bad effect upon the Chinese

---

[147] Chang had in mind Tangyang or Chingmênchou, Hupeh, the former some 120 *li*, the latter some 180 *li*, from Chingchou. To Minister Li, K26/11/13, Chang Chih-tung, *op. cit.*, 170/21.

[148] Chang to the Grand Council, K26/11/10, *Chung Jih Shih Liao*, 59/30; Li Hung-chang, *op. cit.*, " Tien Kao," 30/21.

[149] Decree, K26/11/10, *Ch'ing Tê Tsung Shih Lu*, 475/6a.

[150] To Liu and Shêng, K26/11/17, Chang Chih-tung, *op. cit.*, 170/23.

plenipotentiaries.[151] Liu K'un-i objected to moving the negotiations, whether to Shanghai or Nanking. He pointed out that great difficulties would arise if the Court " shows any lack of confidence in the two plenipotentiaries." [152] Under such objections the idea of moving the negotiations from Peking was dropped.

In a telegram of January 4, Li Hung-chang answered Chang Chih-tung's observations on the Joint Note. The foreign troops to be maintained in the metropolitan area, Li pointed out, would not be as many as Chang asserted. The legation guards of all the Powers would consist of not more than a few hundred. The number of troops to be stationed from Taku to Peking was to be specified, and in no case would come to as many as 5,000 to 6,000. As to the neutralization of the occupation zone in the event of conflict between China and some individual Powers, it was hard to mention it at a time when the Powers were united against China. The statement in the Joint Note that the attacks upon the legations were made by regular troops " who obeyed orders of the Court emanating from the Imperial Palace " was made by the foreign ministers to vent their feelings, Li declared. The foreign ministers had never mentioned it in the conferences; " if we find fault with such wording and phrasing, we only create trouble for ourselves." Lastly, the suggestion that a place in the upper Yangtze Valley be selected as a temporary capital where the foreign envoys would reside was " a nonsensical idea and a distorted view." The Imperial Court certainly could not move at random, nor would the foreign envoys move at the direction of the Chinese Government. The telegram concluded with the following remark: " It is surprising that Viceroy Chang, after serving in the provinces for many years and having had some experience, should still maintain the academic way of thinking which he had acquired twenty years ago in Peking. Those who are not responsible can make comments easily." [153]

---

[151] To Lu, K26/11/17, *ibid.*, 170/23.
[152] From Liu, K26/11/18, *ibid.*, 170/24.
[153] To the Grand Council, K26/11/14, Li Hung-chang, *op. cit.*, " Tien Kao," 30/23. Li's attack immediately drew a retort from Chang Chih-tung. " Somebody has accused me of being academic," he wired Liu K'un-i, Yüan Shih-k'ai, and Shêng Hsüan-huai. " Very true. But the academic way of thinking is better than the bureaucratic way of

As the Imperial Court wavered because of Chang Chih-tung's objections,[154] Li Hung-chang on January 6 sent in another memorial urging the signing of the Twelve Articles presented in the Joint Note. The demands therein, he pointed out, " are not open to discussion; any argument would only lead to the rupture of the negotiations. . . . A decree has been issued ordering acceptance; if we do not sign, they would consider the Court breaking its word and the plenipotentiaries possessing no authority. In that eventuality not only would it be impossible to request them to withdraw their troops, but also impossible to stop their military advance." [155]

On January 10 the Imperial Court ordered that the Twelve Articles be signed. For the details which remained to be settled, the plenipotentiaries were directed to argue " article by article " so as to " forestall any future troubles." Careful consideration should be given to all the decrees concerned as well as to the various suggestions from the officials.[156] On January 16 the Chinese plenipotentiaries signed the protocol containing the Twelve Articles.[157]

---

doing nothing " (K26/11/21, Shêng Hsüan-huai, *op. cit.*, 49/14). He was immediately comforted by Liu, Yüan, and Shêng, who, besides eulogizing the patriotic statesmanship of the Hankow viceroy, expressed their earnest hope that, in an unprecedented crisis like this, all would suppress their personal feelings and contribute their utmost to the country (*ibid.*, 49/14, 16, 21).

[154] Chang to the Grand Council, K26/11/10, *Chung Jih Shih Liao*, 59/29b; Grand Council to Ch'ing and Li, K26/11/13, *ibid.*, 59/31; Decree, K26/11/12, *Ch'ing Tê Tsung Shih Lu*, 476/7a.

[155] To the Grand Council, K26/11/16, Li Hung-chang, *op. cit.*, " Tien Kao," 30/24a.

[156] Decree, K26/11/20, *Ch'ing Tê Tsung Shih Lu*, 475/13a.

[157] *Foreign Relations of the United States*, 1901, Appendix, p. 65.

8

Russia Acts in Manchuria

OCCUPATION OF MANCHURIA

SINCE THE RUSSIAN OCCUPATION of Port Arthur in 1898 there had arisen an anti-Russian sentiment in south Manchuria. The population particularly disliked the building of the South Manchurian Railway.[1] When the Boxer movement spread to the metropolitan area of Peking, agitation found its way to south Manchuria. Yet up to June 15 no disturbances were reported in Fêngt'ien, although the Boxers began to appear and rumors of various kinds circulated. On that day the foreign missionaries and residents as well as the foreign employees of the South Manchurian Railway began to move to Yingkow. On June 23, after hostilities had broken out in Taku, an Imperial decree was issued ordering Tsêng Ch'i, Tartar General of Fêngt'ien, to organize the Boxers so as to reinforce the troops in their resistance to foreign aggression. It was also directed that, if there was any movement of Russian troops, the Tartar General should destroy the railway at Chinchow and stop their advance.[2] Two days later the troops under Chin Ch'ang, Vice-Commander of the Fêngt'ien army, destroyed the railway bridges around Shaho and killed a Russian officer.[3] By the end of June the Boxers intensified their activities. The Protestant missions of Mukden were destroyed by a mob on June 30. The French mission at Mukden was attacked and burnt on July 2. In the early part of July the Russian railway employees and guards were attacked at several points along the railway. The Russian railway guards took up the challenge: they, too, attacked

---

[1] Count Witte, *Memoirs*, ed. by Abraham Yarmolinsky (New York: Doubleday, 1921), p. 110.

[2] Decree, K26/5/27, *Chung Jih Shih Liao*, 53/20.

[3] Memorial by Tsêng Ch'i, K26/intercalary 8/25, *Ch'ing Chi Wai Chiao Shih Liao*, 144/22.

and burned and soon came into conflict with the Chinese troops. The situation was so confused that all the missionaries fled to the treaty ports.[4]

Upon report from Yang Ju, Chinese Minister at St. Petersburg, that the situation in Manchuria might lead to serious consequences, Li Hung-chang telegraphed the Tartar Generals of the three northeastern provinces on June 29, urging them to make the utmost efforts to suppress the disturbances and protect the railway and the foreigners.[5]   The Chinese Minister at St. Petersburg also wired the Tartar Generals directly, advising them that Russia had concentrated in Vladivostok and Port Arthur large forces which could reach Manchuria within a day's time, and that to protect the railway the Russians would occupy Manchuria and might not withdraw.[6]

The advice of Li Hung-chang and Yang Ju, however, was of little effect because of the strong antiforeign sentiment in the area and because of the Imperial decrees which, one after another, ordered the mobilization of the Boxers and resistance against any advance of foreign troops.[7]   The result was that most stations of the South Manchurian Railway, such as K'uanch'êngtzŭ, Mukden, and Liaoyang, were seized by the rioters.[8]

For the time being the disturbances were confined to the province of Fêngt'ien, the situation in the provinces of Kirin and Heilungkiang being largely brought under control.   Ch'ang Shun, Tartar General of Kirin, reported at the beginning of July that the railway under his jurisdiction remained intact and that he would assume full responsibility for protecting it.[9]   In the early part of July, Shou Shan, Tartar General of Heilungkiang, still took measures to protect the railway within his province, and assured the Russian authorities of Kharbarovsk and Amur, as well as the

[4] British Parliamentary Papers, China No. 1 (1901), p. 190.

[5] From Li, received K26/6/5, Tung San Shêng Tien Pao, p. 100; to Shêng, K26/6/4, Shêng Hsüan-huai, Yü Chai Ts'un Kao Ch'u K'an, 37/26.

[6] From Yang Ju, received K26/6/5, Shêng Hsüan-huai, op. cit., 23/8.

[7] Decrees, K26/6/13, K26/6/14, K26/6/16, Chung Jih Shih Liao, 53/42, 44; 54/12.

[8] Aleksei N. Kuropatkin, The Russian Army and the Japanese War (London: J. Murray, 1909), I, 154-55.

[9] To Yang, K26/6/8 (July 4, 1900), Li Hung-chang, Li Wên Chung Kung Ch'üan Chi, "Tien Kao," 23/15b. From Li, K26/6/10, Tung San Shêng Tien Pao, p. 102.

Russian Railway Director at Harbin, that he would continue to do so.[10] Both Tartar Generals wired Li Hung-chang to request the Russian Government not to send any troops to the provinces.[11] Li Hung-chang lost no time in taking action: telegrams were sent to Yang Ju asking him to urge the Russian Government, particularly Count Witte, to stop the dispatch of Russian troops. But the appeal of Li proved of no avail, for the Russian Government had decided to advance into Manchuria.[12]

At the first news of the Boxer uprising, General Kuropatkin, Russian Minister for War, had told Count Witte that " this will give us an excuse for seizing Manchuria " and turning it into " a second Bokhara."[13] The grandiose plan conceived by Count Witte for Manchuria was an expansion under the guise of " pacific penetration " by railroads, banks, etc.[14] The success of this plan depended upon the maintenance of peace rather than war. Accordingly Count Witte at first made an effort to stay Kuropatkin's hand, but as " the riots in Manchuria assumed a threatening character," he, too, urged the dispatch of Russian troops from the Amur region to Manchuria.[15]

On July 11, 1900, Count Witte informed the Chinese Minister at St. Petersburg that the dispatch of Russian troops into Manchuria was indispensable. He declared, however, that its purpose was the suppression of the " rioters " and that, if the Tartar Generals of the three provinces agreed to cooperate, the Russian forces would be withdrawn as soon as the disturbances were quelled.[16] This information was related to the Tartar Generals, who were urged by Li Hung-chang not to engage in any hostilities against Russia.[17]

But before the message could reach the Tartar Generals, hostilities had already broken out in Heilungkiang. General Shou Shan

10 From Shou, K26/6/9, *Tung San Shêng Tien Pao*, p. 101; Ch'êng Tê-ch'üan, *Kêng Tzŭ Chiao Shê Yü Lu*, 31b, 5b.
11 To Yang, K26/6/8 (July 4, 1900), Li Hung-chang, *op. cit.*, " Tien Kao," 23/15b.
12 To Tsungli Yamen, K26/6/17, *ibid.*, 23/31b.   13 Witte, *op. cit.*, p. 109.
14 Roman R. Rosen, *Forty Years of Diplomacy* (New York: Knopf, 1922), I, 196.
15 Witte, *op. cit.*, p. 109.
16 Yang to Li, K26/16/15, *Tung San Shêng Tien Pao*, p. 108.
17 To the Tartar Generals, K26/6/17, Li Hung-chang, *op. cit.*, " Tien Kao," 23/32.

had made efforts to protect the railway, but he was determined that, if the Russian troops encroached upon the territory under his jurisdiction, he would resist with force. " Even if disturbances occur in China," he wired Yang Ju, " there is no need for the Russians to suppress them for China. . . . What status do they accord China when they say they will protect our country with all their military might after the riots are suppressed? " [18]

Accordingly he sent three telegrams to the Russian authorities of the Amur region, warning them that if the Russian warships sailed southward into the province of Heilungkiang, the Chinese forces would open fire.[19] He did not neglect to escort the 6,000 to 7,000 Russians safely out of his province.[20] On July 13, in spite of General Shou Shan's warning, eleven ships bearing Russian troops, escorted by seven warships, sailed southward. To avoid hostilities General Shou Shan let them pass, but warned again that any further reinforcement would be met by gunfire. On July 14 another convoy of Russian ships sailed down the river. They were stopped by Chinese forces at Aigun, and hostilities instantly broke out.[21]

The Chinese armies were in no position to withstand the Russian attacks. On July 23 Aigun fell; on August 16 the Peita Ridge, the strategical pass to Tsitsihar, was taken by the Russians.[22] The following day Mergen fell, and Burdo was in confusion.[23] On August 19 General Shou received a telegram from Yang Ju advising him that the Russian Government had declared that the purpose of the Russian expedition was to suppress the disturbances. As the disturbances were quickly suppressed, the Tartar Generals of the three provinces might appropriately request the Russian commanders to stop advancing any further.[24] The same day General Shou instructed Ch'êng Tê-chüan, his deputy at the front, that if the Chinese armies could no longer make any stand he should negotiate with the Russian commander for a truce.[25] The

18 From Shou, K26/6/16, *Tung San Shêng Tien Pao*, p. 113.
19 From Shou, K26/6/17, *ibid.*, p. 115.   20 *Ibid.*, p. 116.
21 From S'iou, K26/6/20, *ibid.*, p. 120.
22 Ch'êng Tê-ch'üan, *op. cit.*, 1-2.   23 *Ibid.*, 2-6.
24 From Shou, K26/7/25, *ibid.*, 11.
25 *Ibid.*

Russian commander, however, refused to halt his troops.[26] On August 28 General Shou committed suicide. On August 30 the Russian troops entered Tsitsihar.[27]

After hostilities broke out on July 14 the Russians resorted to atrocities against the Chinese civilians. On July 17 several thousand Chinese living in Blagoveshchensk were either killed or driven into the river to be drowned. In Harbin numerous Chinese were burned to death.[28]

Simultaneously with the advance to Heilungkiang, the Russians attacked the province of Kirin in two directions: (1) from Khabarovsk the Russian troops sailed up the Sungari River under the escort of warships, taking Ilan on July 30 and Alechuka on August 17; (2) from Vladivostok they attacked Hunch'un and Ningkuta, taking the latter stronghold on August 29. After that the Tartar General of Kirin thought it futile to resist any longer. He arranged with the Russian commander that "when the Russian troops come, the Chinese troops will hoist a white flag and both sides will not fire." Actually the Chinese forces were disarmed, and the provincial treasury was placed under Russian control. The Chinese officials were permitted to continue their civil administration, but were required to supply the Russian army with provisions. On September 21 the Russian army entered the capital of Kirin.[29]

As regards the province of Fêngt'ien, the Russians advanced from Port Arthur, taking Hsiungyo on August 1 and Yingkow on August 4. The Tartar General of Fêngt'ien sent a delegation to Yingkow to seek a truce, but the Russians refused to negotiate. On September 28 the Russians attacked Liaoyang and defeated the Chinese army. On October 1 they entered Mukden.[30] Thus in less than three months the three provinces of northeast China were occupied by the Russians.

---

[26] *Ibid.*, 22-27.　　　　　　　　　　　　　　　　　　　[27] *Ibid.*, 66.
[28] From Shou, K26/6/26, *Tung San Shêng Tien Pao*, p. 123; from Liu, K26/7/3, Li Hung-chang, *op. cit.*, "Tien Kao," 24/5a; Rosen, *op. cit.*, I, 200.
[29] *Chung Jih Shih Liao*, 59/19.
[30] *Ibid.*

CHINA OPENS NEGOTIATIONS

The Russian advance into Manchuria immediately gave rise to grave concern in Japan. On the eve of the fall of Peking, the Chinese Minister at Tokyo was approached unofficially by a Japanese politician who urged that China must resist the Russian aggression, for if the northeastern provinces were seized by Russia, other Powers would take other territories and thus partition of China would begin. If China decided to fight Russia, Japan would supply arms and ammunition, and army officers could be sent over to assist the Chinese army. If China transferred her troops from the metropolitan area of Peking to Fêngt'ien, it would have the support of Britain, Japan, and America, and there would not be much difficulty in resolving the crisis in Peking. The Chinese Minister was much convinced. He wired Shêng Hsüan-huai and requested him to advise Li Hung-chang, Jung Lu, and the two Yangtze viceroys of the Japanese suggestions. " The Japanese Government entertains similar ideas," added the Chinese Minister, " only it finds it inconvenient to express them officially." [31]

When the report was forwarded to Li Hung-chang, he was not convinced. He told Shêng Hsüan-huai not to forward the message to Jung Lu, as the generalissimo " is too occupied to be of any assistance." [32] Actually it was Li's belief that Russia would not occupy permanently the three provinces and that he could settle the problem with Russia by diplomatic means.[33] As pointed out by Shêng Hsüan-huai, the Chinese armies had just suffered severe defeats from the Allies; they could hardly be expected to fight another formidable enemy immediately.[34] Moreover, the Russian Government had recently offered to persuade the other Powers to agree to a truce in the Peking area.[35] It was more logical for China to request Russia to withdraw her troops from Manchuria than to fight her in accordance with the Japanese suggestions.

On August 13 the Imperial Court had ordered Li Hung-chang

[31] From Minister Li, K26/7/20 (August 14, 1900), Shêng Hsüan-huai, op. cit., 39/12.
[32] To Minister Li, K26/7/21, ibid., 39/12.
[33] See Chang Chih-tung, Chang Wên Hsiang Kung Ch'üan Chi, 166/37b.
[34] To Minister Li, K26/7/21, Shêng Hsüan-huai, op. cit., 39/12.
[35] Grand Council to Li, K26/7/19, Chung Jih Shih Liao, 55/29b.

to request the Russian Government to withdraw its troops from the three northeastern provinces.[36] The Imperial order was transmitted to the Chinese Minister at St. Petersburg by Li Hung-chang on August 15.[37] As the Russian Government declined to give an immediate reply, Li telegraphed again on August 22. He urged the Russian Government to halt the military advance in Manchuria and promised severe punishment of the Chinese officials who were responsible for the disturbances in the three provinces.[38] In reply the Russian Government declared that the Russian troops in Manchuria could not be withdrawn before order was restored to the area and before Russia was assured that no troubles would occur in the future.[39]

Toward the end of August the Chinese defenses in Manchuria rapidly collapsed before the Russian advance. About that time the Russian Government proposed to the other Powers that the Allied troops be withdrawn to Tientsin. Taking advantage of the professed good will of Russia, Li Hung-chang memorialized the Throne on September 3 advising the punishment of Shou Shan, Tartar General of Heilungkiang, and Chin Ch'ang, Vice-Commander of the Fêngt'ien army, as a preliminary step for opening negotiations with Russia on the withdrawal of her troops from Manchuria.[40] Li's proposal was promptly approved by the Imperial Court, which ordered the dismissal of Shou Shan and Chin Ch'ang pending investigation and further punishment.[41]

On October 23 the Russian Government indicated to Chinese Minister Yang Ju that it was willing to return the three provinces to China, but part of the Russian force had to remain for the protection of the railways.[42] When Li Hung-chang received this report from Yang Ju, he immediately wired the Imperial Court that this was a good chance to get back Manchuria. He recommended that Ch'ang Shun, Tartar General of Kirin, and Tsêng

[36] Ibid. [37] Li Hung-chang, op. cit., " Tien Kao," 24/32a.
[38] From Li, K26/7/28, Tung San Shêng Tien Pao, p. 127.
[39] To Li, K26/7/29, ibid., p. 127.
[40] From Li, K26/7/29, ibid., p. 130. At that time Li had not learned of Shou Shan's death.
[41] Decree, K26/8/19, Ch'ing Tê Tsung Shih Lu, 469/6b.
[42] To Li, K26/9/1, Tung San Shêng Tien Pao, p. 2.

Ch'i, Tartar General of Fêngt'ien, be appointed to receive their respective provinces back from the Russians. As to Heilungkiang, since Tartar General Shou Shan had committed suicide, Li recommended that Ch'o Ha-pu be sent there for the purpose.[43] All the recommendations were approved by the Court on October 28.[44] As communication between China proper and Manchuria had been disrupted, the Russian Government was requested to forward the orders of the Chinese Government to Tartar Generals Tsêng Ch'i and Ch'ang Shun with regard to their new assignments.[45]

THE TSÊNG-ALEXEIEFF AGREEMENT

Before the Imperial decree reached Manchuria, Tsêng Ch'i had started negotiations with Admiral Alexeieff, the Russian Governor-General of the Liaotung Peninsula. After the defeat at Liaoyang on September 28, the Fêngt'ien army could offer no more resistance. It evacuated Mukden on October 1. In the meantime General Tsêng Ch'i had received a telegram from Prince Ch'ing reporting the fall of Peking and pointing out that, if fighting was not stopped, no negotiations could be opened. Taking the precedents of Heilungkiang and Kirin, where delegates had been sent to the Russian headquarters to arrange for a truce, Tsêng Ch'i decided to do the same. In Hsinmin he met a former *taotai* by the name of Chou Mien, who had come from Heilungkiang. Chou claimed a knowledge of Russian affairs, and he was appointed " Commissioner Plenipotentiary " to negotiate with the Russians for a truce. The word " Plenipotentiary " was inserted because it was feared that without this title he would not be received by the Russian authorities. In his memorandum to Admiral Alexeieff, Tsêng Ch'i did not neglect to declare that with regard to peace negotiations he had to await orders from the Imperial Court, and that the present parleys were confined to local affairs and matters pertaining to the railway. As Chou Mien did not return after some time, Tsêng Ch'i telegraphed Alexeieff that he would like to postpone the parleys until he himself arrived in Mukden.

[43] To the Grand Council, K26/9/14, Shêng Hsüan-huai, *op. cit.*, 44/5.
[44] *Ch'ing Tê Tsung Shih Lu*, 472/6b.
[45] Li to Giers, K26/9/13, Li Hung-chang, *op. cit.*, " Tien Kao," 28/23a; Yang to Lamsdorff, K26/9/16, *Tung San Shêng Tien Pao*, p. 4.

No reply was received from the Russian Admiral, while Tsêng Ch'i was prevented by the Russian troops from going to Mukden.[46] On November 19 Chou Mien returned to Hsinmin from Port Arthur, bringing back with him an agreement which he had signed with the Russian representative Korostovitch on November 10. The agreement consisted of nine articles:

Art. 1. Upon resumption of office General Tsêng will undertake to protect the province and pacify it so that the construction of the railway can proceed without obstruction or destruction.

Art. 2. Russia will keep troops in Fêngt'ien for the protection of the railway and for the pacification of the province. The Tartar General and the local officials will treat kindly the Russian officials and assist them with all efforts in matters such as lodging and provisions.

Art. 3. The Fêngt'ien troops have collaborated with the rebels and destroyed the railway. The Tartar General must disarm and disband all troops, who will be pardoned for their offense if they do not resist the disarmament. All equipment and munitions of war in the arsenals not already occupied by the Russians will be delivered to the Russian officials.

Art. 4. The various forts and defenses in Fêngt'ien not occupied by the Russians, and all powder magazines not used by the Russians, will be dismantled in the presence of Russian officials.

Art. 5. Yingkow and other places are to be administered temporarily by the Russians. They will be restored to Chinese civil administration when the Russian Government is satisfied that order and peace have been effectively reestablished in Fêngt'ien.

Art. 6. For the various towns and localities in Fêngt'ien, infantry and cavalry police will be organized under the Tartar General. The size of the police and the weapons they carry will be determined later.

Art. 7. A Russian Resident will be stationed in Mukden to take charge of the communications and negotiations between the Tartar General and the Governor-General of Liaotung. The Resident must know all the important measures adopted by the Tartar General.

Art. 8. Should the infantry and cavalry police to be established by the Tartar General in Fêngt'ien be insufficient in any emergency, whether along the borders or in the interior, the Tartar General will communicate with the Resident and request the Russian commanders to give assistance.

Art. 9. The Russian text should be the standard in case of disagreements.[47]

---

[46] Tsêng Ch'i's Memorial, K27/4/24, Ch'ing Chi Wai Chiao Shih Liao, 146/26-30; from Tsêng, K26/12/18, Li Hung-chang, op. cit., "Tien Kao," 31/26b.

[47] Ch'ing Chi Wai Chiao Shih Liao, 144/18. An English version, consisting of ten articles, was printed in William W. Rockhill (ed.), Treaties and Conventions with or concerning China, 1894-1904 (Washington: Government Printing Office, 1904), pp.

Upon examination of the agreement, General Tsêng Ch'i found it highly unsatisfactory. Admiral Alexeieff, however, assured the Tartar General that the agreement, being provisional in character, could be revised later, but that it had to be signed before the Tartar General could return to Mukden. Afraid that his refusal to sign would lead to the rupture of the negotiations and considering that an agreement would have no binding force if the person signing it went beyond his powers, Tsêng Ch'i decided to sign with reservations.[48] On November 30 he notified Admiral Alexeieff that some articles in the agreement required further discussion. For Article 3, which provided for the disarming of the Fêngt'ien troops, it was necessary that a detailed and satisfactory arrangement be worked out so as to avoid evil consequences. As to Article 5, General Tsêng pointed out that the " other places " needed to be specified, and that the administration of Yingkow involved customs and tax revenues which belonged to the jurisdiction of the Viceroy of Chihli. " As I have not been appointed a plenipotentiary, nor received any information of the peace treaty under negotiation, I am unable to make any decision on these matters and should have waited for Imperial orders before signing them." But " since Your Excellency states in your telegram that this is only a provisional agreement that can be revised later, I hereby affix my signature with the understanding that the document will be reported to the Imperial Court for approval and that amendments and additions to the agreement will be negotiated after I return to the capital of the province." [49]

The Tsêng-Alexeieff Agreement was first published in the Lon-

---

201-2, under the title of " Agreement between Tseng Ch'i . . . and Admiral Alexeieff . . . Signed at Port Arthur, January 30, 1901," and with a footnote stating, " The original convention bears date November 11, 1900." It was reprinted in John V. A. MacMurray (ed.), *Treaties and Conventions with and concerning China* (New York: Oxford University Press, 1921), I, 329. Rockhill did not indicate the source of his text. It is now evident that neither his version nor his dates are correct. The version reported by M. Servan de Bezaure, French Consul General at Shanghai, to his Government on January 9, 1901 (in Ministère des affaires étrangères, *Documents diplomatiques français, 1871-1914* [Paris, 1930], 2nd Series, I, 18-19), though different from that of Rockhill's is also incorrect.

[48] Tsêng Ch'i's Memorial, K27/4/24, *Ch'ing Chi Wai Chiao Shih Liao*, 146/26-30.
[49] Tsêng to Alexeieff, K26/10/9, *ibid.*, 144/19.

don *Times* on January 3, 1901. It was reported by the paper's Peking correspondent in a telegram dated December 31.[50] The text given in a condensed form is on the whole correct except for Article 7, which was translated as follows: "A Russian political Resident with general powers of control shall be stationed at Mukden, to whom the Tartar General must give all information respecting any important measure." [51] It was upon the basis of this translation that the correspondent made this comment: "The functions given to the Russian Resident are similar to those of the Russian Resident at Bokhara or of the British Residents in the native states of India." [52] Similarly, the *Temps* of Paris interpreted the instrument as tantamount to the establishment by Russia of a complete protectorate over the southern province of Manchuria, for "a Resident is the cornerstone of the whole protectorate system." [53] According to the Chinese text, there was no provision that the Resident was to have "general powers of control," although Article 7 undoubtedly bespoke sinister aims.

On January 3, the day when the agreement was published in the *Times*, Lord Lansdowne wired the British envoys at Peking and St. Petersburg to ascertain the truth with regard to the instrument.[54] On January 4 Sir Ernest Satow, British Minister at Peking, replied that the report as telegraphed to the *Times* was authentic. "Full text of the Russo-Chinese Agreement has been sent from here by the bag on the 2nd January." [55]

Strangely enough, the Tsêng-Alexeieff Agreement was not reported to the Chinese Court until as late as January 15. It is true that as early as November 13, 1900, Li Hung-chang had received a telegram from Chou Mien, the official who concluded the agreement with the Russians. But the telegram, which was dated Port Arthur, November 11, was a short one: "A provisional agreement of nine articles has been concluded by Fêngt'ien. I suppose the Russian consul and minister will communicate it to Your Excellency." [56] Thereafter, for two months, no mention of the agree-

[50] *Times*, London, January 3, 1901, p. 3.
[51] *Ibid.*
[52] *Ibid.*
[53] *Ibid.*, January 5, 1901, p. 3.
[54] *China No. 6* (1901), p. 2.
[55] *Ibid.*, p. 3.
[56] From Chou, K26/9/22, Li Hung-chang, *op. cit.*, "Tien Kao," 38/37b.

ment appeared in Li's correspondence as published in his *Complete Works*,[57] or in other collections of documents. It is evident, however, that during this interval Li had heard from Tsêng Ch'i about the agreement.[58] According to the report of Satow, a Chinese text of the agreement had been sent to Li Hung-chang by Chou Mien from Port Arthur on November 11.[59] It was this text which the British Minister sent to Lord Lansdowne " by the bag " on January 2, 1901." [60] The condensed version published in the London *Times* was apparently based upon the same text. But if it is established that Li Hung-chang had received a report from Tsêng Ch'i and the text from Chou Mien before December 31, it is not known why he did not immediately forward them to the Imperial Court. At any rate it was Yang Ju, Chinese Minister at St. Petersburg, who was the first to call the attention of the Chinese Government to the agreement. On January 8, after reading the agreement in the " foreign newspapers," [61] he called on Count Witte and had it confirmed.[62] On the 10th he wired Li Hung-chang the agreement, which in the form of nine articles was similar to the version reported in the London *Times*.[63] On January 15 Li Hung-chang forwarded the report to the Imperial Court at Sian.[64]

When the Court read the agreement it was as surprised as it was indignant. General Tsêng Ch'i had been ordered to receive the province of Fêngt'ien back from the Russians; he was not expected to conclude any agreement. Tsêng Ch'i had never memorialized the Throne before the signing of the agreement; in fact, the Imperial Court knew nothing of the agreement until it had been widely reported in foreign countries. There was no reason, de-

---

[57] *Li Wên Chung Kung Ch'üan Chi.*
[58] See Li's Memorial, K26/11/25, *ibid.,* " Tien Kao," 30/32a.
[59] Satow to Lansdowne, January 2, 1901, *China No. 6 (1901)*, pp. 72-73.
[60] *Ibid.*
[61] " No mention of the report in the ' Times ' had appeared in the Russian press, and it was, therefore, only on the receipt of foreign newspapers on the 6th and 7th instant that the existence of this report and the alleged details of the Agreement were known to the general public." Scott to Lansdowne, St. Petersburg, January 8, 1901, *China No. 6 (1901)*, p. 11.
[62] *Chu O Shih Kuan Tang An*, in Wang Yün-shêng (ed.), *Liu Shih Nien Lai Chung Kuo Yü Jih Pên*, IV, 65.
[63] Yang to Li, K26/11/20, *Tung San Shêng Tien Pao*, p. 13.
[64] To the Grand Council, K26/11/25, Li Hung-chang, *op. cit.,* " Tien Kao," 30/32a.

clared the Imperial decree, that Tsêng Ch'i should appoint a *taotai* who had been deprived of office long ago to be a " Commissioner Plenipotentiary." There was no reason that this dismissed official should conclude an agreement with a foreign country, even though it was provisional in character. Accordingly it was ordered that Tsêng Ch'i be handed to the proper board for severe punishment. Li Hung-chang, " who had concluded a secret treaty with Russia, should review the whole situation and correspond with Yang Ju for a solution, so that the three provinces be returned without the loss of civil or military powers." [65]

Upon the advice of the Board of War a decree was issued ordering that General Tsêng Ch'i be deprived of his office.[66] The Russian Government, however, intervened. Count Lamsdorff notified the Chinese Minister at St. Petersburg that any punishment of General Tsêng would be regarded as an insult to Russia, for the agreement was signed by Admiral Alexeieff " in accordance with the order of the Tsar." [67] The Russian Minister at Peking, M. de Giers, warned that any punishment of the Tartar General would affect the negotiations regarding Manchuria.[68] As a result, the Imperial Court rescinded the decree of punishment and ordered Tsêng Ch'i to remain in office.[69]

[65] Decree, K26/11/28, *Tung San Shêng Tien Pao*, p. 19.
[66] *Ch'ing Tê Tsung Shih Lu*, 475/21a.
[67] From Yang, K26/12/17, Li Hung-chang, *op. cit.*, " Tien Kao," 31/24b.
[68] To the Grand Council, K26/12/13, *ibid.*, 31/17a.
[69] To Yang, K26/12/18, *ibid.*, 31/24b.

9

Diplomacy in St. Petersburg

CHINESE PLENIPOTENTIARY AND RUSSIAN MINISTERS

THE CHINESE GOVERNMENT, as noted above, had ordered the
Tartar Generals of Manchuria to take over the three provinces to
be handed back by the Russians, supposing, apparently, that the
restoration would not require much negotiation. It soon turned
out, however, that it was not the intention of Russia to return
those important provinces without conditions. To discuss these
conditions the Russian Government proposed that negotiations be
commenced in St. Petersburg and that Yang Ju, the Chinese
Minister to Russia, be appointed the plenipotentiary.[1] The Russian
Government was desirous of having the negotiations carried on in
St. Petersburg, because it wanted a separate agreement with China
apart from the general agreement which was being negotiated in
Peking, and because it thought Yang Ju, who had a pleasant per-
sonality, would not be too hard to handle.[2] Accordingly it requested that the broadest power for negotiation be given Yang Ju,
and the Russian Minister at Peking, Michael de Giers, intimated to
Li Hung-chang that Yang Ju should be the only person to take
charge of the negotiations.[3] Li Hung-chang preferred to have the
negotiations carried on in Peking, not with Giers, of whom he had
a very poor opinion, but with Prince Uktomski, personal friend
of the Tsar and Director of the Chinese Eastern Railway, who had
shown a more friendly attitude toward China.[4] But he accepted
the Russian proposal, although he seemed to sense the dangers in
the Russian request that Yang Ju be given the widest discretion,

---

[1] To the Grand Council, K26/11/10, Li Hung-chang, *Li Wên Chung Kung Ch'üan Chi*, " Tien Kao," 30/16a.
[2] *Ibid.*, 29/19a; *Tung San Shêng Tien Pao*, p. 11.
[3] From Li, K26/11/21, *Tung San Shêng Tien Pao*, p. 11.
[4] From Li, K26/10/6, *ibid.*, p. 7.

for he advised the latter to request Imperial instructions at any time in the course of negotiations.[5]

On January 3, 1901, the Imperial Court appointed Yang Ju Chinese plenipotentiary to negotiate with the Russian Government for the return of the three northeastern provinces. He was ordered to consult Li Hung-chang and Prince Ch'ing by telegraph with regard to the negotiations.[6] Giers promptly objected that consultation with Li and Ch'ing would delay the negotiations and limit the power of Yang Ju.[7] Count Witte, upon reading the Imperial decree on Yang Ju's appointment, also complained that the power given to the plenipotentiary was insufficient.[8] But as Yang Ju declared that the negotiation was too important for his judgment alone, and as Li Hung-chang explained that Yang could directly request Imperial instructions without consulting Prince Ch'ing and himself,[9] the Russian Government raised no more objections.

On the Russian side, the return of Manchuria was a problem involving three ministries: War, Foreign Affairs, and Finance. As early as October 31, 1900, the heads of the three ministries had agreed upon the "Principles of the Russian Control in Manchuria," which, proposed by Kuropatkin and developed by Witte, were in substance the same as the Tsêng-Alexeieff Agreement. They all now agreed that the annexation of Manchuria was undesirable, but it was held that the "Principles of Control" must be maintained in the forthcoming negotiations, and Count Witte was particularly interested in completely excluding foreign capital not only from Manchuria but from all the area beyond the Great Wall. This program of negotiations was approved by the Tsar on December 13, and it was on the basis of this imposing program that the Russian Government commenced negotiations with the Chinese Minister at St. Petersburg.[10]

The negotiations were carried on in behalf of Russia by Count

[5] From Li, K26/11/21, *ibid.*, p. 11.

[6] Li Hung-chang, *op. cit.*, "Tien Kao," 30/21b.

[7] To Yang, K26/11/20, *ibid.*, 30/29a.

[8] To Li, K26/11/24, *Tung San Shêng Tien Pao*, p. 13.

[9] To Yang, K26/11/20, Li Hung-chang, *op. cit.*, "Tien Kao," 30/29a.

[10] See J. J. Gapanovich, "Sino-Russian Relations in Manchuria," *Chinese Social and Political Science Review*, XVII (1933), 459-60.

Lamsdorff, Minister for Foreign Affairs, and Count Witte, Minister of Finance. According to Count Lamsdorff, it was War Minister Kuropatkin and Finance Minister Witte who " considered the immediate conclusion of a separate treaty with China necessary in order to extend and confirm the provisional agreements already existing between the Russian authorities and the Tartar Generals." The Minister for Foreign Affairs " never considered it very wise to conclude an independent agreement with China on the Manchurian question until a normal state of affairs had been restored in the Celestial Empire, since such negotiations would only be possible with a completely independent and responsible government." [11] It was probably because of Lamsdorff's lukewarm attitude and of the fact that Count Witte had had a keen interest in Manchuria since the secret treaty between Russia and China in 1896 that Witte rather than Lamsdorff played the major role in the negotiations with the Chinese Minister.

WITTE'S THIRTEEN POINTS

Having received his appointment, Yang Ju proceeded to open negotiations with the Russian Government. As Count Lamsdorff was away from St. Petersburg, Yang Ju called on Count Witte on January 4. The Russian Minister declared that Russia had no territorial ambitions in Manchuria and that Russian troops would be withdrawn sooner or later. But " as long as there is no guarantee against a recurrence of disturbances in the three provinces, the Russian troops cannot be withdrawn. In view of the great damage suffered by the Manchurian railway, the Russian Government cannot act like a child by dispatching troops today, withdrawing them tomorrow and dispatching them again day after tomorrow." However, continued Witte, the Russian Government was ready to negotiate, particularly with His Excellency the Chinese Minister, whom both the Foreign Minister and himself admired. He only

[11] Confidential Letter from Minister for Foreign Affairs to Minister for War, June 18 (July 1), 1901, *Krasnyi Arkhiv*, II (63), 30. The Russian documents on the Manchurian question as published in the *Krasnyi Arkhiv*, Vol. II (63) have been translated into English in the *Chinese Social and Political Science Review* (Peiping), Vols. XVIII (1934-35) and XIX (1935-36). The quotations from the *Krasnyi Arkhiv* in the present work are based upon the translation in the *Review*.

regretted that the Imperial appointment did not expressly state that an agreement signed by the Chinese Minister would be recognized by the Chinese Government.[12]

On January 17 Yang Ju called on Count Witte again to inquire about the Russian proposals. Witte said the Russian proposals had to be drafted by the Minister for Foreign Affairs, but since the Chinese Minister and himself were good friends, he would confidentially give him the outlines. He then enumerated the following thirteen points:

1. Indemnity for military expenses to be adjusted in Peking; damage to the railway to be determined separately.

2. Russia and China to agree upon the strength of the police force to be maintained in Manchuria.

3. Tartar Generals of the Manchurian provinces to be appointed with previous consent of Russia.

4. Russia to appoint two officials to the staff of each Tartar General: one to supervise the police force, the other to take charge of railway affairs.

5. No concessions in Manchuria, Mongolia, and the northern provinces to be granted to other Powers.

6. No railways in Manchuria and Mongolia to be built by China.

7. Chinchow to be included within the leased territory of Liaotung.

8. Customhouses in Manchuria to be administered by Russia, with Chinese officials checking the revenues.

9. Goods imported through the land routes to be exempted from inland taxes after payment of customs duties.

10. The interest on the Sino-Russian loan of 1895 to be paid monthly instead of semiannually.

11. Before payment of all the war indemnity China has no right to buy back the Chinese Eastern Railway.

12. Russia is desirous of purchasing the Shanhaikwan-Yingkow Railway, the cost of the purchase to be deducted from the amount to be claimed as war indemnity. The balance and interest of this to be paid from the customs revenues in Manchuria.

13. Manchuria to be evacuated by Russian troops by degrees.

The Chinese Minister observed that such an arrangement would be equivalent to Russia's protectorate over Bokhara and Britain's over India. Count Witte replied that the Chinese Minister " seems

[12] *Chu O Shih Kuan Tang An*, in Wang Yün-shêng (ed.), *Liu Shih Nien Lai Chung Kuo Yü Jih Pên*, IV, 65-67.

to regard Russia as an idiot. Russia has lost so much in Manchuria, with so many of her people killed. To withdraw her troops now without any precautionary measure—there is no such idiot in the world! " The Chinese Minister then pointed out that Russia had repeatedly declared that she had no selfish ambitions with regard to China. " Now all countries, particularly Britain, Japan, Germany, and France, which have large business in China, are watching keenly the Sino-Russian negotiations. Russia not only should think of the position of China but also should consider the opinions of other Powers." When Witte asserted that no other Power could interfere with the negotiations of two states, Yang Ju said: " Other countries may not interfere with the negotiations, but afterward may follow the example of Russia. Russia now proposes to take all the rights and interests in Manchuria. What would become of China if Britain does the same in the Yangtze Valley or Yunnan, Germany in Shantung, France in Kwangsi, Japan and other Powers in some other places? " The Finance Minister dryly observed that if the Chinese Minister worried like this, nothing could be accomplished.[13]

On January 18 Yang Ju reported the conversation and the Thirteen Points to the Chinese Government. He added the following observation: " It is apparent that Russia will seize this occasion to realize her designs in China. Our sovereignty will be impaired if one of the following powers is lost: the military, the industrial, and the appointing powers. But now all three would be lost. The situation will be unbearable if we are deprived of all our rights in Manchuria. But now it would involve also Mongolia and the northern provinces. If one country does this, others will follow. How could China be preserved? " He therefore advised that unless Russia changed her attitude, the negotiations should be postponed.[14]

The advice was endorsed by Li Hung-chang, who quoted the Japanese Minister's statement that if Manchuria was returned to China under the conditions prescribed in the Tsêng-Alexeieff

[13] *Ibid.*, IV, 69.
[14] Li's Memorial, K26/12/3, Li Hung-chang, *op. cit.*, " Tien Kao," 31/4a.

Agreement, Britain, Germany, and Japan would follow suit by seizing Chinese territory.[15] Accordingly the Imperial Court ordered on January 27 that the negotiations be deferred.[16]

CANCELLATION OF THE TSÊNG-ALEXEIEFF AGREEMENT

When the news of the Tsêng-Alexeieff Agreement reached Japan, an intense agitation flared up against the Russian move, which was regarded as tantamount to making Manchuria a Russian protectorate. Soon the Japanese Government bestirred itself to action. During Prince Ch'ing's visit on January 16 the Japanese Minister at Peking, Jutaro Komura, took the occasion to point out that Count Witte had stated to a friend at St. Petersburg [17] that Russia would withdraw her troops from Manchuria and return it to China. Some Russian troops, however, must remain to protect the railway which was being built with Russian money, Komura said. But the number of these railway guards must be limited; otherwise Manchuria, in spite of its restoration, would be in fact under occupation. If Manchuria were taken by Russia, Komura continued, other Powers, particularly Britain and Germany, would follow suit under the principle of equal opportunity. Japan, though having no territorial ambitions in China, would under those circumstances be forced to join the Powers.[18] The following day Komura called on Li Hung-chang and made the same arguments. He offered to exchange information with the Chinese Government on the matter and hoped that the two countries would confer with each other sincerely.[19] The gist of the conversations was telegraphed by Li Hung-chang to Yang Ju, who was instructed to question the Russian Government along the line of the Japanese suggestions.[20]

On January 21 Yang Ju called on Count Witte, who admitted that the Russian proposals were drafted by himself. The Finance Minister now proposed that the damage to the railway might be

---

[15] Ibid. [16] Decree, K26/12/8, Ch'ing Tê Tsung Shih Lu, 776/5b.
[17] M. Komura was referring to the conversation between Count Witte and the Japanese Chargé d'Affaires at St. Petersburg.
[18] Ch'ing Chi Wai Chiao Shih Liao, 145/7. [19] Ibid., 145/9.
[20] From Li and Ch'ing, received K26/12/1, Tung San Shêng Tien Pao, p. 18.

reimbursed out of the gold and coal mines near the railway. Yang Ju immediately protested that if Russia seized concessions like this in Manchuria, other Powers would follow suit in the various areas of China. He particularly objected to the appointment of the Tartar Generals with the consent of Russia and to the appointment of two Russians to the staff of each Tartar General. He stressed that the Russian demands, which extended to Mongolia and the northern provinces, would violate all Russian declarations to uphold China's independence and would greatly impair the sovereignty of China. The Russian arrangement for Manchuria was nothing other than occupation in disguise. To this Count Witte replied that China had been defeated by Russia and that, if no agreement could be reached, the Russians would continue the occupation, which would not be of any advantage to China. The Chinese Minister then requested that the Tsêng-Alexeieff Agreement be canceled. At first Count Witte argued that an agreement already signed should be ratified by the two countries; but as Yang Ju declared that the Chinese Government would under no circumstance ratify the instrument, which was signed without the knowledge and without the authorization of the Imperial Court, the Russian Finance Minister finally said he would give the problem further consideration.[21]

In the meantime the Japanese Government took up the problem with the Russian Government. On January 17 the Russian Minister at Tokyo, M. H. Isvolsky, was told by M. Kato, Japanese Minister for Foreign Affairs, that Japan preferred to postpone the negotiations with Russia concerning the neutralization of Korea until such time as " the fate of Manchuria has finally become apparent." [22] Kato frankly expressed his fear that if the Japanese Government now entered into a new agreement with regard to Korea, such action would be taken as implying that it had already reconciled itself to the Tsêng-Alexeieff Agreement concerning Manchuria.[23] On January 22 the Japanese Minister at St. Peters-

---

[21] *Chu O Shih Kuan Tang An,* in Wang Yün-shêng, *op. cit.,* IV, 80.

[22] In later communications to the Russian Foreign Office, the phrase " until the *status quo ante* has been restored " was used. *Krasnyi Arkhiv,* II (63), 8, 11.

[23] Isvolsky to Lamsdorff, January 4 (January 17), 1901, *ibid.,* II (63), 8.

burg informed the Russian Minister for Foreign Affairs that the present Russian position in Manchuria might very well cause alarm if Russia did not give some positive assurance of her intention to evacuate the area.[24]

The determined opposition of the Chinese Government, the strong reaction from Japan, and the provisional character of the instrument which would have been superseded by some other arrangement may have been good reasons for Russia not to insist upon the ratification of the Tsêng-Alexeieff Agreement. On January 22 Count Lamsdorff had said to Yang Ju that if Count Witte "thinks the agreement may not be ratified, it will be all right." [25] But if the Russian Government had decided to give up the agreement, Count Witte was too shrewd to say so. On January 23, when Yang Ju called on him in his office, the argument on why the Tsêng-Alexeieff Agreement should or should not be ratified was started all over again. Witte acted as if he were in great difficulty, but at last he said to Yang Ju: " If Your Excellency would not make difficulties in the forthcoming negotiations, I would compromise at present and have the ratification dropped." The Russian Finance Minister was anxious to trade the Tsêng-Alexeieff Agreement for the demands he was drafting, but .the Chinese Minister was well on his guard. " If the proposals are reasonable," Yang said, " they surely can be discussed; but their acceptance will depend upon the Imperial Government." After all the wrangling Count Witte finally declared that the Tsêng-Alexeieff Agreement might not be ratified. He reiterated the hope that the Chinese Minister would not create difficulties in the forthcoming negotiations.[26]

RUSSIA'S TWELVE ARTICLES

While Count Witte and General Kuropatkin were working on the Russian proposal to be presented to China, Count Lamsdorff maneuvered to prepare the Chinese Minister for it. During Yang

---

[24] Communication from Japanese Ambassador, January 9 (January 22), 1901, *ibid.*, II (63), 9.

[25] *Chu O Shih Kuan Tang An*, in Wang Yün-shêng, *op. cit.*, IV, 83.

[26] *Ibid.*, IV, 87-88.

Ju's visit to him on February 10 he had called the Chinese Minister's attention to the assistance which Russia rendered to China in the negotiations between the Chinese plenipotentiaries and the foreign ministers at Peking.[27] The following day, when Yang Ju paid him another visit, Lamsdorff emphasized again Russia's goodwill by citing Russia's opposition to Prince Tuan's execution and the withdrawal of all Russian troops from Chihli.[28] It was apparent that the Russian Minister for Foreign Affairs expected the assistance which Russia rendered to China in Peking to bear fruit in the negotiations at St. Petersburg. Lamsdorff also urged that China should keep secret all the negotiations in the Russian capital.[29] He was evidently apprehensive lest other Powers might interfere and foil the Russian scheme; for besides Japan's strong reaction against the Tsêng-Alexeieff Agreement, Britain had also inquired about " the actual facts with regard to the alleged agreement." [30]

On February 16 Count Lamsdorff handed Yang Ju the Russian proposal of twelve articles:

1. The Emperor of Russia, being desirous of giving evidence of his friendly feeling toward China and willing to forget the hostile acts committed in Manchuria, agrees to hand back all Manchuria to China, its administration to be carried on as before.

2. Under Article 6 of the Contract for the Chinese Eastern Railway, the Railway Company is authorized to maintain troops for the protection of the line. The provinces, however, being at present in an unsettled condition, and such troops being few in number, a body of Russian troops must be maintained until order is restored and until China has carried out the provisions of the last four articles of the present agreement.

3. In the event of grave disturbances the Russian garrisons will afford China every assistance in suppressing the same as far as lies in their power.

4. Chinese troops having taken a prominent part in the recent attacks against Russia, China agrees, pending the completion of the railway line and its opening to traffic, not to maintain troops [in Manchuria]. The number of troops to be maintained subsequently will be determined after consultation with Russia. The importation of munitions of war into Manchuria is prohibited.

27 *Ibid.*, IV, 92.   28 *Ibid.*, IV, 95.   29 *Ibid.*
30 Scott to Lansdowne, February 6, 1901, *British Parliamentary Papers, China No. 6 (1901)*, p. 39.

5. With a view to safeguarding the peace and order of the territory, China will, on representations being made by Russia, at once deprive of office any Tartar General or high official whose conduct of affairs proves incompatible with the maintenance of friendly relations with Russia. A police force, consisting of mounted and unmounted units, may be organized in the interior of Manchuria. Its numbers shall be determined after consultation with Russia, and from its armament artillery shall be excluded. The subjects of any other Power shall not be employed in its service.

6. In conformity with the undertaking previously given by China, she will not employ the subjects of any other Power in training her military and naval forces in north China.

7. In the interest of peace and order, the neighboring authorities will draw up new special regulations for the neutral zone treated in Article 5 of the lease agreement [relating to the Liaotung Peninsula, March 27, 1898]. The autonomous rights of Chinchow, provided in Article 4 of the Special Agreement [of May 7, 1898], are hereby abrogated.

8. China shall not, without the consent of Russia, grant to any other Power, or the subjects thereof, privileges with regard to mines, railroads, or other matters in coterminous [i.e., with Russia] regions, such as Manchuria, Mongolia, and places in Sinkiang known as Tarbagati, Ili, Kashgar, Yarkand, and Khoten. Nor shall China, without Russia's consent, build railroads there herself. Except for Newchwang, no lease of land shall be granted to the subjects of any other Powers.

9. As China has to pay Russia's war expenses and the claims of other Powers, arising out of the recent troubles, the amount of the indemnity for Russia, the period within which it will have to be paid, and the security therefor will all be arranged in concert with the other Powers.

10. The compensation to be paid for the destruction of the railway lines, for the robbery of property belonging to the Railway Company and its employees, as well as claims for delay in carrying on the construction of the lines, will be arranged between China and the Company.

11. The above-mentioned claims may, by agreement with the Company, either in part or in whole, be commuted for other privileges. The grant of such privileges may take the form of amending the previous agreement or may be in the form of new concessions.

12. In conformity with the undertaking previously given by China, a line will be constructed by Russia from either the trunk line or the branch line of the [Chinese Eastern] Railway in the direction of Peking up to the Great Wall, its administration to be governed by the railway regulations at present in force.[31]

---

[31] Li Hung-chang, *op. cit.*, " Tien Kao," 32/11-12; cf. G. P. Gooch and Harold Temperley (eds.), *British Documents on the Origins of the War, 1898-1914* (London: His Majesty's Stationery Office, 1927), II, 38-39. The assertion in Article 2 that " under

The above proposal was a revised form of Witte's draft which, in its original form, consisted of two parts: a general agreement between the two governments and a special agreement between China and the Chinese Eastern Railway Company. The special agreement, according to Witte's plan, would comprise the following demands:

1. All gold mines in the province of Fêngt'ien shall be granted to the Railway Company, as well as the petroleum mines in the three Manchurian provinces.

2. All coal mines within five miles on both sides of the Railway shall be granted to the Railway Company.

3. The forest rights in the Yalu Valley shall be ceded to the Railway Company, which also will have the right to build highways.

4. The land within five miles on both sides of the Railway, be it public domain or private property, shall be granted to the Railway Company.

5. Russia may establish settlements in Chinwangtao and at the mouth of the Yalu River for the purpose of building godowns, oil stations, and residences.

6. A branch line may be constructed by Russia from the South Manchurian Railway to Yingkow.[32]

It was the plan of Witte to make the Chinese Eastern Railway a state trust in Manchuria, holding for Russia the economic monopoly in the area.[33] Probably because of the international concern over the designs of Russia in Manchuria, as a result of the publication of the Tsêng-Alexeieff Agreement in the press, the

---

Article 6 of the Contract for the Chinese Eastern Railway, the Railway Company is authorized to maintain troops for the protection of the line" was a misrepresentation of fact. No such authorization is found in the Contract (signed September 8, 1896). On the contrary, it was provided in Article 5 of the Contract that "the Chinese Government will take measures to assure the safety of the railway and of the persons in its service against any attack" (John V. A. MacMurray (ed.), *Treaties and Agreements with and concerning China* [New York: Oxford University Press, 1921], I, 76). Similar misrepresentations appeared in Articles 6 and 12 of the proposed agreement when the Russian demands were introduced with the phrase "in conformity with the undertaking previously given by China." Actually, Alexander Pavloff, Russian Chargé d'Affaires in Peking, had presented those demands, but they had never been accepted by the Tsungli Yamen (see Li Hung-chang, *op. cit.,* "Tien Kao," 32/17a).

    32 B. A. Romanov, *Rossiia v Manchzhurii, 1892-1906* (Leningrad, 1928), pp. 284-87; see Yang Shao-chên, "Kêng Tsŭ Nien Chung O Tsai Tung San Shêng Chih Ch'ung Tu Chi Ch'i Chieh Shu," in *Ch'ing Hua Hsüeh Pao* (The Tsing Hua Journal), IX (1934), 69-126.

    33 Gapanovich, "Sino-Russian Relations in Manchuria," *Chinese Social and Political Science Review,* XVII (1933), 460-61.

second part of Witte's draft was dropped in the proposals presented to the Chinese Minister on February 16. Instead, there was Article 11 which, couched in vague terms, was intended to be the basis upon which the " special agreement " between China and the Railway Company was to be arranged.

Compared with the Thirteen Points orally presented by Count Witte on January 17, the Twelve Articles embodied several changes. There was now no demand for the appointment of the Tartar Generals with the previous consent of Russia, nor for the appointment by Russia of two Russian officials on the staff of each Tartar General. Instead, the Tartar Generals were to be dismissed upon Russian complaints. The former demand with regard to the administration of the customhouses by Russia and the exemption of Russian goods from inland taxes was also dropped. On the other hand, the demand with regard to economic concessions was now specifically extended to Sinkiang; and, instead of buying the Shanhaikwan-Yinkow Railway, Russia now demanded the construction of a line connecting the Manchurian Railway with the Great Wall. Furthermore, Article 11 as now presented was pregnant with far-reaching consequences.

FINAL REVISION OF THE RUSSIAN DEMANDS

The Japanese Government understood that to checkmate Russia the support of other Powers was necessary. " The immediate object of the Japanese Government," reported the Russian Minister at Tokyo, " is to bring about a combination against Russia, like the one as a result of which Japan, after the war with China, was prevented from establishing herself on the Liaotung Peninsula." [34] On February 5 the Japanese Government proposed to Britain that the two countries warn China not to conclude any such agreement as that reported to have been concluded by General Tsêng and Admiral Alexeieff.[35] The British Government, considering the move " might have a useful effect in encouraging the Chinese to hold their own," thought it advisable to meet the wishes of the

[34] Isvolsky to Lamsdorff, February 9 (February 22), 1901, *Krasnyi Arkhiv*, II (63), 15.
[35] Gooch and Temperley, *op. cit.*, II, 35.

Japanese Government, and approached Germany for similar action.[36] On February 13, while the Japanese Government told the Chinese Minister at Tokyo that any territorial cession or cession in disguise would be taken as a precedent by other Powers for similar demands and that the same would apply to any grant of economic privileges,[37] Lord Lansdowne informed the Chinese Minister at London that " any such Agreement as that reported to have been concluded with regard to Manchuria would, in the opinion of His Majesty's Government, be a source of danger to the Chinese Government, and that no Agreement affecting territorial rights in the Chinese Empire ought to be concluded between the Chinese Government and any one of the Powers." [38]   On February 17 the German Government intimated to the Chinese Minister at Berlin that China should not conclude with any Power individual treaties of a territorial or financial character before she had concluded the collective agreement with all the Powers.[39]   At Japan's suggestion, the United States, Austria, and Italy made representations to China in the same vein.[40]

The two viceroys of the Yangtze provinces were strongly opposed to the Russian demands. They maintained close contact with the Japanese consuls, who were eager to secure the viceroys' support as a counterbalance to the influence of Li Hung-chang.[41] On February 24 Chang Chih-tung telegraphed to the Sian Government that acceptance of Russia's Twelve Demands would immediately lead to partition of China. He urged that the Russian demands be rejected and that the Russian Government be informed that other Powers were opposed to individual agreements with any

[36] *Ibid.*, p. 35. The Anglo-German Agreement of October 16, 1900, provided that " in case of another Power making use of the complication in China in order to obtain territorial advantages, the Contracting Parties would come to an understanding as to the steps to be taken to protect their own interests." MacMurray, *op. cit.*, I, 203.

[37] From Minister Li, K26/12/27, Li Hung-chang, *op. cit.*, " Tien Kao," 31/47a.

[38] *China No. 6* (1901), p. 41.

[39] *Ibid.*; Li Hung-chang, *op. cit.*, " Tien Kao," 32/14b.

[40] From Minister Wu, received K27/1/4 (February 22, 1901), Li Hung-chang, *op. cit.*, " Tien Kao," 32/1a; from Liu, K27/1/7, *ibid.*, 32/18b; Li to the Grand Council, K27/1/6, *Chung Jih Shih Liao*, 60/24.

[41] *Chung Jih Shih Liao*, 60/22a; Li Hung-chang, *op. cit.*, " Tien Kao," 32/18b.

single Power.[42]   Liu K'un-i joined in the advice against acceptance. He urged that rejection of the Russian demands was less dangerous than their acceptance, for rejection could result only in conflict with one country, whereas acceptance would lead to demands for Chinese territory by all the Powers.   Furthermore, with world opinion on China's side, Russia would hesitate to act recklessly.[43] Yüan Shih-k'ai also considered the Russian demands unacceptable, for they would mean the giving up of " more than half of China's sovereignty " over Manchuria.   He did not believe that Russia would annex Manchuria if her demands were rejected, for she would be deterred by the opposition of other Powers.[44]

In the meantime Yang Ju suggested that the negotiations be transferred from St. Petersburg to Peking.   It would be too late now, he said in a telegram to Li Hung-chang on February 20, to stop the negotiations with the Russian Government, for the proceedings had gone so far that any such action would lead to the rupture of relations between the two countries.   Since Japan and Britain had suggested that the Manchurian problem be discussed in the general conference between China and the Allied Powers at Peking, and Germany had opposed the conclusion of any individual treaty, Russia, under the pressure of the three Powers, might agree to the transfer to the Peking conference.[45]   The proposal, however, was opposed by Li Hung-chang, who thought it impossible to deprive Yang Ju of his plenipotentiary power at this stage, when the Russian proposals had already been handed to the Chinese Minister.[46]

In fact, it was the belief of Li Hung-chang that the Manchurian provinces could only be restored through an agreement with Russia.   He was afraid that rejection of the Russian demands would lead to the rupture of Sino-Russian relations.   The temporary occupation of Manchuria by Russia would then become permanent.   The opposition of the Powers, said Li in the memorial

---

[42] Chung Jih Shih Liao, 60/25b.
[43] From Liu, K27/1/9, Shêng Hsüan-huai, Yü Chai Ts'un Kao Ch'u K'an, 51/31.
[44] From Yüan, K27/1/8, ibid., 51/29.
[45] To Ch'ing and Li, K27/1/2, Tung San Shêng Tien Pao, p. 34.
[46] To the Grand Council, K27/1/6, Li Hung-chang, op. cit., " Tien Kao," 32/15b.

of February 27, was instigated by Japan; and Liu K'un-i and Chang Chih-tung, having been close to Japan and Britain, were subject to their influence. But Japan was misinformed as to the contents of the latest Russian demands. She mistook the Tsêng-Alexeieff Agreement for what was now under negotiation. Except for Article 8 relating to concessions in Mongolia and Sinkiang, the Russian proposals " are not all obnoxious," Li asserted. The other Powers might have " ulterior intentions "; for instead of taking up the matter with the Russian Government, they " only rattle at us." How could Manchuria be restored without an agreement? It might well be the intention of these Powers to spoil China's opportunity to arrange the restoration of Manchuria with Russia, so that they would have a pretext for seizing Chinese territory themselves.[47]

It was rather unusual that a veteran diplomat like Li Hung-chang should believe that the " ulterior intentions " of the other Powers were to seize Chinese territory at that time. But there were good reasons for him to say that if China did not conclude an agreement with Russia, the Manchurian provinces would never be restored. The threat of Russia was indeed menacing. On February 23 Count Witte warned the Chinese Minister at St. Petersburg that if the Russian proposals were not quickly accepted, the military men in Russia would demand the incorporation of Manchuria. There were two alternatives for China, he declared. Either China signed the agreement and obtained the assistance of Russia, or she broke the negotiations and let Russia help herself.[48] On February 25 the Russian Minister at Peking delivered a similar threat to Li Hung-chang. He further asserted that no Power had made any representation to the Russian Government on the Manchuria negotiations and that China should pay no attention to outside interference.[49]

On the other hand, Li Hung-chang had no assurance that other Powers would come to China's aid should she break the negotiations with Russia. The Powers told the Chinese Government that

[47] Li to the Grand Council, K27/1/9, *Chung Jih Shih Liao*, 60/30.
[48] *Chu O Shih Kuan Tang An*, in Wang Yün-shêng, *op. cit.*, IV, 113.
[49] To the Grand Council, K27/1/7, Li Hung-chang, *op. cit.*, " Tien Kao," 32/17a.

it was dangerous to conclude separate agreements with Russia, but they said nothing as to what they would do if Russia did not return Manchuria to China. When on February 27 the Japanese Minister at Peking was asked by Li Hung-chang why the Powers did not take up the matter directly with the Russian Government, he begged the question by saying that the Chinese Government could instruct its envoys abroad to communicate the request to the foreign governments.[50]

Between the position of Li Hung-chang and that of the viceroys, the Imperial Court took a somewhat middle course. Its policy was summarized in these words: " Not to incur the wrath of Russia, nor to arouse the indignation of the Powers." The Russian Government was to be requested to modify its terms, while the other Powers should be approached to work out a " satisfactory arrangement." [51] In the decree of March 1 the Chinese plenipotentiaries were ordered to urge modification of the Russian proposals along the following lines:

1. Articles 6, 8, and 12 must be modified, particularly the provision for a line from the Manchurian railway to the Great Wall in the direction of Peking.

2. The provision in Article 4 that China will not maintain any Chinese troops in Manchuria should be confined to the areas near the railway. The prohibition of importation of munitions of war should be limited to the same length of time as will be provided in the general agreement between China and the Allied Powers at Peking.

3. Article 7 providing for the abolition of Chinchow's autonomous rights should be rejected not because of the importance of the isolated city but because of the danger that other Powers might seize China's territory by taking the case as a precedent.

4. Article 8 should not apply to cases where China exploits the mines or constructs the railways herself. It may be provided that if China concludes loans for the above purposes, preference will be given to Russia.

5. As to Article 11, it should be made clear that any privileges granted must not be incompatible with the interests of other Powers.[52]

[50] *Ibid.*, 32/22b; see also Chang Chih-tung, *Chang Wên Hsiang Kung Ch'üan Chi*, 171/4a.

[51] Decree, K27/1/7 (February 25, 1901), *Ch'ing Tê Tsung Shih Lu*, 478/8b.

[52] Decree, K27/1/11, *ibid.*, 478/13a. Yang Ju was Chinese plenipotentiary for the Manchuria negotiations; Prince Ch'ing and Li Hung-chang were plenipotentiaries for negotiating the collective agreement in Peking.

As to invoking the assistance of other Powers, an Imperial decree was issued to Liu K'un-i and Chang Chih-tung on February 27, ordering them to request the foreign governments to intervene with Russia so that the Manchurian problem could be satisfactorily solved.[53] The following day a decree was issued to the Chinese ministers abroad, instructing them to ask the respective foreign offices for mediation, so that the issue might be peacefully settled to the benefit of all nations.[54]

The appeal of the Chinese Government brought forth the following responses from the Powers. On March 1 Lord Lansdowne replied to the Chinese Minister at London that the alleged agreement on Manchuria was a matter of very serious consequence. He hoped to have a copy of the official text, and would then have to confer with the other Powers whose mediation had been invited by China. He assumed that China would not commit herself in the meantime, and that she would await the answer to her request for mediation before she took any further steps.[55] On March 5 the Japanese Government through its Consul-General at Shanghai informed Liu K'un-i that Russia was too strong to be opposed by a single power. China was weak; it was necessary to secure the support of other Powers. As the Manchurian problem concerned not only China and Russia, the Japanese Government had instructed the Japanese ministers abroad to confer with the various foreign offices.[56]

In the meantime the Russian Minister at Peking tried to threaten China to come to terms. Giers refused to have any more negotiations with Li Hung-chang. He sent Pokotiloff, Director of the Russo-Chinese Bank, to inform Li that the Russian Government would limit the time for the signing of the agreement. Should China fail to sign within the time limit, more demands would be added. And if China continued to procrastinate, Russia would break off the negotiations.[57] The threat had its effect on Li Hung-chang, who memorialized the Imperial Court to make a quick de-

---

[53] *Ibid.*, 478/11b.   [54] *Ibid.*, 478/12a.

[55] *China No. 6* (1901), p. 94; *Chung Jih Shih Liao*, 60/33a.

[56] Liu to the Grand Council, K27/1/15; *Chung Jih Shih Liao*, 61/1.

[57] To the Grand Council, K27/1/16, Li Hung-chang, *op. cit.*, " Tien Kao," 33/1a.

cision. The British Government, asserted Li, merely said it would confer with the other Powers but did not promise that it would mediate. Even if it mediated, Russia would certainly not yield, and so again there would be no solution. Any delay in signing the agreement with Russia would only strain the relations between the two countries.[58]

But the Imperial Court refused to take hasty action. In a decree issued on March 7 the Chinese plenipotentiaries were ordered to modify the Russian demands in accordance with the decree of March 1, so that when the agreement was signed other Powers would not create any trouble.[59] Next day another decree was issued, reiterating the same theme. It was pointed out that Article 8, which involved railway and mining privileges not only in Manchuria but also in northwest China, was particularly obnoxious. The provision in Article 12 for a railway line to the Great Wall in the direction of Peking was highly dangerous and must therefore also be amended.[60]

On March 5 Yang Ju had called on Count Lamsdorff and urged modification of the proposed agreement along the lines indicated in the Imperial decree of March 1.[61] On March 11 he called on the Russian Foreign Minister again and stated that, if the Russian proposals were not modified, he would resign the office of plenipotentiary and request the Chinese Government to appoint another negotiator.[62] The persistent refusal of the Chinese Government to sign the agreement as it stood compelled the Russian Government to revise its demands. On March 12 Count Lamsdorff handed Yang Ju the following amendments to the proposed agreement:

Article 4. . . . China shall, after consultation with Russia, determine the number of Chinese troops and the places where they are to be stationed in Manchuria. The prohibition of importation into Manchuria of arms and ammunition will be regulated in accordance with the general agreement to be concluded with the Powers. In the meantime, China shall, of her own accord, prohibit such importation as a temporary measure.

58 *Ibid.*　　　　　　　　　　　59 *Ch'ing Tê Tsung Shih Lu*, 479/1b.
60 *Ibid.*, 479/2b.
61 *Chu O Shih Kuan Tang An*, in Wang Yün-shêng, *op. cit.*, IV, 119.
62 *Ibid.*, IV, 127.

Article 5. In order to secure peace in Manchuria, any Tartar General or high local official who has acted improperly in regard to foreign relations shall at once be removed to another post upon a representation made by Russia. Except for the areas under the administration of the Railway Company, China may maintain infantry and cavalry for police purposes, the strength of which is to be determined in consultation with Russia until the complete pacification of Manchuria; but no artillery shall be permitted, and only Chinese shall be employed in those functions.

Article 7. The local authorities in the vicinity of the neutral zone, provided in Article 5 of the Convention of March 27, 1898, for the lease of territory in Liaotung, shall make special regulations to maintain peace and order.

Article 8. China shall not, without previous consultation with Russia, grant to any other Power, or its subjects, railway and mining concessions or any commercial privileges in the whole territory of Manchuria.

Article 10. The indemnities to be paid in compensation for the destruction of the railway and the property of the employees of the Railway Company, and also for the losses from the delay of work, shall be adjusted between China and the Railway Company, in accordance with the principles of assessment to be agreed upon between the foreign representatives at Peking and to be approved by the Powers.

Article 12. The building of a railway into Manchuria from Shanhaikwan to Newchwang and Sinmint'ing with money borrowed from a private company on October 10, 1898, is in contravention of the previous agreement between China and Russia. As compensation for this breach and in order speedily to restore tranquillity in Manchuria, China shall concede to the Chinese Eastern Railway Company the right to build a railway from the main or branch line of its railway, extending it to the Great Wall on the boundary between Manchuria and Chihli.

Articles 1, 2, 3, 9, and 11 are maintained as originally drafted, while Article 6 is entirely eliminated.[63]

In handing the amended text to the Chinese Minister, Count Lamsdorff declared that the present proposals, having been revised in accordance with the order of the Tsar, were final in form and would admit of no further changes. He would withdraw the draft if it were not signed within fifteen days.[64]

---

[63] *Ibid.*, IV, 131; Gooch and Temperley, *op. cit.*, II, 47.
[64] *Chuh O Shih Kuan Tang An*, in Wang Yün-shêng, *op. cit.*, IV, 131.

10

Agony of Decision

ON MARCH 13 Yang Ju reported the amendments to the Chinese Government. He observed that except for Article 11, which remained unchanged, and Article 12, which the Russian Government refused to withdraw, the rest of the draft had been revised more or less along the lines indicated in the previous decrees. There was improvement even in Article 12. The phrase " in the direction of Peking " was deleted, and the stipulation that the right to construct the line was conceded as compensation in connection with the Shanhaikwan Railway would deprive Russia of any pretext for buying the line in the future. Article 4 no longer prohibited China from maintaining troops anywhere in Manchuria, and thus did not conflict with the Imperial instructions that the prohibition should be confined to the vicinity of the railway. The prohibition of importation of arms and ammunition in accordance with the collective agreement to be concluded with the Powers was not unreasonable. It was significant that Articles 6, 7, and 8 were amended or deleted " in accordance with our proposals." Article 10 was amended to bring the railway indemnities within the principles of the collective agreement. In short, asserted Yang Ju, the present text had changed more than one half of the former draft. It not only gave no pretext to other Powers for similar demands but also kept Mongolia and Sinkiang out of the arrangement. The Chinese Minister was so gratified with the amendments that he concluded his observations with these remarks: " Thanks to the great fortune of the Throne, I have been able to achieve a little in the battle of lips and tongue. This indeed is beyond my original expectations." [1]

[1] To Ch'ing and Li, K27/1/23, *Tung San Shêng Tien Pao*, p. 52; to the Grand Council, K27/1/25, Li Hung-chang, *Li Wên Chung Kung Ch'üan Chi*, " Tien Kao," 33/15b.

On March 14 Yang Ju telegraphed Li Hung-chang that there was no assurance that the other Powers would intercede with Russia. If China waited for the mediation of other Powers, he feared that Russia might not yield any more, while the other Powers might demand compensation for their services.[2] Two days later Yang in reply to Liu K'un-i further developed his arguments for the amended agreement. There was no sign, he said, that other Powers would intervene on China's behalf, and even if they did, Russia would not be stopped by anything short of war. But war would only accelerate the partition of China. " The present text has accepted five of the seven counterproposals ordered by the Court as well as some suggestions made by myself. Our more important proposals have been accepted; those that are rejected are not very important." As to the fear that other Powers would follow suit, it would be better to set a precedent involving only small concessions than to break off negotiations with Russia and lose all Manchuria, for the latter case would create a precedent that would inevitably lead to the partition of China.[3]

On March 17 Yang received a telegram from Chang Chih-tung urging that the Russian proposal should not be accepted, for " if Russia becomes angry, we would lose only the three Eastern provinces; but if all the other Powers become angry, the eighteen provinces would at once be lost." [4] In reply Yang maintained that mediation by other Powers was unreliable. By the Agreement of 1899 Britain had engaged not to interfere with Russia in north China.[5] The German Chancellor had just declared in the Reichstag that the Anglo-German Agreement had no reference to Manchuria.[6] The American Ambassador at St. Petersburg had said

---

[2] To Ch'ing and Li, 27/1/24, *Tung San Shêng Tien Pao*, p. 55.

[3] To Liu, K27/1/26, *ibid.*, 59.

[4] To Yang, K27/1/24, Chang Chih-tung, *Chang Wên Hsiang Kung Ch'üan Chi*, 171/8b.

[5] The Russo-British Agreement of April 28, 1899, provided: " (1) Russia engaged not to seek any railway concessions in the Yangtze basin and not to place obstacles either directly or indirectly in the way of railway enterprises in that region supported by the British Government. (2) Similar engagement, *mutatis mutandis*, by Great Britain with regard to railway concessions north of the Great Wall." G. P. Gooch and Harold Temperley (eds.), *British Documents on the Origins of the War, 1898-1914* (London: His Majesty's Stationery Office, 1927), I, 41.

[6] *British Parliamentary Papers, China No. 6* (1901), p. 132.

that it was difficult for the Powers to support China at a time when peaceful relations were not yet reestablished. Japan was too small to fight a great Power. And now that the text had been amended, it would not be easy for the other Powers to make similar demands.[7]

In spite of his arguments, however, Yang Ju was not sure that the agreement should be accepted. On March 18 he telegraphed to Li Hung-chang about his worries: " Although the amended text is quite different from the former draft, there are still disadvantages. But if Russia occupies Manchuria permanently, I wonder whether the other Powers would intervene against Russia or would follow Russia's example and seize our territory. Upon this hinges our preservation or extinction. . . . I worry and think day and night, but I find no safe solution." [8]

VICEROYS VERSUS LI HUNG-CHANG

It was the opinion of Li Hung-chang that the amended agreement was acceptable. On March 16 he telegraphed to Yang Ju that as the objectionable clauses had been abolished, the agreement could now be concluded without evil consequences. He was worried that the Imperial Court might be influenced by the Japanese propaganda which, carried through Liu K'un-i and Chang Chih-tung, was severely attacking the agreement. He hoped that Yang Ju would sent more telegrams to Sian to " explode the illusions of those people." [9]

The same day Li Hung-chang was visited by Giers, the Russian Minister, who emphasized that the amended text would admit of no further change and that there could be no extension of time. Should China fail to sign it within the specified time, Russia would have liberty to action with regard to Manchuria. Giers also declared that no other Power could intervene against Russia, which would pay no attention to any interference. In reporting the conversation to the Imperial Court, Li Hung-chang maintained that the amended text would have no evil consequences. He urged that

---

[7] To Chang, 27/1/27, *Tung San Shêng Tien Pao*, p. 62; Chang Chih-tung, *op. cit.*, 171/9a.

[8] To Ch'ing and Li, K27/1/28, *Tung San Shêng Tien Pao*, p. 63.

[9] To Yang, K27/1/26, Li Hung-chang, *op. cit.*, " Tien Kao," 33/20.

orders be promptly given for its conclusion so that the grave situation could be resolved.[10]

The amended agreement was, however, regarded as unacceptable by the Yangtze viceroys. In a lengthy memorial to the Throne on March 19, Chang Chih-tung insisted that what had been amended was unimportant. Although in Article 8 the clause relative to Mongolia and Sinkiang was struck out, the insertion of the new phrase " or any commercial privileges " was of far-reaching significance. Article 12 conceded to Russia the right to construct a railway to the Great Wall; Article 4 required consultation with Russia as to the number of Chinese troops to be stationed in Manchuria; Article 2 permitted Russian troops to be retained; Article 1 spoke of the restoration of administration but said nothing of the political, military, and commercial rights; all these articles remained intact in all important provisions. The change from " deprived of office " to " removed to another post " in Article 5 was only verbal. The stipulation that only Chinese should be employed in the police was hardly different from the stipulation that the subjects of any other Power should not be employed. Article 6 was abolished, but if there had been an " undertaking previously given by China," as claimed by Russia, the abolition would make no practical difference. In short, except for Article 7 concerning Chinchow, the rest of the amendments were only made to deceive China. If such an agreement were signed, all of Manchuria would belong to Russia, just as India belonged to Britain and Indo-China to France. Other Powers would necessarily follow suit and make similar demands. Thus China would perish, " not because of the attacks made by the Allied Powers, but because of the precedent set by Russia." [11]

To resolve the situation Chang Chih-tung proposed three measures:

1. To request the British, Japanese, American, and German governments to apply to Russia for extension of time so that the agreement could be further considered. The request might be

---

[10] *Hsi Hsün Ta Shih Chi*, 6/1-2.

[11] To the Grand Council, 27/1/29, Chang Chih-tung, *op. cit.*, 171/11; received K27/2/2, *Chung Jih Shih Liao*, 61/18.

made with reference to the statement of Lord Lansdowne, who had advised that China should await the answer to her request for mediation before taking further steps.

2. To open Manchuria to international trade and let subjects of all Powers have equal opportunity with regard to mining, commercial, and resident privileges, provided Britain, Japan, the United States, and Germany would help China resist the Russian demands. This would be a measure not only to develop the Manchurian resources through the use of foreign capital but also to preserve the three provinces from Russian encroachment by invoking the influence of the Powers.

3. To engage British and Japanese officers to train Chinese naval and military forces in the north as a countermeasure against the Russian demand for a railway line to the Great Wall. The Russians might withdraw the demand in exchange for China's abandoning this measure; if not, the modern-trained forces in the north would serve as a bulwark against the Russian designs.[12]

A telegram recommending the first two points was also sent on March 20 in the name of Liu K'un-i, Chang Chih-tung, and Shêng Hsüan-huai.[13]

THE COURT FALTERS

Upon receipt of Yang Ju's report on the amended agreement, the Imperial Court issued its instructions in a decree dated March 17. Although Russia had showed her friendly disposition in the amendments, the Court declared, there were still some clauses which might form a bad precedent. Article 1, which provided for the restoration of civil administration but said nothing about commercial and military rights, should be amended to the effect that the *status quo ante* was to be restored. In Article 2 the phrase " until China has carried out the provisions, etc." should be changed to " until China carries out the provisions, etc." Article 8, which was still broad in scope and subject to the opposition of the Powers, should specify that it would not apply to cases in which China herself constructed the railways or exploited the mines.

[12] Chang Chih-tung, *op. cit.*, 171/11.
[13] Received K27/2/2, *Chung Jih Shih Liao*, 61/17; Chang Chih-tung, *op. cit.*, 171/13.

The Chinese plenipotentiaries were directed to examine carefully the agreement to see if there were some other objectionable clauses. As the other Powers might make similar demands if China signed the agreement without awaiting their reply with regard to mediation, the plenipotentiaries should request Russia to extend the time within which the proposed agreement might be signed.[14]

On March 18 there arrived Yang Ju's telegram of March 16 suggesting the futility of awaiting the mediation of the Powers. The Court, however, still stuck to the policies laid down in the decree of the day before. In reply to Yang the Court pointed out that it was not so much the waiting for the mediation as the danger of other Powers following suit that rendered necessary the extension of time and further amendment of the agreement.[15] But the Court began to waver on March 20 when it received the telegram of Li Hung-chang reporting the conversation with Giers and urging that orders be promptly issued for the conclusion of the agreement. On that day the following decree was issued to Li Hung-chang and Prince Ch'ing:

Your telegram of March 18 has been 'received. The stipulated time for signing the agreement will soon expire. It would be better if the agreement could further be amended along the lines indicated in our telegrams of the 17th and 18th instant. You have said in the telegram that the conclusion of the present agreement will not lead to any evil consequences. If you are sure of this, you can conclude the agreement. Since Lord Lansdowne has advised that China should take no action pending his reply, it is feared that the Powers may blame us for secretly concluding the agreement. It seems better that Britain and other Powers be notified in advance of our action. In short, the present agreement is of such immense importance that Prince Ch'ing and Li Hung-chang must compare its advantages and disadvantages, and consider carefully in making the decision.[16]

Upon receipt of the telegrams of Chang Chih-tung and Liu K'un-i on March 21, the Court became more undecided between the opposite opinions. On the one hand, it was threatened by the Russian Government and warned by Li Hung-chang that if the

[14] Decree, K27/1/27, Ch'ing Tê Tsung Shih Lu, 479/9a.
[15] Decree, K27/1/28, ibid., 479/10b.
[16] Decree, K27/2/1, ibid., 480/1b.

agreement was not signed, Russia would break off the negotiations and Manchuria would never be restored. On the other hand, it was warned by Japan and Britain [17] and vehemently urged by the viceroys that if the agreement was concluded, it would form a bad precedent and lead to the partition of China. Confronted with such a dilemma, the Court was at a loss what to do. At last it chose to act upon the recommendations of the viceroys but leave the decision with regard to the agreement to the plenipotentiaries.

On March 21 a decree was issued to the Chinese ministers abroad ordering them to request the Japanese, British, American, and German governments to apply to Russia for an extension of time so as to allow proper arrangement to be made for further changes in the agreement. The ministers were also to inform the various foreign offices secretly that if the Powers could help China work out a satisfactory arrangement with regard to Manchuria, the Chinese Government would, after restoration of the provinces, confer with the Powers with a view to opening Manchuria to international trade and investment under the principle of equal opportunity.[18] The same day the Grand Council telegraphed Prince Ch'ing, Li Hung-chang, and Yang Ju as follows:

If Russia can extend the time for signing the agreement, so much the better. If not, it is hoped that the agreement can further be amended so that other Powers would not have any pretext for making similar demands. If both are impossible and the stipulated time is expiring, we can but request the plenipotentiaries to make the decision. The Imperial Court is unable to decide from a distance.[19]

YANG JU DECLINES THE RESPONSIBILITY

Thus the Imperial Court, unable to make the decision itself, passed on the responsibility to the plenipotentiaries, namely, Prince Ch'ing, Li Hung-chang, and Yang Ju. As Prince Ch'ing had long preferred a quiet role, the responsibility in fact fell upon Li and

[17] Satow to Lansdowne, March 6, 1901, Gooch and Temperley, *op. cit.*, II, 37; Shêng Hsüan-huai, *Yü Chai Ts'un Kao Ch'u K'an*, 52/26.

[18] Decree, 27/2/2, *Ch'ing Tê Tsung Shih Lu*, 480/2a; *Chung Jih Shih Liao*, 61/20b.

[19] Grand Council to Li, etc., K27/2/2, *Chung Jih Shih Liao*, 61/21b; received K27/2/4, *Tung San Shêng Tien Pao*, p. 79.

Yang. On March 22, in communicating to Yang Ju the decree of March 20 which ordered that the plenipotentiaries could conclude the agreement if they were sure that there would be no evil consequences, Li told Yang to sign. " The attitude of the Court has softened," said Li. " You should inform the British and other envoys at St. Petersburg that under the great difficulty it is impossible not to consent. At the same time you should consider and sign it. Don't fail." [20]

The decision to sign or not to sign was thus left with Yang Ju alone. Since the receipt of the decree of March 17 he had tried to see the Russian Minister for Foreign Affairs, but he had not been received. The Russian Foreign Office refused to accept any communication from him, so it was impossible to negotiate for an extension of time.[21] The Chinese Minister was worried and disturbed, but he made the decision that he was not going to sign the agreement without an express order from the Imperial Court. On March 23 he telegraphed the Grand Council that " whether lesser or graver evils will result from signing or not signing will depend upon the future actions of Russia and other Powers. As I have not received the decree for signing it, I dare not take the liberty." [22] The same day he wired Li Hung-chang that the signing of the agreement " requires an unequivocal decree that can serve as a credential." [23]

Yang Ju's decision not to sign became the more determined on March 24 when he received a severe warning from Liu K'un-i, Chang Chih-tung, and Shêng Hsüan-huai. " There is strong opposition by the Powers against the Russian agreement," telegraphed the three southern officials, " and they are ready to make similar demands. The Chinese gentry has severely criticized Your Excellency, and the Imperial Court has no definite policy. If the agreement is signed and the other Powers create trouble, all the attacks will be centered on you, and we are fearful for your safety.

---

[20] To Yang, K27/2/3, Li Hung-chang, op. cit., " Tien Kao," 34/3a.
[21] To Ch'ing and Li, K27/2/1, Tung San Shêng Tien Pao, p. 70.
[22] To the Grand Council, K27/2/4, ibid., p. 79.
[23] Received K27/2/6, Li Hung-chang, op. cit., " Tien Kao," 34/12a.

We hope you will consider the whole situation and be especially careful." [24] The same morning Yang telegraphed Li Hung-chang and the Imperial Court to explain his position. After quoting the telegram from the three southern officials, Yang wrote:

If the conclusion of the agreement would be beneficial to the country, I should not care about my own safety nor mind the attacks from other people. But opinion in and out of China has maintained that other Powers are ready to follow suit, and the gentry throughout the country have arisen to oppose the agreement. Residing in China, the viceroys must have a solid basis for their statement. The Imperial Court, in consideration of popular sentiment, will not lightly act against the public opinion. In conducting state affairs abroad, I really dare not ignore the opinion of the great majority and arbitrarily conclude the agreement. It is a small thing to have the blame heaped upon oneself; it is a great guilt if calamity be brought to the country. Now that the agreement will not be signed within the stipulated time, the mouths of the Powers should be silenced and the hearts of the Chinese gentry gratified. It is hoped that Russia will not break off the negotiations, and all will be well. Should the situation lead to the permanent occupation of Manchuria, it is requested that the Court order all the ministers of the state to deliberate on remedial measures. [25]

It was with such determination that Yang Ju went to see Count Witte in the afternoon of March 24. The Russian Minister for Foreign Affairs, Count Lamsdorff, had refused to see Yang Ju or to receive his communication concerning the extension of time; but now upon report from Peking that Yang Ju had been instructed to sign the agreement, Count Witte tried to induce the Chinese Minister to sign. Yang admitted that he had received telegrams from the Grand Council and Li Hung-chang instructing him to consider and sign the agreement; but he pointed out that this was not full power for signing. Count Witte, after reading the translation of the telegrams concerned, maintained that the phrases " the plenipotentiaries to make the decision " and " you should consider and sign it " could be regarded as full powers for the purpose. He urged the Chinese Minister to sign. When Yang Ju observed that the Chinese Government surely would not ratify

[24] *Tung San Shêng Tien Pao,* p. 82.
[25] To Ch'ing and Li, K27/2/5, *ibid.,* p. 83; Li Hung-chang, *op. cit.,* "Tien Kao," 34/14b.

an agreement that was signed without instructions, Witte replied that if the agreement was not ratified later on, it could be canceled. This argument being of no avail, Count Witte declared that should the Chinese Minister be punished by the Chinese Government because of his signing the agreement, Russia would extend him protection. Upon this Yang Ju could control himself no longer. "How could Your Excellency say that?" said he. "I am a Chinese official; what a shame if I requested the protection of Russia! If I behaved like this, there would be no room for me to stand in China." [26]

The conversation ended without Yang Ju's signing the agreement. But in China the Yangtze viceroys were seriously worried that Yang might have signed. When Liu K'un-i learned of Li Hung-chang's telegram advising Yang to sign, he suggested to Chang Chih-tung that the viceroys should take two actions: (1) to notify the Powers that the agreement was signed " contrary to the Imperial decrees " and so could not be recognized by the various provinces; and (2) to memorialize the Throne to dismiss Yang Ju and notify the Russian Government that the agreement was to be negotiated anew by another Chinese minister.[27]   Yüan Shih-k'ai had the same opinion.[28]   As Yang Ju had not signed the agreement, no communication to the Powers in the sense of point (1) was necessary.   But in a memorial sent on March 25 the viceroys still recommended that, should Yang Ju sign the agreement, China should denounce it on the ground that it was signed in violation of the decrees of March 23 and 24.[29]

THE COURT DETERMINES NOT TO SIGN

While Yang Ju refused to sign the agreement on his own responsibility, telegrams poured into Sian from various provinces urging refusal.   On March 22 and 23 the Grand Council received telegrams from Liu K'un-i, Yüan Shih-k'ai, T'ao Mo,[30] and Wang

[26] *Chu O Shih Kuan Tang An*, in Wang Yün-shêng (ed.), *Liu Shih Nien Lai Chung Kuo Yü Jih Pên*, IV, 138.
[27] From Liu, K27/2/5 (March 24, 1901), Chang Chih-tung, *op. cit.*, 171/24b.
[28] From Yüan, K27/2/5, Shêng Hsüan-huai, *op. cit.*, 53/12.
[29] *Chung Jih Shih Liao*, 61/33.   For the two decrees concerned see below, pp. 201-2.
[30] Viceroy at Canton.

Chih-ch'un,[31] all arguing for the rejection of the agreement.[32] Personal telegrams were sent to Jung Lu by Yüan Shih-k'ai and Shêng Hsüan-huai urging him to stop the signing of the agreement.[33] The arguments of the objectors centered on these points: (1) If the agreement was signed regardless of the warning of the other Powers, similar demands would be presented by them and partition of China would begin.[34] (2) If the agreement was rejected in accordance with the advice of the Powers, there would be no reason for them to follow the Russian example in Manchuria and occupy Chinese territory.[35] (3) If the agreement was signed, it would mean that Manchuria was given up by China herself, and no Power could intervene for its restoration. On the other hand, if the agreement was not signed, China still had the right to demand its return and the other Powers could still render their assistance.[36] (4) If the agreement was not signed, Russia might not be able to occupy Manchuria permanently. The Russian Government had declared that it would restore Manchuria to China; under the pressure of Japan and Britain, it was hardly possible for Russia to annex Manchuria.[37]

Reports from foreign countries tended to support these arguments of the provincial officials. On March 23 the Court received the report from the Chinese Minister at Tokyo about his conversation with the Japanese Minister for Foreign Affairs, M. Kato. The Japanese Foreign Minister strongly advised against the Manchurian agreement, as it would necessarily lead to similar demands by other Powers. He did not believe that Russia would resort to hostilities if China refused to sign the agreement. On the other hand, if Russia did not evacuate Manchuria after the conclusion of the collective agreement in Peking, the Powers would then intervene

31 Governor of Anhui.

32 *Hsi Hsün Ta Shih Chi*, 6/11; *Chung Jih Shih Liao*, 61/21, 22, 24.

33 To Jung, K27/2/2, Shêng Hsüan-huai, *op. cit.*, 52/30; from Yüan, 27/2/3. K27/2/4, *ibid.*, 53/1, 11.

34 From T'ao Mo, K27/2/3, *Chung Jih Shih Liao*, 61/22a; from Liu K'un-i, K27/2/3, *ibid.*, 61/21; Yüan to Jung, K27/2/3, Shêng Hsüan-huai, *op. cit.*, 53/1.

35 From Liu K'un-i, K27/2/3, *Chung Jih Shih Liao*, 61/22a; Shêng to Jung, K27/2/2, Shêng Hsüan-huai, *op. cit.*, 52/30.

36 Yüan to Jung, received K27/2/4, Shêng Hsüan-huai, *op. cit.*, 53/11.

37 Yüan to Jung, received K27/2/3, *ibid.*, 53/1.

for China.[38]   The same day the Court received the report from the Chinese Minister at London that Lord Lansdowne advised again that China should not enter into separate agreement with Russia before the collective agreement had been concluded in Peking. Britain would extend China " full support " if his advice was taken.[39]

The foreign consuls at the Yangtze ports were particularly active in counseling against the agreement.   The British, American, and Japanese Consuls-General at Shanghai expressed to Shêng Hsüan-huai the opinion that the signing of the agreement would necessarily lead to the partition of China.   If it was not signed, Russia would have no right to occupy Manchuria.   Although the Powers might not oppose Russia by force, their moral support would be on China's side.   There would be no reason for their seizing Chinese territory, and they would assuredly evacuate Peking and Chihli.[40] Shêng's report of the conversation reached the Court on March 22. The same day the Court received a report from Chang Chih-tung about his conversation with a Japanese consul who came to see him from Shanghai.   The Japanese consul informed Chang that his government had approached the British, German, and American governments to advise China against the signing of the Manchurian agreement, and that Britain had consented to such a measure.[41]   On March 23 the Court received two telegrams from Liu K'un-i reporting two communications from the Japanese Consul-General at Shanghai.   After relaying the message from the Japanese Minister for Foreign Affairs that China must not sign the agreement, the Japanese Consul-General vehemently argued against the agreement.   He asserted that, if China rejected the agreement and if Russia continued to occupy Manchuria in violation of her previous declaration that she would return the provinces, the Powers would not tolerate such aggression by Russia.   Russia, not willing to be regarded by the other Powers as an aggressor, would

---

[38] From Minister Li, received K27/2/4, *Chung Jih Shih Liao*, 61/27b.
[39] From Liu, received K27/2/4, *ibid.*, 61/25.   Cf. Lansdowne to Satow, March 20, 1901, *China No. 6 (1901)*, pp. 135-36.
[40] Received K27/2/3, *Chung Jih Shih Liao*, 61/22.
[41] *Hsi Hsün Ta Shih Chi*, 6/12.

alleviate its demands if China resolutely refused to sign the agreement. The Japanese Consul-General emphasized that the agreement not only sapped the strength of China but also violated her treaties with the other Powers, which, in order to protect their rights and to maintain the principle of equal opportunity, would seize Chinese territory. The partition of China would then become a reality.[42]

Confronted with this massive opinion in and out of China against the agreement, the Imperial Court, wavering and yielding the day before, began to stiffen. On March 22 there were indications that the agreement might not be signed. That day a decree was issued declaring that, if Shêng Hsüan-huai's report was true, by rejecting the agreement, China would incur the anger only of Russia, while by concluding it she would incur that of all other Powers. The Chinese ministers abroad were ordered to confirm with the foreign governments that, if China refused to sign the agreement and thus incurred the anger of Russia, the other Powers would intercede with Russia and guarantee not to break off the present peace negotiations in Peking.[43] On March 23 another decree was issued ordering Yang Ju not to sign the agreement. After noting that numerous telegrams had been received from the provincial officials and from the Chinese ministers abroad advising against the conclusion of the agreement, the Court declared:

Since the opinion is unanimous, it is difficult to sign the agreement lightly. . . . The impact of this case is too far-reaching. As there is no perfect solution, the lesser evil should be taken. . . . It is directed that Yang Ju should inform the Russian Minister for Foreign Affairs and Minister of Finance that under the pressure of international opinion, the agreement cannot be signed unless properly amended.[44]

The following day another decree was issued ordering Li Hung-chang to inform the foreign ministers at Peking of the above decision and to request them to negotiate the collective agreement first. Yang Ju was ordered again to inform the Russian Govern-

[42] *Ibid.*, 6/13, 15; *Chung Jih Shih Liao*, 61/25a.

[43] Decree, 27/2/3, *Ch'ing Tê Tsung Shih Lu*, 480/4a.

[44] Decree, K27/2/4, *Ch'ing Tê Tsung Shih Lu*, 480/4a; received K27/2/5, Li Hung-chang, *op. cit.*, " Tien Kao," 34/6a; received K27/2/8, *Tung San Shêng Tien Pao*, p. 87.

ment that China could not sign the agreement unless it was amended to conform with the collective agreement.[45]

Thus, after much wavering and hesitation, the Court at last decided not to sign the agreement. The opinion against the agreement was indeed overwhelming. Of all ministers in and out of Sian, Li Hung-chang was practically the only one that continued to favor its conclusion. Even Yüan Shih-k'ai and Shêng Hsüanhuai, regarded as his protégés, were against him. Li was so piqued by Shêng's opposition that he telegraphed the latter on March 23 to "keep quiet and watch with calm the development of events."[46] Singlehanded, he fought the battle to the end. In all those memorials recommending the acceptance of the agreement, he put down the name of Prince Ch'ing along with his own. Actually he never consulted his colleague plenipotentiary before making those recommendations.[47] As late as March 28 he still maintained in a memorial that the only way to save the situation was to order Yang Ju to sign the agreement.[48] He did not think that Japan would go to war with Russia, and he was angry that the viceroys should have been under the influence of the Japanese.[49] He seemed to be completely overcome by the threats of the Russian Minister and believed that, if the agreement was not signed, Russia would break off the negotiations and never restore Manchuria to China.[50]

CHINA SEARCHES FOR A SOLUTION

After the Court had decided not to sign the Manchurian agreement, it issued a decree to Li Hung-chang on March 25 giving him the following instructions: (1) The separate agreement with Russia should be negotiated after the conclusion of the collective agreement with the Powers. (2) Li should explain China's difficulties to the Russian Minister and ask for his understanding, but if the

[45] Decree, K27/2/5, Ch'ing Tê Tsung Shih Lu, 480/5a; received 27/5/6, Li Hung-chang, op. cit., "Tien Kao," 34/16a; received 27/5/7, Tung San Shêng Tien Pao, p. 87.
[46] From Li, K27/2/4, Shêng Hsüan-huai, op. cit., 53/5.
[47] Prince Ch'ing's Memorial, K27/2/8, Chang Chih-tung, op. cit., 172/19.
[48] To the Grand Council, K27/2/9, Li Hung-chang, op. cit., "Tien Kao," 34/24a.
[49] From Li, K27/2/4, Shêng Hsüan-huai, op. cit., 53/5; to Shêng, K27/2/5, Li Hung-chang, op. cit., "Tien Kao," 34/11a.
[50] From Li, K27/2/8, Hsi Hsün Ta Shih Chi, 6/32.

Russian Minister refused to see the Chinese plenipotentiary, the Manchurian problem should be submitted to *kung tuan* (arbitration) by the United States or the Netherlands.[51] The same day another decree was issued ordering Li Hung-chang to notify the foreign envoys at Peking of those provisions of the proposed agreement that would affect the treaty rights of the Powers, and to request their *kung i* (common deliberation).[52] It seems that the Chinese at that time did not know exactly what arbitration as an international procedure meant. They sometimes used *kung tuan* and *kung i* interchangeably, and so when they said *kung tuan* it is possible that they only meant common deliberation.[53] Anyway, the idea of submitting the Manchurian problem to the common deliberation or arbitration of the Powers was conceived also by the viceroys and governors as the logical consequence after China's refusal to sign the agreement.[54] When Liu K'un-i learned that Japan had proposed to Russia that the agreement be considered by the Powers acting together at Peking, he memorialized the Throne that China should make the same proposal.[55] Chang Chih-tung and Wang Chih-ch'un also urged that common deliberation by the foreign envoys in Peking was the only way to satisfy the other Powers and to curb the Russian ambitions by invoking their influence.[56] In recommending the submission of the Manchurian problem to the conference of the foreign ministers, it was also the opinion of Liu K'un-i that such a move would serve the additional purpose of preventing Li Hung-chang from making any deal with the Russian Minister at Peking.[57]

If the proposed agreement was to be submitted to the consideration of the Powers, it was necessary that they be informed of the

51 *Chung Jih Shih Liao*, 61/32b.
52 *Ibid.*, 61/32a.
53 See, for instance, Wang Chih-ch'un's telegram, received K27/2/1, *ibid.*, 62/2; from Chang Chih-tung, K27/2/10, *ibid.*, 61/38b.
54 From Liu K'un-i, Chang Chih-tung, T'ao Mo, and Yüan Shih-k'ai, K27/2/7 (March 26, 1901), *Hsi Hsün Ta Shih Chi*, 6/29.
55 Liu to the Grand Council, K27/2/8 (March 27, 1901), *Chung Jih Shih Liao*, 61/37b.
56 Chang to the Grand Council, K27/2/9 (March 28, 1901), Wang to the Grand Council, K27/2/9 (March 28, 1901), *ibid.*, 61/38b, 62/2.
57 Shêng Hsüan-huai, *op. cit.*, 53/20, 26.

text. As early as March 5 Chang Chih-tung, upon the suggestion of the German Consul, had advised that the Chinese Government should communicate the agreement to the Powers and request them to intercede with Russia.[58] Then on March 9, upon the suggestion of the British Consul, Chang proposed again that the text be communicated to the Powers so that they could take action upon the basis of the official document.[59] The proposal was vehemently opposed by Li Hung-chang, who declared that international practice forbade any disclosure of an agreement pending its conclusion, not to mention its communication to the Powers.[60] In spite of Li's stern position, the British Minister at Peking, Sir Ernest Satow, was able to obtain a copy of the Chinese text and to send its translation to the British Foreign Office on March 6.[61] After the text had been amended by the Russian Government, Chou Fu, one of Li's aides, privately informed Satow on March 17 of the amendments, but did not give all details.[62] When Liu K'un-i and Chang Chih-tung learned of this from the British consuls, they considered it the intention of Li Hung-chang to lure the British Minister into acquiescence by purposely concealing from him the clauses that affected China's sovereignty or the treaty rights of the Powers. They protested accordingly to the Grand Council.[63] In the meantime the Japanese had copied the amended text, probably by courtesy of Chang Chih-tung,[64] and communicated it to the British Government on March 19.[65] After the Court had decided not to sign the agreement, the viceroys and governors in the telegram of March 25 urged again that the amended text be communicated to the other Powers, so that the foreign envoys could consider it at Peking.[66] On March 30 the Grand Council replied to

[58] Jung Lu to Li, K27/1/15, *Chung Jih Shih Liao*, 60/33.

[59] Li Hung-chang, *op. cit.*, " Tien Kao," 33/14b.

[60] To the Grand Council, K27/1/18 (March 8, 1901), Li Hung-chang, *op. cit.*, " Tien Kao," 33/5a.

[61] Gooch and Temperley, *op. cit.*, II, 38.

[62] See Satow to Lansdowne, March 17, 1901, *China No. 6 (1901)*, p. 131.

[63] Chang to Lu, K27/2/1 (March 20, 1901), Chang Chih-tung, *op. cit.*, 171/14b; Liu to the Grand Council, K27/2/3 (March 22, 1901), *Chung Jih Shih Liao*, 6/16.

[64] From Chang, K27/2/4 (March 23, 1901), Shêng Hsüan-huai, *op. cit.*, 53/8.

[65] Lansdowne to MacDonald, March 19, 1901, Gooch and Temperley, *op. cit.*, II, 47.

[66] Memorial by Liu, Chang, T'ao, and Yüan, K27/2/6, *Chung Jih Shih Liao*, 61/33.

the viceroys that such publication of the text would be considered by Russia a *casus belli,* and so the Court had to be cautious. The viceroys, however, might deliberate carefully and hand secretly to the British, Japanese, and American consuls a summary of the important points of the text and request the foreign governments to consider it jointly.[67] On March 31 Liu K'un-i wired Shêng Hsüan-huai to hand secretly to the British, Japanese, American, and German Consuls-General at Shanghai the full text of the Manchurian agreement.[68] As Shêng declined the mission, Liu had the text secretly handed to the various consuls on April 1.[69]

On April 5 Lord Lansdowne informed the Chinese Minister at London that the British Government would not suggest arbitration, but if China would invite the Powers to " examine conjointly any Agreements of the sort," the British Government would instruct its minister at Peking to join in considering it and the action which China should take.[70] No further action, however, was taken to submit the agreement to the consideration of the Powers, for in the meantime Russia had decided to abandon the agreement.

INTERNATIONAL ALIGNMENT

Throughout the negotiations for the Manchurian agreement, France gave Russia a kind of quiet support that was worthy of a faithful ally. France asked Russia no questions about the agreement,[71] and as the other countries, including China, avoided her in their diplomatic maneuvers against Russia,[72] the French Government was most ill-informed about the Manchurian negotiations.[73] And yet in Peking the French Minister declared to Li Hung-chang that France would be glad to see the Chinese plenipotentiary settle

[67] Grand Council to Liu, Chang, and Shêng, K27/2/11, *ibid.,* 62/4b.

[68] Shêng Hsüan-huai, *op. cit.,* 53/31.

[69] From Liu, 27/2/14, Chang Chih-tung, *op. cit.,* 171/33b; Liu to the Grand Council, 27/2/14, *Chung Jih Shih Liao,* 62/12; see also to Liu, K27/2/16, Chang Chih-tung, *op. cit.,* 171/36a.

[70] Gooch and Temperley, *op. cit.,* II, 51.

[71] Montebello to Delcassé, March 2, 1901, Ministère des affaires étrangères, *Documents diplomatiques français (1871-1914),* 2nd Series (Paris, 1930), I, 177.

[72] Delcassé to Montebello, March 6, 1901, *ibid.,* I, 160.

[73] The several texts reported by the French Minister at Peking and the French Consul-General at Shanghai were either incorrect or incomplete. See *ibid.,* I, 18, 168, 192.

the problems with Russia,[74] while in Tokyo the French Minister did his utmost to help his Russian colleague.[75]

The American government viewed the Manchurian agreement with apprehension and expressed " its sense of the impropriety, inexpediency, and even extreme danger to the interests of China, of considering any private territorial or financial arrangements, at least without the full knowledge and approval of all the Powers now engaged in negotiation." [76] But the American Government would not intercede with Russia; [77] nor did it take up the suggestion of the British Government and propose that all the Powers should not " recognize the validity of any private arrangement made separately between China and individual Powers until it had been referred to the representatives of all the Powers." [78]

Of all the Powers that were opposed to the Manchurian agreement, Japan was the most vigorous. Ever since the news of the alleged Manchurian agreement reached Japan, the Japanese Government had protested to Russia, warned China of partition, and sought common action of the other Powers. As Russia pushed ahead in spite of its protests, Japan was considering war. It was the opinion of the Japanese Government that Japan could certainly cope with the Russian forces on land but would be inferior at sea to the combined Russian and French fleets.[79] Should Russia invade Korea, Japan would not remain indifferent. But unless the French fleet could be kept in check, unaided Japan had no intention of going to war over the Manchurian question.[80]

Consequently the Japanese Government was eager to know what support Germany and Britain could give Japan in the event of a Russo-Japanese war. As early as the middle of February, Baron Hayashi, Japanese Minister at London, had approached Baron Eckardstein, First Secretary of the German Embassy, on the sub-

---

[74] Pichon to Delcassé, March 24, 1901, *ibid.*, I, 194.
[75] Harmond to Delcassé, January 31, 1901, *ibid.*, I, 80-82.
[76] Memorandum handed to Chinese Minister at Washington, February 19, 1901, *China No. 6 (1901)*, p. 108.
[77] From Minister Wu, 27/2/5, Li Hung-chang, *op. cit.*, " Tien Kao," 34/18.
[78] Lansdowne to Pauncefote, March 6, 1901, *China No. 6 (1901)*, pp. 111-12.
[79] Lascelles to Lansdowne, March 10, 1901, Gooch and Temperley, *op. cit.*, II, 42.
[80] MacDonald to Lansdowne, March 22, 1901, *ibid.*, II, 48.

ject.[81] The German Government did not consider Germany's interests in Manchuria so important as to justify its taking an active part and engaging in war with Russia,[82] but it thought it might well take the opportunity, in case matters came to a crisis, of embarrassing the Russo-French Alliance.[83] On March 6 the German Vice-Minister for Foreign Affairs informed the Japanese Minister at Berlin that as the German Government was well aware of the vital importance of the Manchurian question to Japan, Germany would observe " benevolent neutrality " in case matters should come to a crisis. He added that this attitude of Germany would keep the French fleet in check, while England would probably support Japan.[84]

Having obtained the above reply from Germany, the Japanese Government raised the following question with the British Government on March 9: " How far may Japan rely upon the support of Great Britain in case Japan finds it necessary to approach Russia? " It was assumed by Baron Hayashi that " approach " in the context meant " resist." [85] The question called for a review of Britain's Far Eastern policy, and in a memorandum dated March 11, Francis Bertie, British Assistant Under-Secretary for Foreign Affairs, set forth the views of the British Foreign Office. If France were allowed to side with Russia, and they crushed Japan, the result might be a renewal of the triple understanding, viz., Russia, France, and Germany. Those three Powers would become supreme in China, and Britain would go to the wall. On the other hand, if Japan defeated Russia, there would not be any grave danger to European interests in the Far East. A great military and naval Power, such as Russia, with unbounded natural resources and an immense population, was not likely to accept defeat permanently. The conflict between Russia and Japan would be an advantage to

[81] Eckardstein to Bülow, February 16, 1901, *Die Grosse Politik der Europäischen Kabinette, 1871-1914: Sammlung der Diplomatischen Akten des Auswärtigen Amtes* (Berlin, 1924), XVI, 324 (cited hereafter as *Die Grosse Politik*).

[82] Hatzfeldt to Minister for Foreign Affairs, February 28, 1901, *ibid.*, XVI, 326.

[83] William II to Bülow, March 5, 1901, *ibid.*, XVI, 334.

[84] Communicated by Baron Hayashi, March 9, 1901, Gooch and Temperley, *op. cit.*, II, 41.

[85] *Ibid.*, II, 41 (No. 51b).

England and Euorpe. " The yellow danger would be kept in check by Russia and the Russian danger by Japan." Britain's line of action was outlined by Bertie as follows:

If Germany and England, in answer to the Japanese Government's in-
quiries, deprecated war, and said that if unfortunately war broke out between Japan and Russia, it would be the object of England and Germany
to restrict as much as possible the theatre of it, and they would consequently remain neutral, so long as no third Power attempted to take part
in it, then I think that such an assurance might be sufficient to satisfy
Japan that France would not be allowed to join with Russia, and that
Japan might fight Russia single-handed.[86]

On March 8 Lord Lansdowne had brought up the subject as " purely academic " with Count Hatzfeldt, German Ambassador at London. The British Minister for Foreign Affairs wished to know the German attitude on two points:

1. Whether Germany was interested in a *protocole de désinté-
ressement,* which, using the Anglo-German Agreement as the basis, would unite certain Powers so that Japan would not have the fear that in the event of a Russo-Japanese war the spoils of victory would be snatched from her as in 1895.

2. Whether Germany would be disposed, in the event of a Russo-Japanese war, to issue with Great Britain a declaration to Paris that the two Powers, in the interest of European peace, wished the war to be localized in the Far East and that they would maintain strict neutrality. If, however, a European Power inter-vened in the war, the two Powers would reconsider their attitude.[87]

The German Government was, however, suspicious of British intentions. On reading a report from Count Hatzfeldt on March 5, the German Chancellor, Count von Bülow, had made an anno-tation to the effect that Britain did not want to fight Russia at any cost, but was simply trying to embroil other Powers with Russia.[88] In a telegram to the Kaiser on March 6 he further developed the theme. Lord Salisbury, he said, remained faithful to the principle which had been the motto of his politics all the time, i.e., Britain

---

[86] *Ibid.,* II, 43.
[87] Hatzfeldt to Minister for Foreign Affairs, March 8, 1901, *Die Grosse Politik,* XVI, 342.
[88] *Ibid.,* XVI, 339.

would be glad to have her interests defended by a third Power, particularly Germany, and if things came to the worst, she would rather have recourse to compensation than to arms.[89] With such a conception of the British policies, it was but natural that the German Chancellor should view the British proposal with distrust. With regard to point 1, wrote Bülow, a declaration made to Japan by Britain herself would be sufficient to encourage the Japanese. Nobody in Japan would believe that Germany with her small fleet would snatch Japan's spoils of victory. With regard to point 2, Germany could make the declaration to London or Tokyo but not to Paris, and in no case could Germany make it before the first shot was fired. To Bülow a simple promise made by Britain to Japan about France's neutrality would be sufficient to Japan, and a simple move taken at the opportune time by the British Ambassador at Paris would be sufficient for France. There was no doubt, he observed, that Britain only wanted to push Germany forward without doing anything herself. It was time that England should say definitely what she would do herself, instead of always questioning others.[90] As a result, Count Hatzfeldt was instructed on March 6 to tell Lord Lansdowne that as long as Germany was not certain about the British attitude, it was impossible to answer these questions, which until now had been purely academic.[91]

The German Government then found it necessary to restate its position of "benevolent neutrality," which had been interpreted by the German Vice-Minister for Foreign Affairs as having the effect of keeping the French fleet in check. In reply to an inquiry by the British Government, Herr Mühlberg, acting for the German Minister for Foreign Affairs, informed the British Ambassador on March 14 that "benevolent neutrality" meant nothing more than the observance of "a correct and strict neutrality," favoring neither one party nor the other in any manner.[92] The following day the German Chancellor made his famous speech in the Reichs-

89 *Ibid.*, XVI, 336.
90 *Ibid.*, XVI, 343.
91 Richthofen to Hatzfeldt, March 9, 1901, *ibid.*, XVI, 344.
92 *Ibid.*, XVI, 345.

tag, in the course of which he declared that the Anglo-German
Agreement of October 16, 1900, was " in no sense concerned with
Manchuria," that " there were no German interests of importance
in Manchuria," and that " the fate of that province was a matter
of absolute indifference to Germany."[93]   In a subsequent speech
the German Chancellor repudiated the charge that Germany was
serving the interests of England in China.   He desired to lay great
stress on the fact that Germany was serving only German interests
in China, and that she left to England the safeguarding of British
interests there.[94]

In spite of these speeches, Lord Lansdowne asked Baron Eckardstein on March 18 if there was a chance for common action by
Germany and Britain, so that by bringing pressure to bear upon
France the eventual Russo-Japanese war could be localized.   He
suggested that a defensive agreement be concluded between Britain
and Germany.[95]   On March 23 in a conversation with Ambassador
Hatzfeldt, Lansdowne further dwelt upon the idea and asked
whether in connection with the Far East, Japan could be taken
into consideration.[96]   But Bülow considered that such a pact would
bind the contracting parties to guarantee each other's possessions.
While the German possessions were not subject to any menace, he
calculated, those of the British were extremely so.   And Germany
had no desire to pull Britain's chestnuts out of the fire.[97]   He
therefore proposed that Britain join the Triple Alliance.   As to
Japan, she was bent upon conquest, and so was not of immediate
advantage to a purely defensive alliance.[98]

RUSSIA RETREATS

The response of Germany made it difficult for Britain to give the
necessary support to Japan, and, unaided, Japan was unwilling to
go to war with Russia.[99]   But although Britain and Japan could

93 *China No. 6 (1901)*, p. 132.
94 *Ibid.*
95 *Die Grosse Politik*, XVII, 42.
96 *Ibid.*, XVII, 47.
97 *Ibid.*, XVII, 44.
98 Bülow to Hatzfeldt, March 24, 1901, *ibid.*, XVII, 49.
99 Gooch and Temperley, *op. cit.*, II, 48.

promise no material support to China,[100] their opposition to the draft agreement respecting Manchuria was unequivocal. On March 13 the British Ambassador at St. Petersburg pointed out to Count Lamsdorff that the draft agreement could certainly not be described as of a merely temporary and provisional nature, as claimed by the Russian Foreign Minister, and that there were stipulations in it which undoubtedly affected the British treaty rights in China.[101] On March 25 the Japanese Minister, under instructions of his government, informed Count Lamsdorff that China had asked the Japanese as well as other governments for their good offices in connection with the Manchurian agreement which she was being pressed to sign within a specified time. Some articles appeared to Japan to affect the sovereignty and integrity of China and also certain treaty rights of other Powers. The Japanese Government wished to make the friendly proposal that the draft be considered by the treaty Powers acting together in Peking. It was its hope that the Russian proposals in Manchuria would not be incompatible with the treaty rights of other Powers.[102]

In the meantime, as reported by the Russian Minister at Tokyo, M. H. Isvolsky, agitation against Russia had markedly increased in Japan. It was now carried on not only by the numerous less significant papers but also by the most important organs of the press, including those which were officially connected with the government, as well as by many of the foremost statesmen of Japan, such as the ex-Prime Minister and leader of the Progressive Party, Count Okuma, who had recently expressed his views publicly in a most militant tone. The import of all those speeches and articles was the same: " Six years ago, on the advice of Russia, France, and Germany, Japan had to evacuate the Liaotung Peninsula because in the opinion of those Powers her penetration into this part of China endangered the peace and tranquility of the Far East. Now Russia is not only in command of the said territory but, under the pretext of a friendly agreement with China, is striving to establish

[100] From Minister Li, K27/2/6, Li Hung-chang, *op. cit.*, " Tien Kao," 34/13a; from Minister Lo, K27/2/6, *ibid.*, 34/14a.

[101] *China No. 6 (1901)*, p. 140.

[102] Gooch and Temperley, *op. cit.*, II, 49.

her political and military domination throughout Manchuria. This not only runs counter to the rights and interests of Japan in this Chinese region, but also threatens the independence of Korea, a country that is of the utmost importance to Japan. Japan must exert all her strength to prevent this, and with this end in view must make up her mind to resort to arms even if no support from other quarters is forthcoming." Isvolsky also noted that the Japanese Admiralty, in spite of the huge supplies of coal that it already had in store, was still placing urgent orders. Although no special preparations were as yet seen in that quarter, Isvolsky reminded his government that the Japanese navy had only recently been formed and did not by any means stand in need of any such preparations. It was in almost full fighting order and was already distributed among the southwestern ports lying nearest to the arena of possible hostilities. To sum up the situation, Isvolsky added: " The foreign representatives in Tokyo are very carefully observing the excitement that has been aroused here, and nearly all of them agree with me in my estimation of its gravity and extent." [103]

Under these circumstances, although Count Lamsdorff refused to accept officially the communication of the Japanese Minister on March 25 on the ground that he could not recognize the right of a third Power to interfere in a matter about which two independent Powers were negotiating,[104] and although as late as March 28 Count Witte tried to force China into submission by declaring that if China persisted in not signing the agreement Russia would annex Manchuria, the Russian Government realized that it would be difficult to carry out its threat. The Chinese Government, instead of submitting to the threats, had communicated the text of the agreement to the other Powers and requested their joint consideration of the problem. The Japanese Minister for Foreign Affairs told Isvolsky that the Japanese Government was extremely painfully impressed by Count Lamsdorff's refusal to receive the Japanese communication on the proposed agreement, that the assurance on the part of Russia that there was nothing in the agreement con-

103 Letter from Isvolsky to Lamsdorff, March 23 (April 5), 1901, *Krasnyi Arkhiv*, II (63), 24 ff.
104 Report of Conversation, March 12 (March 25), 1901, *ibid.*, II (63), 21.

trary to the rights and interests of other Powers was not compatible with facts that the Japanese Government was aware of, and that Japan would in due course express her views on the subject.[105] On March 29 Count Lamsdorff seems to have begun to consider abandoning the agreement, for he telegraphed the Russian Minister at Peking that " China's course of action, and that of some of the Powers, has presented a very serious obstacle to the realization of the intention expressed by Russia, and this circumstance frees her hands." [106] But it was on April 4 that the Russian Government, after three months of negotiations and three revisions of the text, announced its intention not to proceed further with the agreement, but to await the development of events, " remaining faithful to the program which it has followed from the beginning." [107]

There is no doubt that Count Lamsdorff played an important part in the decision to give up the proposed agreement. On July 1 he wrote the Russian Minister for War:

I have to call your attention in the first instance to the fact that from the political point of view the Minister for Foreign Affairs never considered it very wise to conclude an independent agreement with China on the Manchurian question until a normal state of affairs has been restored in the Celestial Empire, since such negotiations would only be possible with a completely independent and responsible government. Moreover, I have repeatedly pointed out, on the one hand, the danger of concluding such a treaty in view of the protests that would probably be made by the Powers having interests in the Far East, and on the other hand, the small importance that a *written document* has in the eyes of the Chinese, who are always inclined when a convenient moment arrives to repudiate the obligations they have taken on themselves, and the present obligations in any case would not be likely to be taken on by the central Chinese Government.

In my opinion it would have been very much more advisable to wait until the trouble was over and then obtain, by means of bargains with members of the Chinese Government, those favors and privileges which our strategic, political, and economic needs in Manchuria have made necessary.

[105] Letter from Isvolsky to Lamsdorff, March 23 (April 5), 1901, *ibid.*, II (65), 24 ff.
[106] *Ibid.*, II (63), 23.
[107] The Russian communication was handed to the German Foreign Office on April 4, to the British Foreign Office on April 5, and to the Japanese Foreign Office on April 8. *Die Grosse Politik*, XVI, 351-52; *China No. 6 (1901)*, p. 169; from Minister Li, K27/2/20, Shêng Hsüan-huai, *op. cit.*, 54/17.

. . . The War Office and the Department of Finance considered the immediate conclusion of a separate treaty with China necessary in order to extend and confirm the provisional agreements already existing between the Russian authorities and the local Tartar Generals.

Your Excellency is well aware that, only after considerable correspondence and frequent conferences, Infantry General Kuropatkin and State Secretary Witte agreed to make less harsh demands than those with which China was presented in the first instance. But as was to be expected even in the revised form, the proposed agreement on the Manchurian question, which had already been published in Tokyo, having been communicated by the Chinese, gave rise to great agitation on the part of all interested Powers, and especially Japan.

In such circumstances the best thing to do would be to preserve the present *status quo* and abandon for the time being all negotiations regarding a separate agreement with China.

I do not think that we should attribute any importance to the possibility that the Japanese might count this as a gain on their part, for in Europe and America the more farsighted statesmen would see that Russia had taken a very shrewd step in freeing her hands and reserving to herself complete freedom of action.

Whatever this may be from a political point of view, the important thing is that the news that Russia has abandoned all further negotiations with the Chinese on Manchurian affairs has immediately put an end to the very strained state of affairs which would have had disastrous results if, after the proposed agreement had been signed, all the Powers had made official protests and the central Chinese Government had refused to ratify it.[108]

[108] *Krasnyi Arkhiv*, II (63), 30.

11

The International Settlement

ONE OF THE FACTORS that made the Imperial Court hesitate to reject the proposed Manchurian agreement was fear that the exasperation of Russia might disrupt the peace negotiations at Peking. On March 22, the day before deciding not to sign the agreement, the Court telegraphed the Chinese ministers abroad to confirm with the foreign governments that if rejection of the agreement should result in the exasperation of Russia the Powers would continue negotiating the collective agreement.[1] On March 24, the day after Yang Ju had been ordered not to sign the agreement, a decree was issud to Li Hung-chang directing him to negotiate the collective agreement first.[2] The Court's fear that the Peking negotiations would be broken off was superfluous. On March 23 Lord Lansdowne informed the Chinese Minister at London that the British Government would not discontinue the peace negotiations at Peking.[3] A similar assurance was given by the German Government by March 27.[4] As to Japan, she had repeatedly advised China that if the Manchurian agreement was rejected, the other Powers would withdraw their troops from Peking and Chihli and the collective agreement under negotiation at Peking would not be affected.[5] As a matter of fact, the peace negotiations in Peking had never been discontinued, although the Russian Minister often absented himself because of the Manchurian issue.[6] After Russia had announced that it would not proceed further with the Manchurian agreement, the attention of the foreign ministers was soon concentrated on the Peking negotiations.

[1] *Ch'ing Tê Tsung Shih Lu,* 480/4a.   [2] *Ibid.,* 480/5a.
[3] *British Parliamentary Papers, China No. 6* (1901), p. 139. The report reached Sian on March 25. Decree, K27/2/6, *Chung Jih Shih Liao,* 61/32.
[4] Decree, K27/2/8, *Ch'ing Tê Tsung Shih Lu,* 480/7b.
[5] Minister Li to the Grand Council, received K27/2/5, *Chung Jih Shih Liao,* 61/30b; Li to the Grand Council, received K27/2/6, *ibid.,* 61/31b.
[6] From Lu, K27/2/11, *ibid.,* 62/10a.

PUNISHMENT OF THE MINISTERS

As shown in chapter VII, above, the Chinese Court, in anticipation of the Allied demands, had attempted to punish the pro-Boxer ministers itself. On November 13 a decree was issued ordering Princes Tuan and Chuang to be immured for life at Mukden, Princes I and Tsai Ying to be handed to the Clansmen's Court for imprisonment, Prince Tsai Lien to be confined to his house, Duke Tsai Lan to be degraded one degree in rank and be deprived of all his emoluments, Ying Nien to be degraded two degrees in rank, and Yü Hsien to be banished to the most remote frontier at hard labor for life. As to Tung Fu-hsiang, he was by the decree of December 3 deprived of his official rank but allowed to remain in office and was ordered to go to Kansu at once.[7]

The Allies, however, did not consider the punishment adequate or complete. In the Joint Note of December 24, 1900, which was accepted by China on January 16, 1901, it was stipulated that China was to inflict " the severest punishment in proportion to the crimes for the persons listed in the Imperial decree of September 25, and for those whom the representatives of the Powers shall subsequently designate." [8] In pursuance of this stipulation, the foreign representatives informed the Chinese plenipotentiaries that the following personages " deserve death ":

1. Prince Chuang—" Was the official Commander-in-Chief of the Boxers," who as Prefect of Police was " principally responsible for the publication of the poster under the seal of the Chief of Police, promising rewards . . . to any Chinese who should take foreigners . . . prisoners, and who should kill any one protecting foreigners."

2. Prince Tuan—" Was the principal author of the Boxer movement, into which he dragged the Chinese government by persuading them that this was the best means of ridding China of all foreigners. . . . "

3. Duke (Tsai) Lan—" Was one of the official chiefs of the Boxers," who, as Assistant Chief of Police, " was implicated in the publication " of the above-mentioned poster.

4. Ying Nien—Similar position and guilt as Duke Lan.

[7] See above, Chap. VII.   [8] Ibid.

5. Kang I—" Was one of the instigators and advisers of the Boxers, whom he always protected at Court, and for whom he was mainly instrumental in obtaining entire freedom of action."

6. Chao Shu-ch'iao—" One of the leaders of the movement against foreigners," who " went at the beginning of June to meet the Boxers, to whom he promised assistance by lavishing encouragement on them."

7. Yü Hsien—" Renewed and reorganized the Society of Boxers," and " brought about the Shansi massacres."

8. Tung Fu-hsiang—" Elaborated with Prince Tuan, and carried out [sic] at Peking, the plan for the destruction of foreigners in China."

9. Li Ping-hêng—" Employed his influence to get the Boxers recognized as a loyal and patriotic sect, and to induce the government to make use of them for the purpose of exterminating the foreigners. . . . From the 27th July besieged the Legations with the troops which he had brought from Kiangsu, and later fought the allied armies on their way to Peking."

10. Hsü T'ung—" Has always been one of the Mandarins most hostile to the foreigners, whose extermination he advised. . . . Praised the Boxers, whose accomplice he has never ceased to be, and whom he has supported with all his influence in his capacity of a great personage of the Empire and guardian of the heir presumptive."

11. Hsü Ch'êng-yü—" Is equally responsible with his father [Hsü T'ung], in whose plans and acts he constantly took part, and is, moreover, the principal cause of the execution of the Mandarins who had endeavoured to stop the attacks on the Legations."

12. Ch'i Hsiu—" Has been one of the Mandarins most hostile to foreigners, and has employed all his influence, as member of the Tsungli Yamen and Minister of Ceremonies, in the Boxer cause. Took part with those of his colleagues who made bloody reprisals on the party which disapproved of the attack on the Legations." [9]

On February 5 a conference betwen the Chinese plenipotentiaries and the foreign ministers was held at the British Legation. The dean of the diplomatic corps read the indictment against the

[9] China No. 6 (1901), pp. 157-58.

pro-Boxer ministers. The Chinese plenipotentiaries stated that they
had received a decree from the Throne indicating the utmost
length to which it was possible to go in decreeing punishment for
certain personages. The heaviest penalty for Prince Chuang would
be to make him commit suicide. Prince Tuan would be exiled to
Sinkiang and imprisoned for life. Duke Lan was only Vice-President of the Peking Gendarmerie and acted in obedience to orders
received from Prince Chuang, the President of that office. On
this account his guilt was less than that of some others. He would
be degraded and exiled. Chao Shu-ch'iao and Ying Nien had the
same position as Duke Lan; their penalty, the Chinese plenipotentiaries proposed, should be similar to that of the Duke. For Yü Hsien
the death penalty could be carried out. As to Tung Fu-hsiang,
the Chinese plenipotentiaries pointed out that he was in command
of the army and enjoyed great personal popularity among the
Mohammedans. They had every desire to punish him later. The
subordinate position of Hsü Ch'êng-yü, who was only a Vice-
President of the Board of Justice, debarred him from putting forward any proposals which carried weight. The Chinese plenipotentiaries would propose imprisonment in his case and apply for his
degradation. A similar proposal would be made in the case of Ch'i
Hsiu. As to Kang I, Hsü T'ung, and Li Ping-hêng, their deaths
precluded further discussion, but posthumous degradation could be
inflicted.[10]

After the conference with the Chinese plenipotentiaries, the
foreign representatives immediately held a meeting to consider the
final shape of their demands for punishment. With regard to
Prince Chuang, it was decided to accept the proposal of the Chinese plenipotentiaries that he be allowed to put an end to his own
life. In the case of Prince Tuan and Duke Lan there was a difference of opinion among the foreign ministers. At a previous meeting the Japanese, Russian, and the United States representatives had
stated that, while they held that these members of the Imperial
family deserved the death penalty, they were not prepared to insist
on it. On the other hand, five other representatives had voted for

[10] *Ibid.*, pp. 160-63.

that punishment without any reservation. Now the French Minister informed his colleagues that since the occasion in question he had received the instructions of his government to refrain from insisting. Thus there were four who were unwilling to insist, while on the other side there remained the British, German, Austro-Hungarian, and Italian ministers. As it was evidently impossible to obtain unanimity on this point, the British Minister proposed the following compromise:

Prince Tuan: Decapitation. But if subsequently it is commuted as an act of grace, he is to be exiled to the New Dominion (Eastern Turkestan), imprisoned, and never allowed to return.

The Russian Minister objected to the actual use of the word " decapitation." He thought the object might be attained by using the words of the indictment, " deserve death." After much discussion it was decided that the word " decapitation " was to remain but the word " subsequently " was to be replaced by the word " immediately." The same formula was adopted for Duke Lan. In the cases of Li Ping-hêng, Kang I, and Hsü T'ung, who were no longer alive, it was agreed to demand such measures as would produce the same effect on their memory as if they had been actually executed by virtue of an Imperial decree.[11] Finally it was resolved that the demands were to be communicated to the Chinese plenipotentiaries as follows:

1. [The Chinese] proposal relative to an order being given to Prince Chuang to commit suicide is accepted.

2. Prince Tuan and Duke Lan shall be condemned to imprisonment pending their decapitation. If, immediately after being condemned, the Emperor thinks fit to spare their lives, they shall be sent to Turkestan, there to be imprisoned for life, no commutation of the punishment being subsequently pronounced in their favor.

3. Ying Nien shall be sentenced to capital punishment.

4. If Kang I were alive he would have been condemned to capital punishment. Being dead, all the legal consequences of the punishment shall be pronounced against him.

5. The foreign Plenipotentiaries agree to decapitation for Yü Hsien.

6. For Tung Fu-hsiang, the Representatives of the Powers take note of the assurances you have given them on the subject of the penalty to

[11] Satow to Lansdowne, February 6, 1901, *China No. 6 (1901)*, pp. 163-65.

be ultimately inflicted on him. They are of opinion that in view of the execution of this penalty, it is necessary to deprive him as soon as possible of his command.

7. If Li Ping-hêng and Hsü T'ung were still alive, they should have been condemned to capital punishment. As they are dead, all the legal consequences of this sentence shall be pronounced against them.

8. Hsü Ch'êng-yü and Ch'i Hsiu shall be condemned to capital punishment.

The above punishments, the Powers demanded, " should be carried out with the shortest possible delay, and the Representatives of the Powers reserve to themselves the right to control their execution by appointing delegates in Peking or the Provinces." [12]

Upon report from Li Hung-chang of the Allied resolutions, the Imperial Court was surprised that such severe punishments were demanded of so many ministers. It particularly raised the following objections: (1) Ying Nien was only a follower; as Prince Chuang, the principal, had been severely punished, his penalty should be mitigated. (2) Chao Shu-ch'iao returned to Peking two days after he had been sent to investigate the Boxers. In his memorials there was no statement assisting or protecting the Boxers. He therefore did not deserve the death penalty. (3) Li Ping-hêng had come to Peking to " protect the sovereign," and had not participated in the attack on the legations. He as well as Kang I and Hsü T'ung were dead; there was no Chinese law, nor law of Western countries, to punish a minister after death. (4) As to Ch'i Hsiu and Hsü Ch'êng-yü, there was no evidence for their guilt, and it was a breach of China's sovereignty for the Allied forces to arrest and imprison Chinese high officials.[13] They should be released so that the Chinese Government could investigate their cases and, if they were found guilty, inflict the punishment itself. The Chinese plenipotentiaries were ordered to take up the matter and use their utmost efforts with the foreign ministers at Peking.[14] On February 12 Li Hung-chang reported that an interview with

---

[12] Calogan to Chinese Plenipotentiaries, February 6, 1901, *ibid.*, p. 166; to the Grand Council, K26/12/20, Li Hung-chang, *Li Wên Chung Kung Ch'üan Chi*, " Tien Kao," 31/30a.

[13] Ch'i and Hsü were then in the hands of the Japanese military police.

[14] Decree, K26/12/23 (February 11, 1901), *Ch'ing Tê Tsung Shih Lu*, 477/6b.

the British Minister revealed little possibility of mitigating the penalty of the pro-Boxer ministers except for Chao Shu-ch'iao, about whom Sir Ernest Satow agreed to telegraph the British Government for further instructions.[15] On February 13, a decree was issued ordering the following punishments: Prince Chuang was to commit suicide. Prince Tuan and Duke Lan were to be banished to Sinkiang, and there be imprisoned for life. Yü Hsien was to be executed. Ying Nien and Chao Shu-ch'iao were to be " imprisoned awaiting decapitation " (this implied the commutation of the death penalty). Tung Fu-hsiang was to be deprived of his office. Kang I, Hsü T'ung, and Li Ping-hêng were to be posthumously deprived of their office and honors.[16] In another decree issued the same day, Ch'i Hsiu and Hsü Ch'êng-yü were to be deprived of office pending investigation for further punishment.[17] Considering the Chinese plenipotentiaries would not be able to do much with the cases of Chao Shu-ch'iao, Ch'i Hsiu, and Hsü Ch'êng-yü, the Grand Council telegraphed on February 14 the two Yangtze viceroys, "who are respected by Britain and Germany," to urge the foreign governments to agree to the punishment ordered by the Imperial Court.[18]

The death penalty demanded for Chao Shu-ch'iao was especially considered unjust by the Chinese. Twenty-one officials in Sian, together with the representatives of the Kiangsu, Chekiang, Anhui, and Shensi residents in the temporary capital, telegraphed the Yangtze viceroys that no effort should be spared in saving Chao's life.[19] On February 17 Shêng Hsüan-huai had suggested to the Imperial Court that as there was little hope for the Japanese army to release Ch'i Hsiu and Hsü Ch'êng-yü, it would be more practical to accede to the death demand of the Allies with regard to these two as well as Ying Nien, and to concentrate on saving the life of Chao Shu-ch'iao. The idea, however, was discountenanced by the

---

[15] To the Grand Council, K26/12/23, Li Hung-chang, op. cit., " Tien Kao," 31/37b. Cf. Satow to Lansdowne, February 11, 1901, China No. 6 (1901), p. 40.

[16] Decree, K26/12/25, Ch'ing Tê Tsung Shih Lu, 477/9b; Satow to Lansdowne, February 16, China No. 6 (1901), p. 42.

[17] Ch'ing Tê Tsung Shih Lu, 477/11b.

[18] Chang Chih-tung, Chang Wên Hsiang Kung Ch'üan Chi, 170/37b.

[19] From Sian, K27/1/4 (February 22), ibid., 171/1b.

Court, which aimed at saving all four.[20] In the meantime Liu K'un-i and Chang Chih-tung requested the foreign consuls in Nanking, Hankow, and Shanghai, particularly the British and German consuls, to urge their ministers at Peking to reconsider the penalty for the four Chinese ministers.[21] But all effort was of no avail. The British and German ministers replied to their consuls that they could not reconsider their resolutions concerning the punishment of the Chinese ministers. They also warned that any delay on the part of the Chinese Government in inflicting the penalty in accordance with the Allied demands would affect the peace negotiations. Similar advice was given by the Japanese Minister.[22] Under these circumstances the Court telegraphed Prince Ch'ing and Li Hung-chang on February 18 to inquire if the foreign ministers could agree to allowing Ying Nien and Chao Shu-ch'iao to commit suicide and return Ch'i Hsiu and Hsü Ch'êng-yü to be executed by the Chinese authorities.[23] On February 21 the Court received the report of the two plenipotentiaries that the foreign ministers had accepted the proposal with regard to Ch'i Hsiu and Hsü Ch'êng-yü but demanded that Ying Nien and Chao Shu-ch'iao be sentenced to death by strangulation. The Chinese plenipotentiaries observed, however, that if the latter two ministers were ordered to commit suicide, it would not differ much from strangulation.[24] Accordingly a decree was issued on the same day accepting all the Allied demands on punishment with the sole alteration that Ying Nien and Chao Shu-ch'iao were to commit suicide instead of dying by strangulation.[25] This alteration was afterwards accepted by the Allied Powers.[26]

[20] Decree, K26/12/29, Ch'ing Tê Tsung Shih Lu, 477/21a.

[21] To Shêng, K26/12/30, Chang Chih-tung, op. cit., 170/39a.

[22] Ibid., 170/39b. On February 22 the Chinese Minister at Washington reported that the American Government agreed to mitigate the penalty of Chao Shu-ch'iao. But it was too late, and as Li Hung-chang observed, the United States alone could not change the resolution by all the Powers. Li Hung-chang, op. cit., " Tien Kao," 32/9.

[23] Ch'ing Tê Tsung Shih Lu, 477/22a.

[24] Ch'ing and Li to the Grand Council, K27/1/3, Wên Hsien Ts'ung Pien, No. 7 (1937), " Kêng Hsin Tien Pao," 5.

[25] Decree, K27/1/3, Ch'ing Tê Tsung Shih Lu, 478/5a; China No. 1 (1902), pp. 90 ff.

[26] China No. 6 (1901), p. 89.

After the punishment of the principal pro-Boxer ministers had been settled, the foreign representatives presented on March 31 their proposal for the punishment of 142 provincial officials.[27] The personages named in the list ranged from Mongolian princes to local gentry who held no other official honor than passing the provincial examination. The provinces involved included Chekiang, Kiangsi, Hunan, Kweichow, and Szechuan, where no Boxer movement had existed but short-lived riots occurred during the crisis. After much investigation, negotiation, and revision, a final list of local offenders was at last announced by the Imperial Court on August 19. The persons found guilty numbered 119, with 13 more still under investigation. The penalties ranged from capital punishment to mere reprimand.[28]

THE PROBLEM OF INDEMNITY

The problem of indemnity consisted of three parts: (1) What amount was China required to pay? (2) What method of payment was to be adopted? (3) What revenues were to be taken?

The Amount China Was to Pay

At a meeting of foreign ministers held on February 16, 1901, the United States Minister, E. H. Conger, proposed that his colleagues should first ascertain what amount China could afford to pay. When that amount was fixed, Conger explained, it should be claimed on behalf of all the Powers as a joint indemnity and be divided among them in proportion to their actual expenses and losses. If it was less than the sum of the latter, then each Power should abate its claim proportionately, and if there was a surplus it might be repaid to China. The idea, however, did not meet with the approval of the other Powers. The French Minister observed that the proposal of Conger would tend to cause delay rather than to accelerate progress. It seemed to him that the natural order of procedure was to ascertain first what had to be demanded in the way of indemnities and then to seek for the means of meeting that

---

[27] To the Grand Council, K27/2/16, Li Hung-chang, *op. cit.*, " Tien Kao," 35/1.
[28] Decree, K27/7/6, *Tung Hua Hsü Lu*, 168/3; *Li Hung-chang, op. cit.*, " Tien Kao," 40/23b.

demand.   As the German and Russian ministers held similar views, the American proposal was shelved.[29]   The question now was how to fix the indemnities to be claimed by the Powers.   On February 23 a committee consisting of the representatives of Belgium, Germany, the Netherlands, and the United States was appointed to determine principles for the assessment of non-government claims, the military charges being made by each government on principles laid down by itself.[30]   The report of the committee was considered by the diplomatic corps on March 13 and 14, and certain amendments having been introduced, it was finally accepted.   Besides specifying the various cases in which non-government claims might be presented, it provided that " the Representatives of the Powers, after examination of the claims preferred by the persons under their protection, shall make an approximate estimate of their amount, and shall claim the total sum, without giving either details or explanation." [31]

On March 21 W. W. Rockhill, the Commissioner Plenipotentiary of the United States in Peking, was instructed by his government to propose that the total of the indemnity be kept within the limit of £40,000,000, which was believed to represent the extreme ability of China to pay.[32]   The German Government, however, considered that the claims of the Powers were likely to amount to about £63,000,000 and feared that a reduction of this sum to £40,000,000 was too drastic a measure.[33]   At a meeting of the foreign representatives on April 23, the American proposal was brought up for discussion but was not favorably received.   The French Minister declared that China could probably pay more than £40,000,000.   The Russian Minister stated that in principle his government was willing to accept what China was able to pay, but he thought it was premature to discuss the figure until the committee on indemnities had made its report on the subject.   The Japanese Minister also thought it premature to discuss the limit to

[29] China No. 1 (1902), p. 9; Foreign Relations of the United States, 1901, Appendix (Washington: Government Printing Office, 1902), p. 87.
[30] China No. 1 (1902), pp. 45 ff.
[31] Report of the Indemnities Commission, ibid., p. 48.
[32] Ibid., p. 4; Foreign Relations of the United States, 1901, Appendix, pp. 127-28.
[33] Lansdowne to Lascelles, April 17, 1901, China No. 1 (1902), pp. 21-22.

the sum to be demanded, though he believed that the Powers might have to consider a reduction of the indemnity. As a result, it was decided that the report of the committee should be awaited.[34]

In a committee meeting of April 25, the total demands of the Powers were added up to include the cost of occupation up to July 1, 1901. They amounted to over £67,000,000.[35] On May 7 further additions were made which brought the total up to £67,500,000 or 450,000,000 taels.[36] The same day the Chinese plenipotentiaries were notified that the total of the expenses incurred by the Powers, up to July 1, on account both of their expenditures and of losses of foreign organizations and individuals as well as Chinese who had suffered through the fact of having been in the service of the foreigners, amounted to 450,000,000 taels, " a sum which will be considerably augmented should the occupation be prolonged beyond that date." [37]

As early as May 2 the Chinese plenipotentiaries had learned from the foreign representatives that the total indemnity up to July 1 would amount to 450,000,000 taels.[38] Upon receipt of this report the Imperial Court instructed the Chinese plenipotentiaries to urge the foreign representatives to reduce the sum and to be liberal with the mode of payment.[39] Having learned of the proposed sum from the British Minister at an earlier date, Viceroy Liu K'un-i had on April 27 telegraphed the Chinese Minister at London, asking him to urge the British Government to reduce the amount, since China's poverty in consequence of the heavy indemnity would not be of any advantage to Britain, which enjoyed the largest share of the China trade.[40] On April 26 Chang Chih-tung had also suggested, through the British Consul at Hankow, to Sir Ernest Satow that the indemnity be reduced to 400,000,000 taels.[41]

The United States Government consistently held that the total sum should be reduced.[42] Russia and France were inclined to

[34] China No. 1 (1902), pp. 26-27; Foreign Relations of the United States, 1901, Appendix, pp. 141-43.

[35] China No. 1 (1902), p. 34.

[36] Ibid., p. 41.

[37] Ibid., p. 41-42.

[38] To the Grand Council, K27/3/14, Li Hung-chang, op. cit., "Tien Kao," 36/12b.

[39] Decree, K27/3/15, Ch'ing Tê Tsung Shih Lu, 481/12b.

[40] Li Hung-chang, op. cit., "Tien Kao," 36/11.

[41] Ibid., 36/5b.

[42] Foreign Relations of the United States, 1901, Appendix, pp. 158-59.

accept less than 450,000,000 taels.[43] The British Government thought that, while it was unable to support the American proposal to keep the total amount within £40,000,000, it was prepared to concur in a reduction on a more moderate scale.[44] The idea of reducing the amount of indemnity was, however, strongly opposed by the German Government. Seeing that it had met the wishes of the British Government in opposing the Russian proposal with regard to a guaranteed loan and an increase of the Chinese tariff to 10 percent, the German Government requested support of Britain in the matter of indemnity.[45] The British Government agreed. On May 22 Satow was instructed by Lord Lansdowne not to support any reduction of the indemnity below 450,000,000 taels.[46] The same day the German Minister at Peking requested his colleagues to decide " the question as to whether the expenses actually incurred by the Governments, and the losses of Societies and individuals, are to be demanded of China in the form of an indemnity, reserving the question of the advisability of calculating the indemnity to be demanded of China up to the 1st July—that is to say, at the approximate sum of 450,000,000 taels." It was approved by all foreign ministers except the American representative.[47] On May 26 an Imperial edict was issued agreeing to pay the Allied Powers the above sum.[48]

The Method of Payment

As regards the method by which the indemnity was to be paid, a loan jointly guaranteed by all the Powers was advocated by Russia. Since China would be unable to raise the necessary sum for paying the indemnities by any loan without a foreign guarantee, it was thought by the Russian Government that a collectively guaranteed loan would be the simplest solution, as under this scheme the money would be easily and quickly raised in the open market.[49] The proposal was supported by France.[50] The Japanese, Italian, Spanish, and the Netherlands representatives stated in effect

---

[43] Satow to Lansdowne, May 7, 1901, *China No. 1* (1902), p. 41.
[44] Lansdowne to Lascelles, May 20, 1901, *ibid.*, p. 61.
[45] Lascelles to Lansdowne, May 22, 1901, *ibid.*, p. 63.   [46] *Ibid.*, p. 65.
[47] *Ibid.*, p. 64.   [48] Decree, K27/4/9, *Ch'ing Tê Tsung Shih Lu*, 482/5a.
[49] Scott to Lansdowne, May 8, May 15, 1901, *China No. 1* (1902), pp. 58-60.
[50] Lansdowne to Monson, May 20, 1901, *ibid.*, pp. 61-62.

that they would accept the plan if other Powers agreed to it.[51] The proposal was, however, opposed by the United States [52] and strongly opposed by Britain. The British Government considered it inexpedient that Britain should use her credit, which stood higher than that of the other Powers, for the purpose of enabling those Powers to obtain the payment of their demands.[53] It would be impossible for the British Cabinet to ask Parliament to pledge the British credit for so large a sum, so small a part of which would belong to Britain. Moreover, the British Government argued, " many difficulties and long delays, which would in this case be most inconvenient, are involved by the procedure necessitated by a joint guarantee." [54] In view of the British opposition, the Russian Government modified its proposal to the effect that each Power would only pledge its credit for its own individual share of the total indemnity in giving the guarantee.[55] But the British Government considered the plan impracticable. Supposing any default to take place in the Chinese payments, asked Lord Lansdowne, were the creditors to wait till all the governments had forwarded their quotas of the deficiency? The delays would be interminable.[56] Instead of a guaranteed loan, the British Government proposed that China should issue to each of the creditor Powers bonds which at face value would represent the share of indemnity which was due that Power. These bonds were to bear interest at the rate of 3 percent for the first three years and thereafter to increase by ½ percent in each of the two following years, and then to remain permanently at 4 percent. The sinking fund was to commence five years from issue of bonds, and to be at the rate of 1 percent.[57] The service of these bonds was to be effected by the revenues to be agreed upon by the Powers, which would be received and distributed by an international board. This board would have no right of direct interference in Chinese administra-

[51] Satow to Lansdowne, May 23, 1901, *ibid.*, p. 66.

[52] Rockhill to Hay, May 1, 1901, *Foreign Relations of the United States.* 1901, Appendix, p. 145.

[53] Lansdowne to Monson, May 8, 1901, *China No. 1* (1902), p. 43.

[54] Lansdowne to Scott, May 20, 1901, *ibid.*, p. 60.

[55] Scott to Lansdowne, May 25, 1901, *ibid.*, p. 67.

[56] Lansdowne to Scott, May 27, 1901, *ibid.*, p. 70.

[57] Lansdowne to Lascelles, May 24, 1901, *ibid.*, p. 67.

tion or in the imposition or collection of taxes. If default took place, the default would be to the board, and not to any individual Power, and the Powers would jointly concert necessary action.[58] Under this arrangement, the British Government maintained, it would not be possible for a single Power to allow arrears to accumulate with the object of coercing the Chinese Government into preferential advantages to itself.[59]

The German Government at first did not seem to have any objection to a guaranteed loan.[60] But when it learned of Britain's strong opposition, it decided not to encourage the proposal. On May 14, 1901, Baron von Richthofen, German Foreign Minister, informed the British Ambassador at Berlin that the British proposals on bonds furnished a satisfactory basis for negotiation. It considered however that ½ percent for amortization was too little,[61] and that anything under 4 percent interest was unacceptable.[62] In view of Germany's support in opposing the Russo-French proposal for a guaranteed loan and a 10 percent tariff, the British Government decided to meet the German wishes. It assented to 4 percent interest on the bonds and a progressive increase in the sinking fund.[63]

When Chang Chih-tung learned from George Jamieson, British Chargé d'Affaires, that the British Government might suggest to the other Powers a lower rate of interest, he telegraphed the Imperial Court on May 24 that, since there was little hope for a reduction of the indemnity, effort should be made to have the interest reduced.[64] The Chinese plenipotentiaries were accordingly instructed by the Court to negotiate for a lower interest and for a longer period within which to pay the indemnities.[65] It was hoped by the Court that the interest could be reduced to 3.30 percent.[66]

[58] Lansdowne to Satow, May 11, 1901, ibid., p. 45.
[59] Lansdowne to Monson, June 5, 1901, ibid., p. 115.
[60] See Satow to Lansdowne, May 15, 1901, ibid., p. 55.
[61] Lascelles to Lansdowne, May 14, 1901, ibid., p. 51.
[62] Lascelles to Lansdowne, May 26, 1901, ibid., p. 68.
[63] Memorandum to Eckardstein, July 18, 1901, ibid., p. 183.
[64] Li Hung-chang, op. cit., "Tien Kao," 37/15a.
[65] Decree, K27/4/10 (May 27, 1901), Ch'ing Té Tsung Shih Lu, 482/5a.
[66] Li Hung-chang, op. cit., "Tien Kao," 37/19b.

This hope had no chance of realization as Britain had to meet the wishes of Germany, which insisted on 4 percent interest. With Britain and Germany taking the same position toward the method of payment, an agreement was at last reached among the foreign representatives. On June 13 the Russian Government made it known that it was prepared to accept any scheme for the indemnities to which other Powers agreed, whether it be by obligations, loans, or bonds, so long as the whole of the claims would be provided for by the revenues assigned and so long as control of the assigned revenues did not involve interference in Chinese administration.[67] On July 18 the United States representative, who had proposed that the question of indemnity should be submitted to the Hague Arbitration Tribunal if the Powers could not agree among themselves,[68] announced that his instructions allowed him to accept any solution agreeable to the majority.[69] The same day the representatives of all the Powers agreed that the sum of 450,-000,000 taels be fixed as the final amount of indemnity and that payment be made by bonds with interest at 4 percent.[70] As provided in the final protocol, the capital was to be repaid by China in 39 years. The Commission of Bankers at Shanghai charged with the service of the debt was to receive from the Chinese authorities the sum due on the successive dates of payment.[71]

[67] Lansdowne to Satow, June 13, 1901, China No. 1 (1902), p. 139.

[68] Rockhill to Hay, June 8, 1901, Foreign Relations of the United States, 1901, Appendix, p. 226.

[69] China No. 1 (1902), p. 184. Cf. Rockhill to Hay, July 18, 1901, Foreign Relations of the United States, 1901, Appendix, pp. 275-78.

[70] Foreign Relations of the United States, 1901, Appendix, p. 277. On June 15 all the Powers except Japan had voted in favor of the issuance of bonds at par, bearing 4 percent interest. The Japanese Minister pointed out that the last Japanese loan placed on the London market had been at 4 percent and that the bonds at the present time were quoted at 0.78. " If the bonds [for the indemnity] were to bear interest at 4 percent," the Japanese Minister declared, "nothing less than a capital sum which would yield interest equal to 5 percent on the total amount of Japan's claims should be regarded as equivalent to such claims which were calculated on the basis of immediate payment " (ibid., p. 244). On June 18, however, the Japanese Minister announced that he would accept the total indemnity of 450,000,000 taels at 4 percent interest (ibid., p. 277).

[71] Article 6 of the final protocol concerning the indemnities was drafted on August 2 and agreed to on August 12. China No. 1 (1902), pp. 195, 209.

The Revenues

The consideration of the sources from which China could furnish the indemnities to be demanded by the Powers was entrusted to a committee consisting of the British, German, French, and Japanese Ministers.[72] On May 1 the committee presented its report to the diplomatic corps.[73] Among the Chinese revenues the committee chiefly considered those which combined the following conditions: " well-organized collection, assured yield, easy and effective control." The committee advised that, even when they fulfilled these conditions, those revenues should be set aside whose yield was especially devoted to such expenditure as would appear incapable of modification without prejudice to the internal administration of the country. With these explanations the committee recommended that the following resources be taken as security for the indemnity:

1. Maritime customs and the *likin* at that time under foreign control. It was estimated that these two revenues, properly administered, constituted a total of 28,000,000 or 29,000,000 taels, from which must be deducted until 1905 an average of 24,000,000 taels for loans. Out of the balance 3,917,000 taels had to be paid for the administration of the maritime customs, the maintenance of the lighthouses, the Peking College, and the Chinese legations abroad. The available surplus for the payment of indemnity would be 83,000 to 1,083,000 taels. Since, however, the annuities of the existing debt reached their maximum in 1905, decreasing thereafter, the available surplus would augment from that date by 200,000 a year until 1918, when it would amount to more than 5,000,000 taels.[74]

2. Increase of import duties to an effective 5 percent *ad valorem*. The duties received for the year 1899 were equal to 3.18 percent of the value of all merchandise imported; the increase to 5 percent would result in an augmentation of receipts by 2,320,276 to 3,900,311 taels.[75]

[72] Satow to Lansdowne, March 22, 1901, *China No. 6 (1901)*, p. 138.
[73] *China No. 1 (1902)*, p. 37.   [74] *Ibid.*, p. 158.
[75] *Ibid.*

3. Native customs. Duties on merchandise borne on junks were collected by a special native administration according to a special tariff which operated in the open ports alongside the maritime customs and everywhere else on the coasts or in the islands at the stations which the Chinese Government had established since time immemorial. The revenue was valued at 3,000,000 to 10,000,000 taels.[76]

4. Taxation of merchandise imported free at that time. Some articles such as flour, butter, cheese, foreign clothes, soap, candies, spirits, etc., had been exempted from duty at the time when the tariff was drawn up because they were only imported in small quantities for the use of foreigners. But the Chinese had taken to buying them extensively, so that now they represented a considerable value. It was recommended that these goods be subject to the general tariff, with the exception of rice and cereals.[77]

The committee also considered the possible increase of the customs duties to 10 percent and the appropriation of the salt gabelle, but it was unable to reach an agreement.[78] The gabelle was valued at 14,000,000 taels, which would increase to 20,000,000 taels under good administration. M. Pokotiloff of the Russo-Chinese Bank advised against securing control of the gabelle except as a last resource. According to him, this control would necessitate a very complicated organization, which it would be difficult to create and set going, and a foreign staff which was completely lacking. Furthermore, he would consider this control as an interference in the internal administration.[79] At first the Imperial Court was unwilling to set aside the salt gabelle and the native customs as securities for the indemnities, for fear that the foreign Powers would infringe upon the sovereign rights of China.[80] But when Li Hung-chang pointed out that the maritime customs alone was insufficient for the indemnities and that it was not the intention of the Powers to infringe upon the sovereignty of China,[81] the

---

[76] Ibid., p. 159.
[77] Ibid.
[78] Ibid., p. 156.
[79] Ibid., pp. 160-61.
[80] From the Grand Council, K27/3/16, Li Hung-chang, op. cit., " Tien Kao," 36/19a.
[81] To the Grand Council, K27/3/17, ibid., 36/20a.

Court gave its consent.[82]   The British experts were strongly in favor of using the salt gabelle, and they were supported by their German colleague.[83]   At last it was agreed by the Powers that the gabelle be earmarked for payment of the indemnities.[84]

On the proposal to increase the tariff to 10 percent, the Powers were unable to reach an agreement.   The Chinese Government was in favor of the increase and counted upon it as the main source for paying the indemnities.   The increase to 10 percent was favored by Russia and France.[85]   The Japanese Minister would consent to it if the *likin* on imports and exports were abolished.[86]   The American representative declared that he was in favor of the increase on condition that the *likin* on imports was suppressed, the rates of *likin* on exports revised, and certain other commercial improvements introduced.[87]   The 10 percent increase was, however, firmly opposed by Britain.   The British Government insisted that the tariff could be raised only up to 5 percent of the existing values.[88]   It maintained that any increase of the duties beyond 5 percent could only be discussed when the question of commercial reform was dealt with under Article 11 of the Joint Note.[89]   The British Government could not consent to "subjecting British sea-borne commerce, which far exceeds that of all other Powers put together, to customs duties which would exceed Treaty rate of 5 percent, in order that means may be provided to satisfy indemnities which the Powers claim." [90]   The German Government at first advocated the increase of the import duties to 10 percent,[91] but by May 26 it had agreed not to insist upon the proposal in exchange

[82] From the Grand Council, K27/3/18, *ibid.*, 36/12a.

[83] *China No. 1* (*1902*), pp. 160-61.

[84] Lansdowne to Scott, July 12, 1901, *ibid.*, p. 181.

[85] Satow to Lansdowne, May 7, 1901, *ibid.*, pp. 41-42; Lansdowne to Monson, May 20, 1901, *ibid.*, pp. 61-62.

[86] Satow to Lansdowne, March 24, 1901, *China No. 6* (*1901*), pp. 139-40; *China No. 1* (*1902*), p. 68.

[87] Rockhill to Hay, June 11, 1901, *Foreign Relations of the United States*, 1901, Appendix, p. 227.

[88] Lansdowne to Satow, March 27, 1901, *China No. 6* (*1901*), p. 145.

[89] Lansdowne to Satow, March 30, 1901, *ibid.*, pp. 146-47.

[90] Lansdowne to Scott, May 20, 1901, *China No. 1* (*1902*), p. 60.

[91] Satow to Lansdowne, March 24, 1901, *China No. 6* (*1901*), p. 139.

for Britain's support for the 4 percent interest.[92] In view of Britain's strong objection the Russian Government proposed a compromise that, in the event of default on the part of China, the arrears should be secured upon the eventual raising of the import tariff up to 10 percent.[93] But the British Government insisted that the *sine qua non* of a 10 percent tariff was fulfillment of Article 11 of the Joint Note, and that Britain's freedom to utilize the yield of extra duties in connection with commercial reforms must remain unimpaired.[94] Because of Britain's unswerving opposition, the Powers finally agreed on an increase of import duties to an effective 5 percent.[95]

On July 27 the diplomatic corps informed the Chinese plenipotentiaries that they had decided to assign the following revenues as guarantees of the bonds:

1. The balance of the maritime customs augmented by the receipts accruing from the raising to 5 percent effective of the present tariff on importation by sea, inclusive of the articles which until now have entered free of duty, but with certain exceptions, which will be indicated later.

2. The revenues of the native customs, administered by the Imperial maritime customs.

3. The net revenue of the (salt tax) gabelle, with the exception of the fraction previously assigned to other foreign loans.[96]

THE FINAL PROTOCOL

With the problems of punishment and indemnity settled, the peace negotiations moved rapidly to a conclusion. On September 7, 1901, one year and twenty-four days after the Allied forces relieved the legations in Peking, the peace protocol was at last signed by the eleven foreign ministers and the two Chinese plenipotentiaries at the Chinese capital. This final protocol consisted of twelve articles with nineteen annexes. The articles were arranged in the same order as the Joint Note which China had accepted in January, 1901. Article 2 (a), concerning the punishment of the

---

[92] Lascelles to Lansdowne, May 26, 1901, *China No. 1 (1902)*, p. 68.

[93] Satow to Lansdowne, June 7, June 11, 1901, *ibid.*, pp. 118, 137.

[94] Satow to Lansdowne, June 7, 1901, *ibid.*, p. 118; Lansdowne to Satow, July 12, 1901, *ibid.*, p. 180.

[95] Satow to Lansdowne, August 2, 1901, *ibid.*, p. 197.

[96] *Foreign Relations of the United States*, 1901, Appendix, p. 289.

guilty officials, and Article 6, concerning the indemnities, embodied the results of negotiations which have been described in the preceding two sections of this chapter. The rest of the treaty may be summarized as follows:

Article 1. Prince Ch'un was to convey to the German Emperor the regrets of the Chinese Emperor and Government for the assassination of Baron von Ketteler, German Minister. A commemorative monument would be erected on the spot of the assassination of the late German Minister.

Article 2 (b). An Imperial edict promulgated August 9, 1901, ordered the suspension of official examinations for five years in all cities where foreigners had been massacred or submitted to cruel treatment.

Article 3. Na T'ung, Vice-President of the Board of Finance, was to convey to the Emperor of Japan regrets of the Chinese Emperor and Government for the assassination of Mr. Sugiyama, Councellor of the Japanese Legation.

Article 4. China was to erect an expiatory monument in each of the foreign or international cemeteries which had been desecrated and in which tombs had been destroyed.

Article 5. China agreed to prohibit the importation into its territory of arms and ammunition, as well as of materials exclusively used for the manufacture of arms and ammunition. An Imperial edict had been issued on August 25 forbidding said importation for a term of two years. New edicts might be issued subsequently extending this by successive terms of two years in case of necessity recognized by the Powers.

Article 7. China agreed that the quarter occupied by the legations was to be considered as one especially reserved for their use and placed under their exclusive control, in which Chinese were not to have the right to reside, and which might be made defensible.

Article 8. China agreed to raze the forts of Taku, and those which might impede free communication between Peking and the sea.

Article 9. The following points were to be occupied by the Powers for the maintenance of open communication between the capital and the sea: Huangts'un, Langfang, Yangts'un, Tientsin, Chünliangch'êng, T'angku, Lut'ai, T'angshan, Luanchou, Ch'angli, Chinwangtao, Shanhaikwan.

Article 10. China agreed to post and to have published for two years in all district cities the following Imperial edicts:

(a) Edict of February 1, 1901, prohibiting forever, under the pain of death, membership in any antiforeign society.

(b) Edict of August 19, 1901, prohibiting examinations in all cities where foreigners were massacred or subjected to cruel treatment.

(c) Edict of February 1, 1901, declaring all viceroys, governors, and provincial or local officials responsible for order in their respective districts, and that in case of new antiforeign troubles or other infractions of the treaties which were not immediately repressed and the authors of which were not punished, these officials were to be immediately dismissed without the possibility of being given new functions or new honors.

Article 11. China agreed to negotiate the amendments deemed necessary by the foreign governments to the treaties of commerce and navigation, and the other subjects concerning commercial relations with the object of facilitating them.

For the time being China was to assist in the improvement of the courses of the rivers Paiho and Whangpu as follows:

(a) The works for the improvement of the navigability of the Paiho, begun in 1898 with the cooperation of the Chinese Government, had been resumed under the direction of an international commission. As soon as the administration of Tientsin had been handed back to the Chinese Government it would be in a position to be represented on this commission and would pay each year a sum of 60,000 taels for maintaining the works.

(b) A conservancy board, charged with the management and control of the works for straightening the Whangpu and the improvement of the course of that river, was to consist of members representing the interests of the Chinese Government and those of the foreigners in the shipping trade of Shanghai. Expenses for the works were estimated at 460,000 taels a year for the first twenty years. This sum was to be supplied in equal portions by the Chinese Government and the foreign interests concerned.

Article 12. An Imperial edict of July 24, 1901, reformed the Tsungli Yamen on the lines indicated by the Powers, that is to say, transformed it into a Ministry of Foreign Affairs, Wai Wu Pu, which took precedence over the six other ministries of state. China also agreed to modify the Court ceremonial as regards the reception of foreign representatives.[97]

Finally, the protocol provided that, with the exception of the legation guards mentioned in Article 7, the international troops were to evacuate Peking on September 17, 1901, and, with the exception of the localities mentioned in Article 9, to withdraw from the province of Chihli on September 22.[98]

On October 6, after staying at Sian for nearly a year, the Imperial Court started its return journey to Peking. It arrived at the capital on January 7, 1902, having stayed at K'aifêng, Honan, for a month. The situation created by the Boxer disorders was thus terminated except in Manchuria, which was still under Russian occupation. On April 8, 1902, after much negotiation and protest by the other Powers, Russia finally agreed to evacuate Manchuria by zones within a year and a half.[99] But Russia did not live up to the agreement, and it was not until after the Russo-Japanese War of 1904-5 that the Russian troops were at last withdrawn from the three provinces.

[97] The substance of the agreement was embodied in annex 19 to the protocol. Among other things it was stipulated that solemn audiences given by the Chinese Emperor would take place in the hall of the Palace called Ch'ien Ch'ing Kung. On going to these solemn audiences or in returning, the representatives of the Powers would be carried in their chairs as far as the exterior of the gate Ching Yün. There they would alight from the chairs in which they had come and would be borne in small chairs (*i chiao*) as far as the foot of the steps of the gate Ch'ien Ch'ing. When a representative of a Power had to present to the Chinese Emperor his credentials or a communication from the chief of the state by whom he was accredited, the Emperor would have sent to the residence of the said representative, to bear him to the Palace, a sedan chair with yellow upholstery and tassels, such as were used by princes of the Imperial family.

[98] For text of the final protocol and the annexes see *China No. 1 (1902)*, pp. 237 ff.

[99] For the Sino-Russian Agreement of April 8, 1902, see *China No. 2 (1904)*, pp. 35 ff.

12

Conclusion

THE BOXER BANDS were not militia recruited in response to Imperial decrees. They were officially reported to have appeared in Shantung as early as May, 1898, while the first decree ordering the organization of the militia was not issued until November of that year. Our record shows that they began as volunteer associations under the influence of the heretical sects. With the declared aim of fighting the native Christians, they soon became a popular front against foreigners.

The policy of Yüan Shih-k'ai towards the Boxers in Shantung has been a subject of controversy. It has been asserted that Yüan's policy toward the rioters was marked by no greater display of severity than had been shown by Yü Hsien. Actually, as soon as he assumed the acting governorship of Shantung, Yüan was determined to suppress the Boxers. His proclamation ordering the suppression was as vigorous as it was thoroughgoing. It was because of Yüan's strong determination that the Boxer movement was stopped in Shantung.

Viceroy Yü Lu is often described as a pro-Boxer official. Our evidence indicates that at the outset he did order his troops to suppress the Boxers. But his measures were never vigorous, and he must be held responsible for declining the proposal of Yüan Shih-k'ai to jointly memorialize the Throne for a forcible suppression. Had he been as determined as Yüan, the Boxer movement would have been stopped in Chihli at an early stage, as it was in Shantung. Partly because of the weak character of the Viceroy and partly because of pressure from Peking, which was more effectively brought to bear upon the province in which the capital lay, the Boxer movement in Chihli soon became a conflagration blazing toward the capital.

The policy of the Imperial Court toward the Boxers has long

been a subject of guesses and inferences. Our record indicates that as late as April, 1899, when conflicts between the Boxers and Christians were reported, the Court showed sympathy toward the Christians, who were regarded as being maltreated and suffering from injustice. The report of Yü Hsien, then Governor of Shantung, that the Christians domineered in the villages and bullied the good people, must have influenced the attitude of the Court, for henceforth there was an unmistakable change of tone in the decrees dealing with antiforeign riots. Pacification rather than suppression was emphasized. In December Yü Hsien was recalled to Peking under diplomatic pressure. There is no doubt that he had the ear of the Manchu Court, for in March he was awarded a new appointment as Governor of Shansi, while from December 26, 1899, to January 3, 1900, three decrees were issued to Yüan Shih-k'ai ordering him not to resort to force in dealing with the Boxers.

The pacification policy of the Court toward the Boxers culminated in the dispatch of Kang I to Chochou on June 6, 1900, with the mission of appeasing the Boxers. That Kang I, the arch-reactionary, was responsible for the encouragement of the Boxers is beyond doubt. The assertion, however, that the Imperial Court decided to utilize the Boxers and called them into the capital after the return and personal report of Kang I is not correct. Kang I did not leave Chochou for Peking until the midnight of June 14. On June 13 the Boxers had already entered the capital in force.

That the reactionaries, with a deep-rooted hatred against the foreigners, opposed the suppression of the Boxers, there is clear evidence. That the Empress Dowager fell in with them has also been established. But if the Imperial Court was determined not to suppress the Boxers, it was only after the Allied expedition under Admiral Seymour had left Tientsin for Peking on June 10, 1900, that it was prepared for war. In the decree issued to Yü Lu and Generals Nieh and Lo on June 13, the Court explicitly laid down its policy: to resist any further foreign reinforcements and to stop the Allied force from coming to Peking. The several Imperial audiences were summoned to rally the ministers to the

Imperial policy rather than to hear their advice. The Imperial Government indeed had no intention of starting war, and the door of diplomacy was left open. But if the foreign Powers brought up further reinforcements or the Allied forces continued to push toward Peking, war was inevitable.

Our evidence indicates that the attack upon the legations was authorized by the Imperial Court, although it is not so clear why the attack was made. The motives must have been complex. The following are possible explanations: (1) to give vent to hatred and anger; (2) to stimulate the patriotism of the people; (3) to remove the menace constituted by the foreign troops within the capital; (4) to deprive the Powers of witnesses as to what actually was happening and who really was responsible.

The position of Jung Lu during the crisis has been an enigmatic issue. Our record shows that he was opposed to the Boxers and the war. A minister, however, had to obey Imperial orders, and Jung Lu was loyal to the Empress Dowager. Hence his troops participated in the attack upon the legations; but the attacks were never pushed home, for he realized that to avert a national calamity the foreign ministers had to be saved. In the truce and negotiations for the escort of the foreign ministers to Tientsin in the middle of July, Jung Lu took a leading part. It should be noted that the Chinese proposal to escort the foreign envoys out of Peking was sincere, and not a treacherous move to lure them out of the legations and kill them.

The contributions of the southern viceroys in maintaining peace in the southeastern provinces can hardly be exaggerated. They preserved more than half of China from war, and by doing this they created a basis upon which they could work for peace. But while this success is justly attributed to Viceroys Liu K'un-i and Chang Chih-tung, the contribution of Shêng Hsüan-huai has not been sufficiently noted. As Director of Telegraphs he was well informed, and, stationed in Shanghai, he was able to sense the feelings of the foreigners. His resourceful mind was a motivating force in many of the measures taken by the southern viceroys.

The activities of the southern authorities [1] were not confined to the southeastern provinces: they worked hard to resolve the general situation. Their memorials to the Throne urging the protection of the foreign ministers contributed much to the truce and the negotiations for the escort of the foreign ministers to Tientsin. Their advice to the Chinese ministers abroad prevented China from breaking her diplomatic relations with the Powers. Because of their efforts the payment of China's foreign debts was not stopped as ordered by the Imperial Government. Their telegrams to Jung Lu gave the latter support in moderating the war policy of the Imperial Court. The southern viceroys ignored the Imperial decree that declared war against the Powers. They contemplated a *coup d'état* by marching troops to Peking under Yüan Shih-k'ai to overthrow the reactionaries. Chang Chih-tung corresponded with Ito with the hope of securing the assistance of Japan; Li Hung-chang declared to the Powers that the hostilities at Taku had been started without Imperial order. Never in the annals of the Ch'ing Dynasty had the provincial officials played such an active part in the shaping of the nation's foreign policy. It is interesting to note how in a national crisis the southeastern provinces assumed a position of semi-independence.

It was to Li Hung-chang that credit must go for concluding the peace with the Powers. No other person showed greater courage than Li in advising against the Court's wishes. Although he tarried, and that not without reasons, in going up to the north, he lost no time in applying himself to resolving the situation. His policy of treating the hostilities not as a war between China and the Powers but as a combined effort in suppressing the Boxers was a correct and successful one. His dauntless recommendation of severe punishment of the pro-Boxer ministers, which frightened even Chang Chih-tung, was a necessary move for a speedy settlement. To oppose what was impossible and to accept what was in-

---

[1] That is, Liu K'un-i, Chang Chih-tung, Yüan Shih-k'ai, Shêng Hsüan-huai, and, at the early stage, Li Hung-chang. Yüan's province was located in the north rather than in the south, and Shêng was a Railway and Telegraph Director rather than a provincial official. But they were so inseparably connected with the policies and activities of the Yangtze viceroys that they were properly spoken of as belonging to the southern group.

evitable was his guiding principle in the peace negotiations. The recommendation that the Joint Note should be accepted, the advice that the indemnities should be agreed to, and the plea that the demands of the Powers regarding punishment of the ministers should be acceded to are a few of the examples in which the above principle was put into practice. Had it not been for the determination of Li Hung-chang in these and other cases, it would have taken much time for the undecided Court to make up its mind.

The Tsêng-Alexeieff Agreement was signed without the Imperial Court's knowledge. The text printed in William W. Rockhill, *Treaties and Conventions with or concerning China*, and John V. A. MacMurray, *Treaties and Conventions with and concerning China*, is incorrect. So also is the version in the *Documents diplomatiques français, 1871-1914*, 2nd Series, I, 18-19.

In the Manchurian crisis Li Hung-chang's persistent advice that the amended Manchurian agreement be signed was opposed by almost all the high officials of China. The Imperial Court, undecided and wavering, had for some time practically passed on to Yang Ju the responsibility of making the decision. It was the insistence of Yang Ju that he could not sign without an express order from the Court that saved China from signing away its rights over Manchuria. In the Russian scene Kuropatkin and Witte considered the immediate conclusion of a separate treaty with China necessary, while Lamsdorff thought it more advisable to wait until a normal state of affairs had been restored in China. The refusal of Yang Ju to sign helped create a situation where, under the pressure of Japan and Britain, Russia at last decided to abandon the agreement.

The Boxer movement was the last struggle of the Chinese people against foreign imperialism under the rule of the Ch'ing Dynasty. The struggle of the people continued, but the rule of the Dynasty did not last long. The ignorance and folly of the Manchu rulers were fully exposed. There was no hope that they would reform along Western lines,[2] and without a thorough reform China could

[2] On January 29, 1901, anxious to appease public opinion, the Imperial Court issued a decree ordering reforms to make China strong and prosperous. (*Ch'ing Tê Tsung Shih Lu*, 476/8a.) Although the decree declared that the superior qualities of foreign

at best be a pawn in the power politics of the great Powers. People began to turn to another direction for strength and prosperity— a revolutionary movement was under way.[3] But it took ten years before the Manchu rule was at last overthrown.

---

countries should be adopted to remedy the shortcomings of China, the southern viceroys were given to understand that in their proposals for reforms, emphasis should not be placed upon Westernization. (Chang Chih-tung, *Chang Wên Hsiang Kung Ch'üan Chi*, 170/34b, 171/3b, 23a.)

[3] Before 1900, noted Dr. Sun Yat-sen, it was the general opinion of the country that the revolutionists were rebels and traitors from whom people should turn away. After 1900, "condemnation from the common people were seldom heard and among the intellectuals not a few began to show sympathy." Sun Yat-sen, *Chien Kuo Fang Lüeh* (The Program of National Reconstruction), Part I, chap. 8.

Bibliography

Bibliography

The following bibliography is confined to important Chinese sources pretaining to the subject. No attempt is made to include sources in Western languages or in Japanese. Their full names are given in the footnotes when they are cited, and most of them are so well known that they hardly need any annotation here. For works in European languages on the Boxer movement, readers may consult the Bibliographical Note in George Nye Steiger, China and the Occident: The Origin and Development of the Boxer Movement (New Haven: Yale University Press, 1927).

Ai Shêng 艾聲 Ch'üan Fei Chi Lüeh 拳匪紀略 (A Brief Record of the Boxers). 1 book. First published in the Kuang Hsü reign, in Chien Po-tsan 翦伯贊 and others (eds.), I Ho T'uan 義和團 Vol. IV. Shanghai, 1951.

Development of the Boxer movement in Chihli. Conflict between common people and native Christians recorded.

Chang Chien 張謇 Chang Chi Tzŭ Chiu Lu 張季子九錄 (The Nine Works of Chang Chien). 90 books. Shanghai, 1931.

Information on the Hundred Days as well as the southeastern provinces during the Boxer crisis.

Chang Chih-tung 張之洞 Chang Wên Hsiang Kung Ch'üan Chi 張文襄公全集 (Complete Works of Chang Chih-tung). 231 books. Peiping, 1928

Documents on the Boxer crisis, particularly the maintenance of peace in the south. Indispensable records for understanding the Viceroy not only during the Boxer crisis but also in the reform movement.

Chang Hsiao-jo 張孝若 Nan T'ung Chang Chi Chih Hsien
Shêng Chuan Chi 南通張季直先生傳記 (A Bi-
ography of Mr. Chang Chien). Shanghai, 1930.

Stories of Chang Chien in connection with the reform
movement and the Boxer crisis.

Chang Po-chêng 張伯楨 Nan Hai K'ang Hsien Shêng Chuan
南海康先生傳 (A Biography of Mr. K'ang Yu-wei).
1928.

A factual biography by one of K'ang's disciples.

Chang Shên 章梫 I Shan Wên Ts'un 一山文存 (Collected
Writings of Chang Shên). 12 books. 1918.

Sheds light on the status of Yüan Ch'ang's "Memorials."

Chao Shu-ch'iao 趙舒翹 Shên Chai Wên Chi 慎齋文集
(Collected Writings of Chao Shu-ch'iao). 14 books. 1924.

Contains material in defense of Chao's innocence.

Ch'ên Ch'iao 陳鍪 "Wu Hsü Chêng Pien Shih Fan Pien Fa Jên
Wu Chih Chêng Chih Ssŭ Hsiang" 戊戌政變時反變法人物
之政治思想 (The Political Thought of the Anti-Reformists
during the Time of the One Hundred Days), in Yen Ching
Hsüeh Pao 燕京學報 (Yenching Journal of Chinese Studies),
Peiping, No. 25 (1939).

Asserts that Wêng T'ung-ho was at heart opposed to the
reformers.

Ch'ên K'uei-lung 陳夔龍 Mêng Chiao T'ing Tsa Chi
夢蕉亭雜記 (Miscellaneous Notes from Mêng Chiao
T'ing). 2 books. 1925.

Notes on Prince Tuan, Kang I, Tung Fu-hsiang, and Li
Ping-hêng in connection with the Boxer crisis.

Ch'ên Tê-hui 陳德輝 Kêng Tzŭ Ch'üan An Shu Mu 庚子
拳案書目 (Bibliography on the Boxer Movement of
1900), in Wu Shêng-tê 吳盛德 and Ch'ên Tê-hui, Chiao
An Shih Liao Pien Mu 教案史料編目 (Bibliography
of Historical Material on Religious Cases), Appendix II.
Yenching University, Peiping, 1942.

A bibliography of 169 items including documents, treaties, diaries, as well as novels, poetry, and translations of Western works.

Ch'êng Ming-chou 程 明 洲 "So Wei 'Ching Shan Jih Chi' Chê" 所 謂'景善日記' 者 (The So-called Diary of Ching Shan), in Yen Ching Hsüeh Pao (Yenching Journal of Chinese Studies), Peiping, No. 27 (1940).

Casts doubt upon the integrity of Jung Lu.

Ch'êng Tê-ch'üan 程 德 全 Kêng Tzŭ Chiao Shê Yü Lu 庚子交涉隅錄 (Some Records of the Negotiations in 1900). 1909.

Documents on the war and truce in the province of Heilungkiang.

Ch'êng Tsung-yü 程宗裕 (ed.). Chiao An Tsou I Hui Pien 教 案 奏 議 彙 編 (A Collection of Memorials concerning Religious Cases). 7 books. Shanghai, 1903.

Documents concerning religious cases in the Ch'ing Dynasty with accounts of the Boxer uprising.

Chiang K'ai蔣 楷 P'ing Yüan Ch'üan Fei Chi Shih 平原 拳 匪 紀 事 (A Record of the Boxers in P'ingyüan). 1901.

Reliable source for the Boxer movement in Shantung and the policy of Governor Yü Hsien, the author having been a magistrate in the province of Shantung.

Chiang-tung-t'ai-tou 江東太斗 "Ku Hung Mei Ko Pi Chi" 古 紅 梅 閣 筆 記 (Notes from Ku Hung Mei Ko), in Jên Wên Yüeh K'an 人文月刊 Vol. III (1932), Nos. 1, 3, 4.

Account of the Boxer movement and its suppression in Shantung.

Chien Po-tsan 蕑伯贊 and others (eds.). I Ho T'uan 義和團(The Boxers). 4 vols. Shanghai, 1951.

This recent collection contains 48 works on the Boxers.

Chih Tung Tien Ts'un [Full title: Chih Tung Chiao Fei Tien
Ts'un] 直東剿 匪電存 (Telegrams concerning the
Suppression of Boxers in Chihli and Shantung), ed. by
Lin Hsüeh-chên 林學琛 4 books. 1906.

Invaluable collection of documents concerning the Boxer
movement in Shantung and Chihli.

Chin Liang 金梁 Ch'ing Hou Wai Chuan 清后外傳 (Supplementary Biographies of the Ch'ing Empresses). 1934.

____Ch'ing Ti Wai Chi 清帝外紀 (Supplementary Records
of the Ch'ing Emperors). 1934.

____Ssŭ Ch'ao I Wên 四朝佚聞 (Stories of Four Reigns).
1936.

The author, an eminent editor of the official history of the
Ch'ing Dynasty, collects in these three books stories that
are not included in the Ch'ing Shih Kao. While some of these
stories are of highly revealing nature, many others need
verification.

Ch'ing Chi Chiao An Shih Liao 清季教案史料 (Histori-
cal Material concerning Religious Cases in the Latter
Part of the Ch'ing Dynasty). 2 vols. Published by the
Palace Museum, Peiping, 1937.

Documents concerning religious affairs give background
to conflicts between the common people and the native
Christians.

Ch'ing Chi Wai Chiao Shih Liao 清季外交史料 (Historical Material on Foreign Relations in the Latter Part of
the Ch'ing Dynasty), ed. by Wang Yen-wei 王彥威 and
Wang Liang 王亮 255 books. Peiping, 1932-33.

A collection of diplomatic documents covering the period
1875-1911. Some documents relating to the Manchurian
crisis appear here that are not found in the Hsi Hsün Ta
Shih Chi, compiled by the same editors.

Ching Chin Ch'üan Fei Chi Lüeh 京津拳匪紀略 (A Brief
Record of the Boxers in Peking and Tientsin), ed. by
Ch'iao-hsi-shêng 橋析生 and Chin-yün-shih 縉雲氏
12 books. Hong Kong, 1901.

A collection of documents, newspaper reports, and rumors concerning the Boxer uprising.

Ch'ing Shih Kao   清史稿 (Draft History of the Ch'ing Dynasty), ed. by Chao Êrh-sun 趙爾巽 and others. 543 books. Peiping, 1928.

The official history of the Ch'ing Dynasty. Biographies of the ministers contain much material on the Boxer crisis.

Ch'ing Tê Tsung Shih Lu [Full title: Ta Ch'ing Tê Tsung Ching Huang Ti Shih Lu] 大清德宗景皇帝實錄. (True Records of the Ch'ing Dynasty, Reign of Kuang Hsü), in Ta Ch'ing Li Ch'ao Shih Lu 大清歷朝實錄 Ch'angch'un, 1937.

This monumental work, the reign of Kuang Hsü alone occupying 597 books, is the day by day record of state affairs in the Imperial Court. It is the most complete collection of Imperial decrees.

Chu Fei 祝芾 Kêng Tzŭ Chiao An Han Tu 庚子教案函牘 (Correspondence concerning Religious Cases in 1900), 1905, in Chien Po-tsan 翦伯贊 and others (eds.), I Ho T'uan. Vol. IV.

Documents concerning the Boxer riots in Laishui.

Chu O Shih Kuan Tang An 駐俄使館檔案 (Archives of the Chinese Legation in Russia), in Wang Yün-shêng 王芸生 (ed.), Liu Shih Nien Lai Chung Kuo Yü Jih Pên 六十年來中國與日本 Vol. IV. Tientsin, 1932.

Documents concerning the negotiations on the proposed Manchurian agreement at St. Petersburg.

Ch'ü Hung-chi 瞿鴻機 Ên Yü Chi Lüeh 恩遇紀略 (Notes on Imperial Favors). 1920.

___Pao Chih Chi Lüeh 葆直紀略 (Notes on Duties in Court). 1920.

___Shêng Tê Chi Lüeh 聖德紀略 (Notes on Imperial Virtues). 1920.

These notes by a Grand Councillor shed light on the character of the Empress Dowager and the Emperor, as well

as on the relationship between the Grand Councillors
and Their Majesties.

Chuan Chi Hsing Shu Hui Chi　傳記行述彙輯　(A Collection of Biographies and Obituaries). Collected by Columbia University Library. 218 ts'ê or pamphlets.

The biography of Yüan Ch'ang by his sons is of interest.
There is serious doubt, however, whether the "Diary of
Yüan Ch'ang" attached thereto is genuine.

Ch'üan Fei Chi Shih　拳匪紀事　(A Record of the Boxers),
ed. by Sawara Tokusuke　佐原篤介　and Ou-yin　漚隱
6 books. 1901.

Similar in nature to Ching Chin Ch'üan Fei Chi Lüeh but
with some different material.

Chung Jih Shih Liao [Full title: Ch'ing Kuang Hsü Ch'ao Chung
Jih Chiao Shê Shih Liao] 清光緒朝中日交涉史料
(Historical Material on Sino-Japanese Relations in the
Kuang Hsü Reign). 88 books. Published by the Palace
Museum, Peiping, 1932.

In spite of the title, the collection has numerous documents concerning the Boxer crisis.

Han-pin-tu-i-chê (Ku Hung-ming) 漢濱讀易者 (辜鴻
銘) Chang Wên Hsiang Mu Fu Chi Wên　張文襄幕
府紀聞 (Notes from the Office of Viceroy Chang Chih-
tung). 2 books. 1910.

Notes by an eminent philosopher and writer, who for some
time served as secretary to Chang Chih-tung.

Hêng Ch'ien 恒謙 Hêng Ch'ien Shou Cha Ts'an Kao 恒謙
手札殘稿 (Remnants of Hêng Ch'ien's Letters), undated, in Chien Po-tsan 翦伯贊 and others (ed.), I Ho
T'uan 義和團 Vol. IV.

Letters of a contemporary describing the situation in
Peking during the Boxer crisis.

Ho Ch'i 何啟 and Hu Li-yüan 胡禮垣　Hsin Chêng Chên
Ch'üan 新政真詮 (Essentials of Reform). 8 ts'ê. 1901.

The essays criticizing Marquis Tsêng and Chang Chih-
tung are of special interest.

Hsi Hsün Hui Luan Shih Mo Chi 西 巡 回 鑾 始 末 記 (The Western Imperial Tour from Beginning to End), ed. by Yoshida Ryotaro 吉 田 良 太 郎 and Yung-lou-chu-jên 詠 樓 主 人 6 books, 1902, in Chung Kuo Nei Luan Wai Huan Li Shih Ts'ung Shu 中 國 內 亂 外 患 歷 史 叢 書 Vol. XXXIV. Shanghai, 1936.

Similar in nature to Ching Chin Ch'üan Fei Chi Lüeh and Ch'üan Fei Chi Shih, but with material not found in those two.

Hsi Hsün Ta Shih Chi 西 巡 大 事 記 (Journal of the Western Imperial Tour), ed. by Wang Yen-wei 王 彥 威 and Wang Liang 王 亮 12 books. Peiping, 1933.

A collection of decrees, memorials, and other documents sent and received by the Imperial Court during the exile period. Some of the dates assigned to the documents are incorrect.

Hsi-yin 惜 陰 "Kêng Tzŭ Ch'üan Huo Tung Nan Hu Pao Chih Chi Shih" 庚 子 拳 禍 東 南 互 保 之 紀 實 (A True Account of the Maintenance of Peace in the Southeast during the Boxer Disaster of 1900), in Jên Wên Yüeh K'an 人 文 月 刊 Vol. II (1931), No. 7.

The author claims that he suggested to Shêng Hsüan-huai the idea of concluding an agreement with the Powers for the maintenance of peace in the southeast.

_____ "Shu Ho Fei Yi Wên" 書 合 肥 軼 聞 (Stories of Li Hung-chang), in Jên Wên Yüeh K'an 人 文 月 刊 Vol. III (1932), No. 7.

Stories of Li's tarrying in Shanghai and his contact with the Russian Minister.

_____ "Wu Kêng Hsin Chi Shu" 戊 庚 辛 紀 述 (An Account of 1898, 1900, and 1901), in Jên Wên Yüeh K'an 人 文 月 刊 Vol. II (1931), No. 5.

The author finds the cause of the Boxer disaster in the estrangement between the Emperor and the Empress Dowager.

Hsiang Pao Wên Pien 湘報文編 (Essays from the Hsiang Pao). 3 vols.

Essays on reform from the Hunan journal in 1898.

Hsieh Fu-ch'êng 薛福成 Yung An Pi Chi 庸盦筆記 (The Yung An Notes). 6 books. 1898.

Historical notes on the Empress Dowager and other Imperial personages give background to Imperial personalities and palace intrigues.

Hsü Ching-ch'êng 許景澄 Hsü Wên Su Kung I Kao 許文肅公遺稿 (Papers of the Late Hsü Ching-ch'êng). 12 books. 1918.

Contains the "Three Memorials of Yüan Ch'ang and Hsü Ching-ch'êng."

Hsü Pei Chuan Chi 續碑傳集 (Supplement to the Collection of Tablet Inscriptions and Biographies), ed. by Miu Ch'üan-sun 繆荃孫 86 books. 1910.

A collection of tablet inscriptions and biographies of eminent persons from 1821 to 1908, it was intended to be a continuation of Ch'ien I-chi 錢儀吉 Pei Chuan Chi 碑傳集 which covered the period from the beginning of the Ch'ing Dynasty to the reign of Chia Ch'ing.

Hu Ssŭ-ching (T'ui-lu-chü-shih) 胡思敬 (退廬居士) Kuo Wên Pi Ch'êng 國聞備乘 (Notes on National Affairs). 4 books, 1911, in T'ui Lu Ch'üan Shu 退廬全書 1924.

———— Lu Pei Chi 驢背集 (The Lu Pei Writings), 1913, in T'ui Lu Ch'üan Shu.

Notes by a Chinese official on the Boxer crisis, particularly the situation of Peking after the flight of the Imperial Court.

———— Wu Hsü Li Shuang Lu 戊戌履霜錄 (A Record of the Crisis in 1898), 4 books, 1913, in T'ui Lu Ch'üan Shu.

Account of the reform movement by a contemporary who disliked K'ang Yu-wei.

Hua Hsüeh-lan 華學瀾 Hsin Ch'ou Jih Chi 辛丑日記
(Diary of 1901). Shanghai, 1936.

This diary of an official during the year after the Boxer
incident contains information on the Allied occupation.

I Chiao Ts'ung Pien 翼教叢編 (Essays in Defense of Con-
fucianism), ed. by Su Yü 蘇輿 6 books. 1898.

A collection of essays written by the anti-reformists.

Jên Tsung Jui Huang Ti Shêng Hsün 仁宗睿皇帝聖
訓 (Decrees of Emperor Chia Ch'ing), 110 books, in
Shih Ch'ao Shêng Hsün 十朝聖訓 Published in the
Kuang Hsü reign.

Decrees concerning the origin of the Boxers.

K'ang Nien P'u [Full title: K'ang Ch'ang Su Hsien Shêng Nien
P'u] 康長素先生年譜 (A Chronological Sketch
of the Life of Mr. K'ang Yu-wei), compiled by Chao Fung-
t'ien 趙豐田 in Shih Hsüeh Nien Pao 史學年報 Vol.
XXI, No. 1, Yenching University, Peiping, 1934.

Based upon the chronological sketch written by K'ang
himself, this is one of the most important sources about
K'ang and his reform movement.

K'ang Yu-wei 康有為 Pao Kuo Hui Yen Shuo Tz'ŭ 保國
會演說詞 (Speech to the "Society to Preserve the
State"), 1898, in Tso Shun-Shêng 左舜生 (ed.), Chung
Kuo Chin Pai Nien Shih Tzŭ Liao Ch'u Pien 中國近
百年史資料初編Shanghai, 1926.

_____ Nan Hai Hsien Shêng Ch'i Shang Shu Chi 南海先生
七上書記 (The Seventh Petition of Mr. K'ang Yu-
wei). Shanghai, 1898.

_____ Nan Hai Hsien Shêng Ssŭ Shang Shu Chi 南海先生
四上書記 (The Four Petitions of Mr. K'ang Yu-wei).
Shanghai, 1895.

K'ang's four memorials from 1888 to 1895.

_____ Nan Hai Hsien Shêng Wu Hsü Tsou Kao 南海先生
戊戌奏稿 (Memorials of Mr. K'ang Yu-wei in 1898).
1901.

____ Nan Hai Hsien Shêng Wu Hsü Chüeh Pi Shu Po 南海 先生戊戌絕筆書跋 (Postscript to Letter of Suicide in 1898). 1921.

K'ang's reminiscences on his escape from Peking and his decision to commit suicide.

Kao Chi-chien 高紿諫 Kêng Tzŭ Jih Chi 庚子日記 (Diary in 1900). 4 books. 1904.

Situation of Peking during and after the Boxer incident.

Kao Shao-ch'ên 高紹陳 Yung Ch'ing Kêng Hsin Chi Lüeh 永清庚辛紀略 (A Brief Record of Yungch'ing in 1900-1901). 1908.

Arrogance of the Boxers and the conduct of the Allied forces in a Chihli district.

Kêng Tzŭ Chiao Shih Shou Nan Chi 庚子教士受難記 (The Persecution of Missionaries in 1900). Author not given, undated.

Kêng Tzŭ Ching Shih Pao Hsü Lu 庚子京師褒卹錄 (List of the Posthumously Honored in Peking, 1900), ed. by Wang Shou-hsün 王守恂 1920.

List of persons who died because of hostilities of the Allied forces.

Kêng Tzŭ Ching Shih Pao Hsü Lu Chiao Chi 庚子京師 褒卹錄校記 (A Collation of "List of the Post-humously Honored in Peking, 1900," by Lo Chên-yü 羅振玉 2 books. 1921.

A correction of Wang Shou-hsün's work.

Kuan Ho 管鶴 Ch'üan Fei Wên Chien Lu 拳匪聞見錄 (What I Heard and Saw of the Boxers), in Chên Ch'i T'ang Ts'ung Shu Ch'u Chi 振綺堂叢書初集 1911.

Account of the Boxers in Tientsin and the neighboring districts.

Kuang Hsü Chêng Yao 光緒政要 (Important Political Events of the Kuang Hsü Reign), ed. by Shên T'ung-shêng 沈桐生 and others. 34 books. Shanghai, 1909.

Books 24-26 contain documents for the period 1898-1900.

Kuo Pin-chia 郭斌佳 "Kêng Tzŭ Ch'uan Luan" 庚子拳亂 (The Boxer Rebellion of 1900), in <u>Wu Han Ta Hsüeh Wên Chê Chi K'an</u> 武漢大學文哲季刊   Vol. VI (1936), No. 1.

Hatred of Tz'ŭ Hsi against foreigners emphasized. Sources not given.

Lao Nai-hsüan 勞乃宣   Ch'üan An Tsa Ts'un 拳案雜存 (Miscellaneous Papers on the Boxers). 3 books. 1902.

____<u>Fung Chin I Ho Ch'üan Hui Lu</u> 奉禁義和拳彙錄 (A Collection of Documents for the Suppression of the Boxers). 1906.

____<u>I Ho Ch'üan Chiao Mên Yüan Liu K'ao</u> 義和拳教門 源流攷 (Study of the Origins of the Boxer Sect). 1899.

It is in this work that the author expounds the theory that the Boxers were heretical sects or secret societies.

____<u>T'ung Hsiang Lao Hsien Shêng I Kao</u> 桐鄉勞先生遺 稿 (Writings of the Late Lao Nai-hsüan). 9 books. 1927.

Includes a chronological sketch of his life by Lao himself.

Li Hung-chang 李鴻章   <u>Li Wên Chung Kung Ch'üan Chi</u> 李文忠公全集   (Complete Works of Li Hung-chang). 166 books. 1905.

Consists of "Tsou Kao" (Memorials), "Tien Kao" (Telegrams), "I Shu Han Kao" (Correspondence with the Tsungli Yamen), etc. The "Tien Kao" is particularly important to the study of the peace negotiations and the Manchurian crisis.

____<u>Wu Tz'ŭ Wên Ta Chieh Lüeh</u> 五次問答節略 (Minutes of Five Conferences), in <u>Chung Jih Hui I</u> 中日 會議 1896.

Reveals Li's thought about China's reforms and Sino-Japanese relations.

Li Ping-hêng 李秉衡　Li Chung Chieh Kung Tsou I 李忠
節公奏議 (Memorials of Li Ping-hêng). 16 books.
Liaoning, 1930.

Li Ti 李杕　Ch'üan Huo Chi 拳禍記 (A Record of the Boxer Disaster). Shanghai, 1903.

Account of the Boxer movement and the Roman Catholic
Church during the crisis. Includes some important documents.

Liang Ch'i-ch'ao 梁啟超　Li Hung-chang 李鴻章 1901,
in Yin Ping Shih Ho Chi 飲氷室合集　Shanghai, 1936.

A critical study of Li Hung-chang.

____Nan Hai K'ang Hsien Shêng Chuan 南海康先生傳
(A Biography of Mr. K'ang Yu-wei), 1911, in Yin Ping
Shih Ho Chi.

____Wu Hsü Chêng Pien Chi 戊戌政變記 (The Coup
d'État of 1898), in Yin Ping Shih Ho Chi.

Account of the reform and the coup d'état. Should be read
with reservations in view of the writer's strong partisan
standpoint.

Liu Ch'i-tzŭ 柳溪子　Chin Hsi Pi Chi 津西毖記 (Les-
sons from Western Tientsin). 2 ts'ê. 1902.

Notes on western Tientsin under occupation.

Liu Ch'un-t'ang 劉春堂　Chi Nan Chi Pien Chi Lüeh 畿南
濟變紀略 (Coping with the Crisis South of the Capital). 2 ts'ê. 1901.

Biographies of Chinese officials dealing with the Boxer
crisis in Paoting and neighboring districts. Contains an
account of the Boxer uprising in Tientsin and Laishui by
Yüan Kuo-chêng 阮國楨.

Liu K'un-i 劉坤一　Liu Chung Ch'êng Kung I Chi 劉忠
誠公遺集 (Works of the Late Liu K'un-i). 63 books.
1909.

Contains memorials, telegrams, and other documents
concerning the Boxer crisis.

Liu Mêng-yang 劉孟揚 T'ien Chin Ch'üan Fei Pien Luan
Chi Shih 天津拳匪變亂紀事 (A Record of the
Boxer Uprising in Tientsin). 2 books. 1910.

A journal of events in Tientsin from the appearance of
the Boxers to the occupation of the city by the Allies.

Lo Tun-yung 羅惇曧 Ch'üan Pien Yü Wên 拳變餘聞
(Further Stories of the Boxer Crisis), undated, in Tso
Shun-shêng 左舜生 (ed.), Chung Kuo Chin Pai Nien
Shih Tzŭ Liao Ch'u Pien 中國近百年史資料
初編 Shanghai, 1926.

A supplement to the author's following work.

_____Kêng Tzŭ Kuo Pien Chi 庚子國變記 (The National
Crisis of 1900), 1912, in Tso Shun-shêng (ed.), Chung
Kuo Chin Pai Nien Shih Tzŭ Liao Ch'u Pien.

Account of the Boxer crisis upon the basis of notes writ-
ten by a contemporary named Li Hsi-shêng 李希聖.
Part of these notes had been published under the title
Kêng Tzŭ Ch'uan Hsin Lu 庚子傳信錄.

Lü Hai-huan 呂海寰 Kêng Tzŭ Hai Wai Chi Shih 庚子
海外紀事 (A Record of Events Overseas in 1900).
4 books. 1901.

Documents of the Chinese Legation in Berlin concerning
the Boxer incident.

Lu Shu-tê 陸樹德 Kêng Tzŭ Ch'üan Pien Hou Ching Chin
Chien Chih Ts'an Chuang 庚子拳變後京津間
之慘狀 (Terrible Situation between Peking and Tientsin after the Boxer Incident of 1900), undated, in Tso
Shun-shêng 左舜生 (ed.), Chung Kuo Chin Pai Nien
Shih Tzŭ Liao Hsü Pien 中國近百年史資料
續編 Shanghai, 1933.

Lu Wan-t'ien 陸完天 Kêng Tzŭ Pei Ching Shih Pien Chi
Lüeh 庚子北京事變紀略 (A Brief Account of
the Crisis at Peking in 1900). 1 ts'ê. 1901.

An account of the Boxer uprising and the experiences of
the Chinese Christians in the legation quarters during
the siege.

Ma Yü-kuei 馬毓桂 Shou Cho Hsien Chêng Shu 守拙軒
政書 (Political Papers of Ma Yü-kuei). 1 ts'ê. 1902.

Documents of the Hochien district concerning the suppression of the Boxers after the Allies had entered Peking.

Pao Shih-chieh 包士傑 (ed.). Ch'üan Shih Shang Yü 拳時
上諭 (Decrees during the Boxer Crisis), Peking, 1919,
in Chien Po-tsan 翦伯贊 and others (eds.), I Ho T'uan
義和團 Vol. IV.

Some of the decrees collected here are not found in
Ch'ing Tê Tsung Shih Lu, apparently because the Imperial
Court orderd on February 14, 1901, the destruction of
all decrees issued between June 20 and August 14, 1900,
that were favorable to the Boxers or hostile to the foreigners.

Pei Chuan Chi Pu 碑傳集補 (Further Supplement to
the Collection of Tablet Inscriptions and Biographies), ed.
by Min Êrh-ch'ang 閔爾昌 60 books. Yenching University, Peiping, 1931.

A supplement to Hsü Pei Chuan Chi.

Pien Fa Tsou I Ts'ung Ch'ao 變法奏議叢鈔 (A Collection of Memorials on Reforms). 4 books. Undated.

A collection of memorials on the subject of reform in
response to the Imperial decree of January 29, 1901.

Ping-hêng-chü-shih 秉衡居士 "Ho Hsiang Kuan So Yen"
荷香館瑣言 (Trifling Words from the Ho Hsiang
Kuan), in Jên Wên Yüeh K'an 人文月刊 Vol. I (1930),
No. 4.

Suggests that Wêng T'ung-ho was opposed to the reform
in 1898.

Shan Hsi Shêng Kêng Tzŭ Nien Chiao Nan Ch'ien Hou Chi
Shih 山西省庚子年教難前後紀事 (Events
before and after the Massacre of Missionaries in Shansi
in 1900), author not given, undated, in Chien Po-tsan
翦伯贊 and others (eds.), I Ho T'uan. Vol. I.

Account of the massacre in Shansi with documents. It is
interesting to note that an Imperial decree ordered the

foreign missionaries to leave China for their own countries. The ground given by Yü Hsien for the execution
was that the foreigners refused to leave and engaged
themselves to plot against the country.

Shên Wei-hsien 沈維賢 "Chi Yüan Ch'uang Ch'iu Hsien
Shêng Yi Shih" 記袁磢秋先生軼事 (Stories of
Yüan Ch'ang), in Jên Wên Yüeh K'an 人文月刊 Vol.
III (1932), No. 9.

Maintains that the "Three Memorials" were not submitted by Yüan.

Shên Tsu-hsien 沈祖憲 and Wu K'ai-shêng 吳闓生
(eds.). Yung An Ti Tzŭ Chi 容菴弟子記 (Notes by
the Students of Yung An). 4 books. 1913.

Discussion of Yüan Shih-k'ai's suppression of the Boxers
in Shantung.

Shêng Hsüan-huai 盛宣懷 Yü Chai Ts'un Kao Ch'u
K'an 愚齋存稿初刊 (Collected Papers of Shêng
Hsüan-huai, First Issue). 100 books. 1939.

Invaluable material concerning the Boxer uprising, the
peace in the southeastern provinces, and the Manchurian
crisis.

T'ang Yen 唐晏 Kêng Tzŭ Hsi Hsing Chi Shih 庚子西行
記事 (A Record of the Trip to the West in 1900). 1 ts'ê,
1900.

Notes of a Chinese official in his flight to Sian. Social
conditions between Peking and Sian described.

Tsou Wei-san 鄒渭三 and Ling Têng-yo 凌登岳 Yü
Kuan Chi Shih 榆關紀事 (A Record of Events in
Shanhaikwan). 4 books. 1904.

Reliable account of events in Shanhaikwan during the
Boxer crisis.

Tung Hua Hsü Lu, Kuang Hsü Ch'ao 東華續錄 光緒朝
(Records of the Reigning Dynasty, Reign of Kuang Hsü).
220 books. 1909.

Although the Tung Hua Lu is generally less detailed than the Ch'ing Shih Lu (The True Records of the Ch'ing Dynasty), it sometimes includes full texts of the memorials upon which the decrees were based.

Tung San Shêng Tien Pao [Full title: Chung O Hui Shang Chiao Shou Tung San Shêng Tien Pao Hui Ch'ao] 中俄 會商交收東三省電報彙鈔 (A Collection of Telegrams concerning the Sino-Russian Negotiations on the Restoration of the Three Eastern Provinces), ed. by Yang Ju 楊儒 1901 (Reprint, Peiping, 1935).

The editor was the Chinese plenipotentiary during the negotiations in St. Petersburg.

Tung Tso-pin 董作賓 (ed.). Kêng Tzŭ Yi Shih 庚子軼 事 (Stories of 1900), in I Ching 逸經 1937, No. 22.

These notes on the situation in Tientsin during the Boxer crisis are based upon Wang T'ung-ts'ai 汪桐采 Kêng Tzŭ Jih Chi 庚子日記.

Tzŭ Ch'iang Chai Pao Fu Hsing Kuo Lun 自強齋保 富興國論 (Essays on National Prosperity and Rejuvenation), ed. by T'ien-nan-tun-sou 天南遯叟 6 books. Shanghai, 1897.

An early publication on reform by the Ch'iang Hsüeh Hui, a reform organization, in Shanghai.

Wang Chih-ch'un 王之春 Chiao Shêng Tsou I 椒生奏議 (Memorials of Wang Chih-ch'un). 5 books. 1904.

Wang was Governor of Anhui during the Boxer crisis.

Wang Hsiao-yin 王小隱 Hua Hsü Man Lu 華胥漫錄 (The Hua Hsü Notes), in Jên Wên Yüeh K'an 人文月刊 Vol. IV (1923), No. 6.

Story of Prince Tuan attempting to kill Yüan Shih-k'ai during the Boxer crisis.

Wang Hsing-wu 王星五 Luan Chou Kêng Tzŭ Chi Shih 灤州庚子紀事 (A Record of Events in Luanchou during 1900). Published in the Kuang Hsü reign.

Account of Chinese dealing with the Allied forces in northeastern Chihli.

Wang Shu-nan 王樹枏   Tê Tsung I Shih 德宗遺事   (Stories of Emperor Kuang Hsü). 1911.

Not a reliable source.

Wang Wên-shao 王文韶 Kêng Tzŭ Liang Kung Mêng Ch'ên Chi Shih or Wang Wên Shao Chia Shu 庚子兩宮蒙塵紀實 (王文韶家書) (The True Story of the Flight of the Empress Dowager and the Emperor in 1900, or, Family Letter of Wang Wên-shao), 1900, in Tso Shun-shêng 左舜生 (ed.), Chung Kuo Chin Pai Nien Shih Tzŭ Liao Hsü Pien 中國近百年史資料續編 also in Hsi Hsün Hui Luan Shih Mo Chi 西巡回鑾始末記

The authenticity of this "Letter" is questionable. See above, chap. VI, note 9.

Wang Yen-chao 王延釗   Kêng Hsin Chih Chi Yüeh Piao 庚辛之際月表 (A Chronology of Events between 1900 and 1901). 1907.

Wên Hsien Ts'ung Pien 文獻叢編 (Collection of Historical Materials). Published by the Palace Museum, Peiping, Nos. 34-36 (1936), Nos.1-7 (1937), Nos. 44-46 (1942-43).

The sections entitled "Kêng Hsin Tien Pao" 庚辛電報 have much material concerning the Boxer crisis. The five letters called "Chün Chi Ch'u Ch'ih Tu Wu T'ung" 軍機處尺牘五通 in No. 18 (1934) are also of interest.

Wêng T'ung-ho 翁同龢 Wêng Wên Kung Kung Jih Chi 翁文恭公日記 (Diary of Wêng T'ung-ho). 40 ts'ê. 1925.

The role of the author in the reform and some entries in this Diary have been the subject of controversy. See above, chap. I, note 84.

Wu Hsü Liu Chün Tzŭ I Chi 戊戌六君子遺集 (Writings of the Six Martyrs of 1898), ed. by Chang Yüan-chi 張元濟 6 ts'ê. Shanghai, 1917.

Collection of essays and poems of the six reformers who
suffered execution in the <u>coup</u> <u>d'état</u> of 1898. Important
material for understanding the character and thought of
the reformers.

Wu Yung 吳永 <u>Kêng Tzŭ Hsi Shou Ts'ung T'an</u> 庚子西
狩叢談 (Reminiscences of the Western Imperial
Journey in 1900), transcribed by P'i-yüan-chü-shih (Liu
Chih-hsiang) 闢園居士 (劉治襄) 4 books. 1928.
English translation by Ida Pruitt under the title <u>The
Flight of an Empress</u>. New Haven: Yale University
Press, 1936.

Many inaccuracies. For further comments see above,
chap. VI, note 8.

Yang Mu-shih 楊慕時 <u>Kêng Tzŭ Chiao Fei Tien Wên Lu</u>
庚子剿匪電文錄 (Telegrams concerning the
Suppression of the Boxers in 1900), 1915, in Chien Po-
tsan 翦伯贊 and others (eds.), <u>I Ho T'uan</u> 義和團
Vol. IV.

Yang, a commander under General Nieh Shih-ch'êng,
was sent to Laishui to suppress the Boxers in May-June,
1900. He was ordered to leave the area by Kang I.

Yang Shao-chên 楊紹震 "Kêng Tzŭ Nien Chung O Tsai
Tung San Shêng Chih Ch'ung Tu Chi Ch'i Chieh Shu"
庚子年中俄在東三省之衝突及其結束
(Sino-Russian Hostilities in the Three Eastern Provinces
in 1900 and Their Termination), in <u>Ch'ing Hua Hsüeh
Pao</u> 清華學報 (The Tsing Hua Journal), IX (1934),
69-126.

A study of the Russian occupation of Manchuria from
1900 to 1902.

Yeh Ch'ang-ch'ih 葉昌熾 <u>Yüan Tu Lu Jih Chi Ch'ao</u>
緣督廬日記鈔 (Diary of Yeh Ch'ang-ch'ih). 16 books.
Shanghai, 1933.

Some valuable information, but not always accurate.

Yü Yin-lin 于蔭霖 <u>Sung Chai Jih Chi</u> 悚齋日記 (Diary of
Yü Yin-lin), 8 books, in <u>Sung Chai I Shu</u> 悚齋遺書
1923.

The author was Governor of Hupeh during the Boxer crisis. Books 5 and 6 contain material relative to the crisis.

Yüan Ch'ang 袁昶 Yüan Chung Chieh Kung Shou Cha 袁 忠 節公手扎 (Letters of Yüan Ch'ang). 2 ts'ê. Shanghai, 1937.

Material concerning the Boxer movement.

Yüan Shih-k'ai 袁世凱 Wu Hsü Jih Chi 戊戌日記 (Diary in 1898), 1926, in Tso Shun-shêng 左舜生 (ed.), Chung Kuo Chin Pai Nien Shih Tzŭ Liao Ch'u Pien 中國近 百年史資料初編 Shanghai, 1926.

Story of the coup d'état told by Yüan Shih-k'ai. Should be compared with Liang Ch'i-ch'ao, Wu Hsü Chêng Pien Chi.

_____ Yang Shou Yüan Tsou I Chi Yao 養壽園奏議輯 要 (Important Memorials of Yüan Shih-k'ai). 44 books. 1937.

Though not a complete collection of Yüan's memorials, it contains some important documents concerning the Boxer crisis.

Yün Yü-ting 惲毓鼎 Ch'ung Ling Ch'uan Hsin Lu 崇 陵 傳 信 錄 (A True Record of Emperor Kuang Hsü), 1911, in Tso Shun-shêng 左舜生 (ed.), Chung Kuo 中國 Chin Pai Nien Shih Tzŭ Liao Ch'u Pien 近百年史資料初編 Shanghai, 1926.

Valuable account of the palace doings with regard to the Boxer crisis.

Index

Index

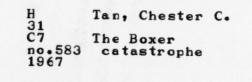

```
H          Tan, Chester C.
31
C7         The Boxer
no.583     catastrophe
1967
```

DATE			